Stolen Voices

Terrie and Paul Duckett

Stolen voices

A sadistic step-father.

Two children violated.

Their battle for justice.

HARPER
element

This book is a work of non-fiction based upon the life, experiences and recollections of the authors. To protect the privacy of certain individuals some names have been changed, locations altered, identifying details blurred and dispersed events collapsed. This is not the whole story, there are many things that simply could not be made to fit within these pages, but it is a true story.

HarperElement
An Imprint of HarperCollins*Publishers*
77–85 Fulham Palace Road,
Hammersmith, London W6 8JB

www.harpercollins.co.uk

and *HarperElement* are trademarks of
HarperCollins*Publishers* Ltd

First published by HarperElement 2014

3 5 7 9 10 8 6 4

A catalogue record of this book is
available from the British Library

ISBN 978-0-00-753223-0

Printed and bound in Great Britain by
Clays Ltd, St Ives plc

MIX
Paper from
responsible sources
FSC™ C007454

FSC is a non-profit international organisation established to promote the
responsible management of the world's forests. Products carrying the FSC
label are independently certified to assure consumers that they come
from forests that are managed to meet the social, economic and
ecological needs of present and future generations.

Find out more about HarperCollins and the environment at
www.harpercollins.co.uk/green

We dedicate this book to each other and to every other brother and sister struggling to survive: with strength, humour and love we came through this together. Our bond is unbreakable.

Prologue
June 2012

'What's up?' I yawned into the phone to my brother Paul. It was almost 1 a.m. and I was feeling bloody tired.

'I've just got off the phone to the police,' Paul blurted out. 'You know they arrested Peter today and searched the house? Well, you're just not going to believe this!' He took a breath. 'Apparently, it's been designated a crime scene and they've left police outside all night, to make sure no one gets in. There was so much evidence they ran out of time and need to go back and collect the rest. They reckon it's an "Aladdin's cave". Their words, not mine.' There was a slight pause. 'I'm gonna drive over. Do you wanna come?'

I didn't even have to think twice. 'Yes! Come and get me. I'll be waiting outside.' I hung up, threw on some clothes and ran outside. I stood waiting impatiently by the side of the road, trying to calm my breathing. A few moments later, Paul's car turned the corner and pulled up next to me. I jumped in and we screeched away.

'Fasten seat belt,' Paul's car lectured me repeatedly in a mechanical monotone.

'All right, all right, shut the fuck up,' I muttered, cutting the car off as I clicked the belt in place. Paul rolled his eyes and drove on.

We drove silently towards our childhood home, lost in our thoughts. We were both feeling numb, not able to believe they had finally arrested him. We had had a couple of intensely stressful weeks waiting for the police to call, and now here we were driving towards the place we had barely survived as children, not knowing quite what to expect.

None of the events of the past few weeks had actually sunk in; whether it was the police telling us it was the worst case they had dealt with in a long time, the pitying looks we had received as we gave our interview, or the fact that we'd been brave enough to tell anyone at all.

My thoughts snapped back into focus as the car turned into Churchill Avenue, an ordinary estate filled with neat council houses; a place we'd avoided for over 10 years because it evoked so many traumatic memories. As the well-trodden pavements swept past, my stomach twisted into a hard knot.

In the distance the familiar silhouette of our childhood home loomed: the box-shaped porch, the white wooden cladding, the thin paving snaking from the public footpath to the front door. Such an innocent-looking house, yet one that hid so many dark secrets. Today Number 59 looked tardy and neglected.

As we approached, we saw a police car parked opposite the house with two men inside it. With a quick glance at Paul, I could tell we both felt weird and in some ways wrong to pass by the empty house. The reality was starting to sink in, and although neither of us was sure how as victims we were meant to act, we knew that together we'd get through it, just as we did through our childhood.

Paul accelerated so that we passed the house at normal speed.

'Well, it looks like we've got the ball rolling now,' breathed Paul as he sucked long and hard on his roll-up.

'I've got a feeling this isn't going to be an easy journey.' I sighed.

'Can't be any harder than what we've been through,' Paul commented.

'Don't you wish we could have told our younger selves how things would work out?'

'I wouldn't change a thing; the struggles we went through have made us the people we are today. I believe if we changed one thing in our past it would change who we are now.'

I glanced at Paul and nodded. 'True.' I was full of apprehension about the days and weeks ahead. I was just glad we had each other.

Chapter 1

'Humble Beginnings'

Terrie

My parents, John and Cynthia, were childhood sweethearts. Their relationship had begun like a storybook romance, but with their marriage their dreams died.

Mum intended to follow in her father's footsteps in Northampton's traditional calling, designing shoes, until she naively showed her designs to a local shoe manufacturer during one lunchtime, who stole them. Dad joined the parachute regiment and aspired to be part of the SAS – until he failed their selection course.

In 1968, with both their dreams in tatters, life was to change irreparably again. Mum discovered she'd accidentally fallen pregnant. To say Dad was not best pleased was an understatement, but in 1968 pregnancy meant marriage and that was that. So Mum abandoned her place in college and went up the aisle – or at least the corridor – of Northampton register office.

She didn't tell her parents, my Nan and Pap – Gladys and George – at first. Not only had she let them down, but they believed she could do better than my dad. However, by the time she told them the damage had been done, and at the very least they felt he'd done the honourable thing.

I arrived on 27 June 1969 in Aldershot, the garrison town where Dad was based. For the first month of my life we lived in married quarters, though Dad was desperate to be released back to Civvy Street, not being able to face being returned to his parachute regiment after failing the SAS selection course. The only way he could be discharged was to buy himself out, so Mum raided her savings and stumped up the required £200 – a prohibitive sum, but a small price to pay to keep her new husband happy.

Mum and I lived my first year with my Nan and Pap in their cosy two-bedroom house. But the first home I remember clearly was a council maisonette in Moat Place. It was a bit sparse; the kitchen and lounge were downstairs and the bedrooms were up a white-painted stairway that had a thin carpet runner tacked loosely to the wood. Two wooden slats ran down the side of the stairs, with a narrow gap between them, so that as a small child I could peer through. I spent a fair bit of time sitting in nervous silence on those stairs, listening to Mum and Dad argue their way through life.

Dad worked away a lot of the time, stopping home for clean clothes and food maybe once a fortnight. When he wasn't there to argue with Mum, I felt happy and relaxed. I had my mum all to myself and we had our routine. We didn't have a lot of money, or many belongings, but she had time for me – even though I could be more of a hindrance than a help, as a simple trip to the shops could turn into an adventure.

At the age of four, whilst I was dawdling back from the shops with a loaf of bread for tea, I thought of Hansel and Gretel. 'I wonder what would happen if I dropped a trail of bread slices?' Imagining a magical creature might appear, I pulled slices of bread out of the bag and began placing them carefully on the pavement. Skipping along, I looked over my shoulder, pleased at the snowy trail … until Mum suddenly appeared, looking up the road for me. 'Terrie!' she cried. 'What are you doing? That's our tea!'

I held a slice of bread mid-air and my face crumpled. 'Sorry, Mummy.'

She scurried to scoop up the slices and put them carefully back into the bread bag for later.

The weekends Dad came home left their impression on me. One such weekend, when I was three, I was sitting in the kitchen waiting for Mum to dish up dinner when he arrived. I looked up as he walked in, but he didn't seem to notice me.

'Hurry up, I'm hungry,' he complained to Mum. Mum seemed flustered and rushed to place the plates of macaroni cheese in front of us. 'Is this it?'

Mum looked up. 'I have some Spam if you'd like some?'

He laughed sneeringly. 'This'll do.'

I was actually relieved. I hate Spam – no, I detest Spam. Poor Mum was running out of new ways to cook it. Fried, battered and deep-fried, diced and sliced. For me any way was disgusting, and I would often gag trying to swallow the pink sludge.

I hated macaroni too. I couldn't stop thinking about slugs as I tried to swallow the slimy pasta pieces. Dad would become frustrated with the faces I was pulling and send me up to my room, telling me not to come back downstairs until they had both finished dinner.

A few minutes later, as I cautiously slid back down the stairs on my bum, I could hear our budgie was squawking loudly. Dad was standing up shouting as Mum turned to look at me. He followed her gaze and saw me. 'Get out! This is adult talk. *Get out, now!'*

I ran and sat on the stairs, scared and alone, peering through the gap.

At three years old, I was confused. I still wanted and needed to be loved by my dad, but I felt anger towards both of

3

my parents for letting him come home and ruining my time with Mum. The rage had to get out somehow, so I began destroying things Mum had lovingly made for me. I picked apart a crocheted waistcoat made with squares of colourful pansies all sewn together. I cut the silky lining out of the green felt coat she'd made. And I carefully hacked my way across my fringe.

Dad's presence at home meant rows and arguments, slammed doors and tears. Mum never really explained why it happened; I just thought it was my fault, because I was stupid and ugly.

It may have been that Dad felt trapped at home and would rather have been back amongst the camaraderie and banter of his army friends. Dad had joined the Territorial Army after being discharged out of the service, as it was more relaxed than the regular army. I enjoyed watching him with his mates in the TA, laughing and joking, so very different to how he was at home. Drill weekends often included family gatherings, lots of delicious food and kids running about, playing games amongst the lorries and heavy gear outside the drill hall.

But Dad did let a glimmer of his home face show there occasionally. Like the time he was supposed to be keeping an eye on me while Mum was inside with the other mums setting up for dinner. I was on my hands and knees pushing my new green plastic train that had two carriages attached. He warned me not to go near a large stack of bricks by the wall, but, me being me, I pushed my train a little hard. It sped off behind the brick stack. The top of the pile was leaning in towards the building, but there was a me-sized gap between the stack and the wall. I squeezed between and reached out for my train. I heard Dad yelling just before the pile fell onto my legs.

As he yanked me out by my arm, I said my leg felt funny and I refused to stand on it. 'You're just being a baby,' he said.

I cried and he yelled for my mum. She gave me a look over and said I needed to get my leg checked. Later that day, as I showed my broken leg, plastered to the knee, to my Nan, she was horrified. She gave me extra cuddles to make up for it.

To me, Nan and Pap were perfect. Their house was an oasis of calm and I loved every brick of it, from the Indian-style felt-covered living room, where Nan saw faces and shapes in the patterns ('Look, Terrie, there's a goat!' she'd laugh), to their conservatory where Pap would proudly show off his small cucumbers hanging around the door.

Nan had blonde wavy hair and sweet, flowery perfumed skin. She was always quick to cuddle me whenever she could. Nothing was ever too much trouble, whether it was cooking up delicious treats in the kitchen, playing pretend games or re-telling every fairy story I could absorb. Nan would pull up a chair in the kitchen, so I could stand and help her make dinner. Afterwards we'd play snap, or she'd get out a big tin of assorted buttons she'd collected over the years and we'd sit and thread them onto coloured cotton.

Pap was as round and cuddly as Nan, and they adored each other. He always had a twinkle in his eyes when he told me stories of when he was a boy and how mischievous he was.

All too soon, it was time to go home.

In late 1973, I was holding Mum's hand as we walked across the Northampton market square, when she turned and knelt in front of me.

'Mummy is going to have a baby.' She looked a little worried, patting her tummy. I'd seen it getting rounder and fatter.

'Okay.' I shrugged, not really understanding. It was obviously something I was thinking about, though, as later that afternoon I pointed to Nan and Pap's tummies. 'Are you both having babies too?' They laughed.

That evening I played with my only dolly, Baby Beans, named because she was filled with dried beans. I could hear Mum and Dad downstairs, and he didn't seem happy. I tried banging my head against the wall to block out the sound of their voices. It didn't work, but I did eventually manage to fall asleep.

When I woke in the morning, Dad had gone again for a few weeks. Mum heard me stir and called me into her bedroom. 'Hey, Ted,' Mum said, using her nickname for me. 'Come and put your hand on my tummy.'

She held my hand firmly to her stomach, and I felt something move under the skin. 'That's the baby's foot,' she said, her face lighting up.

I looked at her big belly in confusion. 'How did it get there?' I pointed to her belly button and she laughed.

A couple of weeks later I was taken to Nan and Pap's. 'The baby is on its way,' Nan said gently, 'so Mummy is in hospital.'

I worried. I didn't really understand what was happening. But the next morning Nan took me on a bus to the hospital and held my hand as she led me to a bed where Mum lay, look-ing exhausted but happy. As we reached the bed, Nan lifted me up so I could look into the crib. There was a little baby with a screwed-up pink face, swaddled in a blue blanket.

'Isn't he lovely?' said Mum. 'His name is Paul. He's your brother.'

I grabbed Nan's hand again. Everything seemed too strange, and I tugged at her to leave. I'd had enough of Paul already. 'I don't really want a brother, thank you,' I said as politely as I could.

Mum was in hospital for a few days, after which Nan walked me back home. I tried not to cry as she knocked on the door to our house. As we entered everything smelled different, the house seemed messier and it didn't feel like home. Nan gave me a kiss goodbye and headed home to Pap. I ran upstairs to my room and cried; I'd desperately wanted to go back with her, but dared not say anything.

The next few weeks were filled with nappies, washing, bottles and crying. Gently I stroked his fuzzy peach scalp while he was asleep. I was growing to like him. He always seemed to like me reading my picture books to him, so perhaps having a baby brother wasn't going to be so bad after all.

Dad hated Paul crying and escaped out with his friends as much as he could. Tired from night feeding, Mum would let me take Paul out by myself in a big second-hand Silver Cross pram she'd borrowed. I proudly paraded him to my friends. 'He's my brother,' I said proudly. 'And it's my job to look after him.'

Starting primary school gave me a chance to show off my reading skills. I loved going to school, though I did hate leaving Mum and Paul alone. I was used to having Mum's time; now all of a sudden I had none.

Eventually we moved to a new council house in Churchill Avenue. Mum wanted us to go to a better school and live in a nicer area. The house was much bigger, with room for Paul and me to run around. By then Mum worked all hours, doing day and night shifts in a shoe factory. She always groaned when the bills arrived, and while Dad worked away we never had much food in the cupboards.

Mum walked me to my first day at lower school, only the second time she ever took me. I hated the mornings before school. My long hair was always knotted and tangled, and Mum had to yank the brush through. By the end of lower school Mum had had enough of the morning battle to brush my hair, so she placed a bowl on my head and cut around it.

I looked like a boy. I hated it. I clutched at my head, wondering what had happened. From that point on my hair was always kept short, Mum cutting it herself in the kitchen. 'I'm not very good at this,' she sighed. 'But it's just easier this way.'

The kids at school laughed at my hairstyle. They taunted me for having a boy's name and tatty hair. At the age of six, I realised I didn't fit in. My clothes were threadbare and my shoes worn to the sole. I was never invited back to anybody's house for tea.

The closest person to me was my little brother, and I loved playing with him. He'd grown into a mischievous, adorable toddler with a mop of blond hair and a cheeky smile. He tried to follow me everywhere on his little red tricycle. He was always looking for attention from Mum – I'd just got used to not having any. In the evenings, if Dad was away, we'd be passed between babysitters and Nan and Pap while Mum worked until 9 p.m. But although Mum worked a lot, she, Paul and I were happy together.

Despite my age I could sense Mum and Dad's marriage was falling apart, but occasionally we were able to pretend we were a happy family. At family barbecues or at TA events, sometimes Dad would chase us around with water pistols, laughing, and for a few minutes I could pretend everything was okay at home. On occasion he would surprise us all. Once he turned up after a few weeks away with a puppy, a beautiful tortoiseshell-coloured mongrel. We decided to name him Sam. We all loved him. Another time he brought us the biggest hand-made Easter eggs I'd ever seen.

I was eight when we met Dad's friend Peter Bond-Wonneberger at one of the TA functions. Peter was in his early thirties, with dark hair brushed to the side and a wiry moustache. A smiling, happy guy, he always seemed up for a joke or laugh. He was married to Anne and they didn't have kids. Anne didn't seem that comfortable with our energy and playfulness, like Peter did.

'Hello, Terrie and Paul!' he beamed and crouched down to our height whenever he saw us. 'Want to have a look at my camera?' Peter was always snapping away.

Sometimes I wished Dad was more like him. Often they went off together to the TA Centre to develop photographs in a lab. Sometimes we were allowed in and saw them hanging on the line, dripping and smelling of chemicals.

Dad had gone off on a trip to Zimbabwe to see an old army friend, and asked Peter to pick him up from the airport. Peter arrived to collect us first. He was in a chatty mood, as usual, pulling on our seat belts, making sure we were comfortable.

'What planes you hoping to spot, Paul?' he asked.

'Big ones!' Paul giggled.

'Great! I'll get a shot of a jumbo for you,' he replied.

It felt good to have an adult, especially a man, showing interest in our lives. On the way back we stopped off at Dunstable Downs for a breath of fresh air when Peter pulled out a cine camera.

'Wow!' said Paul. At four he didn't quite understand it, but was impressed by all the buttons.

'Hey, I know,' said Peter with a huge grin. 'Why don't I take a film of both of you, eh? You can act, can't you? Be fun to see yourself like in the movies!'

Mum and Dad laughed as Peter concentrated through the viewfinder, and Paul and I sprinted off, dancing hand in hand. I was in a light green dress with big sleeves that made me feel girly for once, despite my cropped hair.

That afternoon, Peter captured a rare moment: us, a happy family on film. As our mum and dad held hands, watching their giggling children playing in the fields, for half an hour we were genuinely a family.

Chapter 2

'In the Picture'

Paul

$\mathcal{T}$he summer before I started school, Peter came over, a camera slung around his neck like always. Peter went to chat with Mum in the kitchen and we overheard him.

'We've got more rabbits than you can imagine. Would Terrie and Paul like to come over and choose one?'

I leapt up and down excitedly, clapping my hands with Terrie. Dad didn't like pets, but he hadn't been home for weeks, so maybe we could persuade Mum? We both ran out to the kitchen. The excitement must have been showing all over our faces.

Mum sighed, looking at us both. 'I guess you heard Peter's news.' She paused. 'All right, let's go and see them this afternoon.'

Terrie and I leapt up and down cheering, and Sam joined in, barking loudly.

Peter drove us to his house later that afternoon. It was bigger than ours and had cats everywhere, on every chair, surface and floor.

'It's like a cattery in here,' laughed Peter. 'Would you like a glass of orange squash, kids?'

'Yes please,' we chimed in unison.

We sat at a table sipping our drinks and nibbling a digestive biscuit Anne had offered from an exciting-looking tin. Terrie was pulling funny faces at me while the adults were busy talking. I tried not to laugh as my mouth was filled with squash, but I choked and sprayed squash all over the table.

'Paul!' I heard Mum scold.

'It's okay, Cynth,' Peter said, smiling at me, 'he's just excited. Maybe we should go out into the garden.'

I held Terrie's hand as Peter led us outside into his big grassy garden with a fence around it. There was a small open enclosure in the middle and there were baby rabbits of all colours hopping around. Peter lifted us over and we crouched down. I couldn't believe how small they were.

I felt really excited and I tapped Terrie's arm. 'Can we choose one?' I mouthed silently.

'I think so,' whispered Terrie back.

We started gently stroking them as they jumped past, nibbling grass. My eyes quickly scanned every bunny. I wanted to find mine.

Terrie fell in love with a beautiful fluffy black one. I had my eye on a grey speckled one that was snuffling at my finger. I giggled as the whiskers tickled me.

As we fussed over them, Peter appeared with his camera. Click, click.

'Hey kids, smile for the camera!' he said.

Proud in my favourite Superman T-shirt, I gave him my best grin.

After about an hour of deciding, we finally picked our bunnies. Terrie named hers Sooty and mine was Smokey.

Mum couldn't thank Peter enough. 'You're so kind,' she said repeatedly.

Peter ruffled the top of my head.

'You're more than welcome, Cynth.' He smiled down at us both. 'The look on these twos faces makes it worth it.'

Peter also gave Mum the things we'd need: a small hutch, sawdust, food, hay and a drinking bottle each. We excitedly set up our new pets' home that afternoon.

They were so gentle, and soon grew used to us picking them up and stroking them. Every morning I jumped out of bed and went to poke grass through the wire of the cage as a treat. Then I sat and cuddled mine, rubbing my face against Smokey's silky fur.

A few months after we'd got our new pets, something was wrong with Smokey. He was trying to hop, but looked lopsided. I gently picked him up, but he didn't want to eat any grass and looked miserable.

'Muuuuum!' I cried, calling her to look.

'Hmm,' she said, looking upset. 'He needs to go to a vet.'

We walked to the local vet, carrying Smokey in a box. The vet took one look at his leg and shook his head.

'He's broken it,' he said.

'What?' gasped Mum. 'How did he do that?'

The vet asked if we'd dropped him recently from a height or grabbed his leg in some way. Mum said absolutely not. The vet shrugged and plastered the leg up.

Mum was quiet on the way home. 'Are you sure you haven't been too rough with Smokey?' she asked.

I was completely confused about how Smokey had done this. I kept thinking, maybe it was something I'd done.

My first day at school was traumatic as I hated leaving Mum. The thought of spending all day long without her was too hard and I cried so much in the classroom she had to come and get me. On the second day I was given a pedal bike to race around on in the playground, but when no teachers were looking I pedalled straight out of the gate and home.

'What're you doing here?' asked Mum, her eyebrows shooting up to her hairline.

'I don't like school,' I said simply.

She let me have that afternoon off, but in the morning I was back there. I found it hard to make friends and preferred sitting under a tree or hanging out in the dinner hall, instead of playing tag, or hopscotch or skipping.

My name didn't do me any favours either. 'Duckett, Duckett, there's a hole in my bucket,' kids chanted in the playground if I did dare show my face.

Kids always found it easy to be mean about me. From my scuffed shoes to my second-hand uniform that didn't fit properly. Even the two slices of bread and butter I brought for lunch made kids laugh.

'Is that it?' taunted one little boy, waving a packet of crisps and a Wagon Wheel at me, as he tore off the plastic wrapper of the chocolate biscuit and stuffed it into his mouth.

'Mmmhmm!' he smiled, chomping into the chocolate.

I looked at my soggy white bread and nibbled it miserably. At least I'm not going to be a fat fucker, I thought to myself.

Mum always did her best, but you don't get a lot of choice when you don't have money. Thankfully I started getting free school dinners and quickly learned that making friends with the dinner ladies was the way forward. I loved any food. Lumpy custard with the skin on top was a treat to me.

'Can I have more, please?' I beamed gratefully, as an extra spoonful slopped on my plate.

'You're a good boy,' said the kindly dinner lady. When no one was around I'd get slipped an extra biscuit too; coconut ones with a cherry on top were my favourite.

Having dinner ladies as allies made up for the fact I didn't have many others. While the girls always refused to let me play kiss chase, teachers were more likely to appreciate the nice side of me. I could think up things to get myself out of most sticky situations too.

One escape from school and home was my Nan and Pap's. It was always warm and welcoming, full of hugs, kisses and food, unlike our own. Here I felt loved and normal.

Pap had worked in a shoe factory all his life while Nan kept the house, but she used to tell us all her stories about life in the munitions factory, or when she watched Coventry burning down in a huge bombing raid while close by in the park called 'The Racecourse'.

I could tell Nan loved me by the way her face softened as she looked at me, and how she looked after me and made sure I was never hungry in her house.

'We need to fatten you up, Paul,' she'd frown worriedly. 'You're all skin and bone.'

Nan piled my plate high with favourites like bacon and onion roly-poly, or a dish that was pastry over meat, gravy and veg; I never knew what that was called. Ground rice for afters. Me and Terrie would eat until our stomachs hurt. And Pap was a whiz at making wine; he'd joke he could make anything from the sole of his shoe to potato, raspberry, rose hip, black-berry or any fruit he laid his hands on.

Mum adored her parents as much as we did. Sitting around that table with all of them was the place I felt safest in the world. One person who never came join us there, however, was Dad – something both me and Terrie were glad about.

Dad's own parents, Nin and Bill Duckett, didn't have any more patience for us than he did. They lived just up the road from Nan and Pap, but they couldn't be any more different. When we popped around there we often saw our cousins Nicky and Claire, Dad's sister Ruth's kids, but we all stayed out of Pap's way. He sat by himself in the living room, barking orders at Nan for food or drink. Nan had a terrible temper, too; however, she would at least give us a biscuit when we arrived and she never ever left us alone with Pap Duckett either. Not for a single second.

At the end of November 1979, Dad came home from another working jaunt. For once he came through the door with a proper grin on his face.

'We're going to South Africa on holiday,' he announced. 'It'll be for four weeks over Christmas.'

We both jumped up and down with real excitement. This wasn't something the likes of our family ever did. It seemed too good to be true!

We flew out to Johannesburg and caught a train to Kimberley. It was all scary yet exciting. We stayed with Dad's friends Kevin and Sylvia, who had two kids, James and Anne, a bit younger than us. They showed us the sights, including a diamond mine that completely captured my imagination as we watched the glinting metal sparkle on conveyor belts through metal fences.

Despite being on holiday, Dad was meticulous with time keeping. He was like this at home and now we were away he arranged a very strict schedule. We were up every day for breakfast at 7.30 a.m. on the dot, then out the door by 8 a.m. Dad would time how long everything took. While visiting a museum about the Afrikaaners Dad tapped his watch at the entrance and looked us all individually in the eye.

'You have precisely 40 minutes to look around,' he said.

It wasn't just schedules Dad liked to stick to; the way we looked was important too, despite our hand-me-downs.

'It's not acceptable for girls to slouch or have dangly bits of hair in front of the face, Terrie,' he told her, pulling her shoulders back and yanking back her fringe. 'And when you speak, speak up clear and loudly so we can all hear.'

So her fringe was kept neatly pinned back, and whenever I walked past Dad I'd square my shoulders a little more.

All too soon, we had to go home. Dad was in a foul mood on the trip back. He had been ill most of the holiday. When we arrived back in England, everywhere was covered in snow. Dad didn't talk all the way home. Terrie and me slept most of the way back. As soon as we arrived home we were sent straight to bed. It was so cold.

In the morning Mum said Dad had gone to Portsmouth for work. A few weeks later, when it was the half-term holiday, Mum told us we were going to go and visit him. We had to catch a coach. My insides just clenched at the thought of a coach. I got terribly car sick on the shortest journey and knew I'd end up throwing up on a two-hour trip.

We packed a small bag and set off. I sat next to Terrie. She seemed miserable.

I tried to cheer her up. I patted the seat with my hand. 'Look, bum dust.' I giggled as a cloud of dust erupted from the seat.

She patted her seat, laughing hard. 'Fat bum dust.'

Soon we were lost in laughter and patting seats, when Mum leaned over from behind.

'Pack it in, you two,' she hissed menacingly. 'Just sit quietly.'

'Yes Muuuum,' we chimed in unison, grinning cheekily.

I turned to look at Terrie. She was doing her best not to look at me. I knew all I had to do was catch her eye and she'd start laughing again.

I closed my eyes, trying to sleep, to escape the waves of nausea. I could feel the bile rising just 20 minutes after we set off.

'Oh, not again, Paul,' Mum said as I turned green.

She stood up, wobbling and holding onto seats as she made her way to the driver. 'Excuse me, but my son is going to be sick,' she said.

The driver half turned around.

'Oh,' he said. 'Right, well, grab that newspaper by the side of my seat and make him sit on it.'

'Eh? Sit him on the newspaper?' quizzed Mum with a puzzled look on her face.

The driver gave a laugh. 'Yeah, I don't know why, but it does often stop people feeling sick.'

Willing to try anything, Mum picked up a few sheets and came back.

'Pop this under you, Paul. The driver says it will stop you chucking up.'

She pushed it under my bum. I struggled, thinking I would look silly and not believing for one moment that the paper would make me better. However, the next thing I remember is waking up, having dozed off, the sickness passed as if by magic and I felt much better. When we arrived in Portsmouth we had to stand and wait a few hours before Dad's friend Gerry picked us up.

'Sorry, Cynth.' He looked embarrassed.

He took us to the house where Dad was staying. A few of the construction men rented the place between them. Dad was sitting at the table; he nodded at us both and handed us 50p each. 'Go and entertain yourselves until six.'

Terrie had to check her watch was wound up and said the right time. We both then turned and walked down the hall-way. On the way out we had to walk past a big glass bowl full of 10ps and 50ps. I looked at Terrie and she raised her eyebrow as we both had the same thought: 50p wasn't going to last us eight hours. We'd be starving by the time we got back. Terrie grabbed us a handful of change each and we scurried out of the door.

Side by side we set off for the seafront. First stop was the sweet shop. We filled little white bags with sherbet pips, jawbreakers, fruit salads and chewy peanuts. Then we walked to the seafront 15 minutes away and sat down and gorged ourselves. Next, we went roaming on the rocks, grabbing tiny crabs with our hands and chasing each other. We took off our shoes and socks, rolled up our trousers and ran along the sea edge, splashing each other with the cold salty water.

'I'm cold, Terrie.' I was shivering; I'd got wetter than I had intended. I was also feeling hungry.

'Me too,' agreed Terrie.

We sat on a bench and shared some hot chips. Then we spent the afternoon playing in the amusement arcade.

'Time to go back, Paul,' Terrie said resignedly, looking at her watch. She knew I felt the same and squeezed my hand harder as we trudged back. This time the house was quiet as we turned up. No yelling; that was good.

But as soon as we walked in, one look at Mum, her face red and swollen with tears, told us the visit wasn't going well. Terrie led me off to our room and we quickly got changed. Dad took us to his favourite Chinese restaurant for dinner, but told us we were only allowed crab and sweetcorn soup.

As the pretty Chinese waitress showed us to our seats she looked a bit confused. 'Hello, John,' she smiled, bowing. 'And Karen …?'

Mum visibly bristled, glaring at Dad, as we were ushered to our seats with Dad trying to laugh it off.

I'd heard of Karen a few times by now, but I still had no clue who she was.

Chapter 3

'Last Laugh'

Terrie

$\mathcal{J}$t was in early April 1981, when Dad was away working in Portsmouth, that Mum made an announcement over breakfast.

'We're going to emigrate to South Africa.' She paused, looking at our faces. 'What do you think? It's all happening in September, so Terrie, you won't be starting upper school.'

'Oh, wow!' I was stunned. I glanced over at Paul, trying to read his expression. He was smiling and then began manically leaping around the kitchen. I raised my eyebrow, pretending to look disapproving, and after a few moments joined in.

I was very excited. I'd loved our holiday to South Africa. Anywhere had to be better than grey old Northampton. I wondered if Mum and Dad might be happier in the sunshine too. It also meant a fresh start, maybe a place I could make friends and fit in.

At school, I told all my classmates about it. 'What? The Ducketts are going to live abroad?' laughed one. 'Not that we'll notice you'll be gone.' They just poked fun at me and I could see they didn't really believe that we were moving.

My friend Lisa, who was more of an enemy I kept closer, looked a bit sad when I told her. 'But I thought you were really poor,' she said, looking confused. 'How comes you can afford it?' I shrugged. I didn't actually know the answer to that.

That evening I had a chat with Paul about our fresh start. 'I don't care whether we move or not,' said Paul. 'I don't have many friends anyway and I doubt anyone will miss me.'

'Aww, Paul. What about Mark Millar? I thought he was a friend.' I gave him a hug. But I understood how he felt. I wasn't going to be missed much either. Paul struggled as much as me to fit in; relentlessly bullied about our surname, haircuts and never having the fashionable clothes or the latest toys meant we couldn't join in many games. Thankfully, we had each other, and we enjoyed playing out with bikes and exploring.

That summer, before our emigration, was one of the hottest for years. Dad had flown out to South Africa to try to get a home and job sorted ready for when we flew out, and meanwhile Mum worked all hours to pay the rent and bills. She'd started packing up the house into tea chests, sending what we thought would be important over to South Africa. Other items she sold to friends: the cooker, the sofa, our beds, my lovely bike. Gradually each room in our house became more and more bare as furniture and bits and pieces were shipped off or sold.

'I don't see how I can carry on like this.' Mum was stressed and was sitting chatting to Dad on the phone. He rang once a week, giving her updates on our new life, telling her what needed doing back home in England.

She'd left the shoe company and had got herself a job as a saleswoman for a carpet company called Rainbow Carpets and worked nine to five every day. She couldn't afford childcare so we were left to our own devices all day during the holidays.

Paul and I were getting good at entertaining ourselves. One afternoon Paul, my friend Lisa and myself got hold of a couple of pairs of old tights, cut them at the knee and then pulled them over our heads.

We roared with laughter as we saw each other's squashed noses and hooded eyes. 'Let's pretend to be bank robbers and scare some neighbours,' said Paul, sniggering from behind his tight mask. His nose was puckered upwards like a pig's snout.

At the same time we looked at each other. 'Doris!' we said in unison.

Doris was a little old lady who lived three doors up. She was a proper busybody, always peering out the corner of her window, or twitching her net curtains whenever anyone went past. We crept along to her half-open kitchen window and saw her standing doing some ironing, her head down focusing on the crease she was pressing into a shirt. Arranging our tight masks over our faces we nodded at each other and then leaped up as high as we could. 'Boo!' we yelled.

She screamed and dropped her iron onto the floor in fright, while we ran off around the corner and rolled around on the floor, clutching our stomachs as we laughed hysterically.

Later on in the week rain set in, so we stayed inside to play board games and watch TV. Paul thought it might be fun to make a few prank calls and get a carpet delivered to Mary next door. We'd get a good view from the kitchen window and we could have a laugh at her reaction.

Later, when Mum came home from work, she was not best pleased with us.

'Today my boss stuck the speaker phone on,' she said crossly. 'And I heard two giggling voices ordering a fuzzy blue carpet for Mary next door.'

I tried not to look at Paul. I knew if I just took one look at his face and saw a twitch of his lip or an eye movement I'd laugh.

'My boss asked me if those voices belonged to my kids and I said I was sure it wasn't you as you were with your grandparents all day. But I would know your voices anywhere,' she scolded, a twinkle in her eye.

We all started laughing and we couldn't stop.

'Right,' said Mum, getting her breath back. 'A lock is going on this phone so you won't be able to use it at all.'

'Awwww,' said Paul, realising how much it'd spoiled our fun.

Mum was true to her word. The following day a silver lock was secured into the number one on the dial of the phone. Annoyed at not being able to play wind-ups on the phone any more, Paul started fiddling around with it in the afternoon, pressing the receiver up and down, up and down. Suddenly he froze, the receiver mid-air. I could hear a faint mechanical voice coming from the phone; by this point Paul was staring at it with a wicked grin, which later on I came to recognise as his 'light-bulb' moment.

'Terrie!' he yelled excitedly. 'We can still make calls! Watch this!' He tapped the black plugs in the receiver cradle in a sequence, almost like Morse code, and then I saw it too – the taps corresponded to numbers.

'This is the speaking clock,' I heard the mechanical voice again.

'Paul, guess what?'

'What?' he asked, looking up at me.

'Mary is hungry. I think we need to get her a pizza.'

Giggling our heads off, we called for a pizza for our neighbour Mary and a cab for the lady across the road who seemed to walk everywhere.

When the next phone bill came through, the look on Mum's face was a picture. I felt guilty as I realised our fun had cost her. She was puzzled and had no idea at all how it was so high.

The holidays passed by quickly. We spent hours scrumping fruit from around the estate for lunch; we would antagonise local children and spend hours evading capture, or bike for miles and wander around the estate collecting seeds from weeds like poppies and dandelions to drop into nearby immaculate gardens, just out of boredom. Then we'd walk along to the bus stop just in time to meet Mum getting off, and stop off at the chippy on the way home, where Mum would buy twopence worth of batter bits for us to nibble on.

The date for our emigration drew closer. The worst part of all for me and Paul came about: we had to say goodbye to Nan and Pap. They both held me close, as I breathed in their lovely smell for the last time. I had no idea when I'd see them again.

'Of course we'll come back as often as we can,' said Mum to Nan, cuddling her tightly.

'I wish you could come too, Nan,' I said, tears welling in my eyes.

They would both miss us terribly and vice versa, but I knew we'd write and ring as often as possible. We packed our final personal bits and pieces in a big tea chest to be shipped off to our new home and I said my goodbyes to Lisa. The rooms in our house now echoed as they'd been stripped of everything. All we had left were our suitcases.

On the morning of our flight, Mum clattered about in the kitchen, looking tense. She'd just called South Africa from a neighbour's house as our phone had been disconnected.

Then the doorbell rang. It was Peter. He looked cheery as ever, although his face dropped when he saw how upset Mum appeared.

They spoke in hushed tones, as Mum started weeping.

'Come and use our phone,' he assured her after they'd spoken. Mum left with him and returned looking deathly pale.

She'd been crying. 'We're not going. Not only has your Dad been looking for somewhere for us to live but also his girlfriend Karen. So I've told him we're not coming. Our new life is cancelled.'

We stood in the empty kitchen. Paul and I looked at each other, not quite sure what to do.

'Well, you might as well go to school,' Mum sighed, waving at me. 'Go on, Terrie, get ready.'

She turned and lit up a fag on the gas cooker.

I frowned, upset. The new term had started two weeks earlier. How could I possibly just turn up at school as if nothing had happened when we were supposed to be on our way to the airport, starting a new life?

'But I've not got a uniform,' I began. 'They've all been at school for weeks.'

'Just wear your old one then,' snapped Mum, looking upset.

Peter put his arm around her, so I dropped it. 'Come on,' he said gently. 'Everything will work out. I'll drop Terrie and Paul at their schools if you like.'

Peter dropped me off outside the school gates at 10 a.m. I looked at my reflection in a large window before entering the building. I felt embarrassed. I had last year's uniform on, and my socks looked grey. Then there was my chopped, short, spiky hair. I looked down at my feet and sighed. But I raised my head and took a deep breath as I entered the building. I confidently approached reception but inside my stomach was churning, my heart pounding. Both of my hands were clammy and I was shaking. I explained who I was and why I was there. The receptionist looked at me disapprovingly. I could feel her eyes looking me up and down.

'We have a uniform code. Your Mum should have received a letter.' My anger rose at her nasal tone. 'We have a lost property bin, I suggest you look in there for a jumper.'

She took me to a room where I had to rummage for a jumper that was too big and had worn cuffs, and then she showed me to the classroom for my first lesson. As I walked in alone, I wanted the ground to swallow me up.

'Ah, Terrie Duckett,' sniped the teacher. 'We're honoured by your arrival. You do know term actually started two whole weeks ago and school starts at 8:50?'

Heads swivelled to look at me. I could hear stifled giggles. I blindly found an empty desk to sit at. After class, everyone brushed past me, wearing new cardigans and shiny shoes, looking down their noses at my clothes. Keeping my head down, I found a bench at break time but soon found myself surrounded by kids from the previous school.

'Thought you weren't coming back, Terrie Buckett?'

'Nice hairdo,' one sniggered. 'Did your Mum use a chainsaw?'

'Yeah, you said were going to South Africa. Change your mind, did we?'

'I bet they were too smelly to be let into the country.'

'Terrie is just a little liar. But been caught out now, haven't we?' she smirked.

I ran home in tears. I hated my life, I felt nauseous, my stomach was churning and my head wouldn't stop pounding. Today had been horrendous. How was I going to face them the next day? I didn't understand why Mum had to send me to that hellhole, yet I was happy because I didn't have to leave Nan and Pap. Paul didn't look any happier when he crashed in through the door after school either.

'The kids chanted "pants on fire" all lunch,' he said, miserably.

'I know. We just have to ignore them.'

We sat in my bare bedroom, our voices echoing off the walls.

'I wonder when Dad'll send our stuff back?' said Paul, looking around, lost. 'I've hardly got any toys as it is.'

I gave him a wry smile. Deep down I knew it was unlikely Dad would be worrying about that. Now our belongings had gone I couldn't see him sending them back any time soon.

Mum looked strained when she came home from work. On the verge of tears, she nipped off again to Peter's to use his phone. Then she came back, trembling as she told us to sit down.

'I've told your Dad he's not to come back to this house,' she said, clutching a ball of sodden tissue in her hand. 'I'm divorcing him.'

For most kids it's an earth-shattering statement, but for us it was the one silver lining in this cloud. No more shouting. No more rows.

I suppressed the urge to leap up and punch the air. Paul and I were silent. We looked at each other knowingly. Out of Mum's earshot, Paul and I shared our own reaction to the news.

'Isn't it brilliant?' I squealed to Paul. 'We'll be so much happier without all the arguing.'

Paul shrugged. 'Yeah, I suppose so.'

Despite living in a threadbare house, without the worry of Dad appearing again we felt awash with relief. We played out after school and often came back late for tea. Mum would be standing menacingly at the door, telling us to get inside. We'd have to time running in just ahead of the swipe of the palm of her hand. If we felt like staying up a bit later we did so, reading with a torch under the bedclothes until the early hours of the morning.

Mum sent us on frequent errands.

'Can you go and fill this up?' she'd ask, bringing her empty sherry bottle through to the living room as we watched TV.

Every night either Paul or I would carry the bottle to the off-licence to get a top up and stop at the newsagents for more fags for Mum. After drinking a few glasses Mum nodded off to sleep. Once she'd passed out we'd creep back downstairs from bed to watch TV from the bottom of the stairs, or sit together in my room playing board games and reading books. We were relishing our freedom.

Mum would often kick us out of the house early at the weekends and tell us to come home for tea. We'd get back and she would be passed out drunk on the sofa. Then she started to go out drinking with her friend Cheryl. She'd organise a procession of local teenagers to look after us, as no one would babysit us more than once. We would both slip out of Paul's bedroom window, wobble across the corrugated roof of the shed and walk like cats along the wall before dropping to the grass below. We would then play around the estate for a while and slip back in unnoticed.

Mum would arrive home in the early hours of the morning, a little worse for wear, and wake us up.

'Hey, let's make some crisps!' Mum said, smiling around my doorway.

We rubbed our eyes tiredly, but it was an adventure and we'd join her in the kitchen to slice potatoes super thin and deep-fry them. Mum never had the spare money to buy crisps so it was a big treat as we salted them and sat around munching on them at 2 a.m., giggling. Other times she treated us to 'poor man's doughnuts' – jam sandwiches dipped in batter and fried and then rolled in sugar. They were delicious!

Mum had to work all hours to replace our furniture, as well as pay the rent and bills. The day a second-hand sofa arrived was a big event. The sofa had big soft brown cushions, the kind you can sink into. We were all very excited.

'Wow!' yelled Paul. 'This is great.' He tried to jump up and down on it as Mum told him off.

'Calm down,' she yelled. I understood Paul's excitement. New furniture felt like a new start. Mum decided to pop over to Cheryl's two doors away for a cup of tea and a chat, waving to Jim the council man as she left. It didn't take long for Paul, still hyper from the excitement of the sofa, to start chasing me around with his stretchy Thomas the Tank Engine belt with a metal S buckle.

He whirled it like a lasso above his head. We were both laughing loudly as we dashed about the house. I dived at Paul, making a grab for the end of the belt and just catching it with the tip of my fingers. The belt pinged from his hand, catapulting into the living-room window.

'Paul, look what you've done!' He turned worriedly, looking at the chip in the window. We knew any damage done to our council house had to be paid for.

I looked out the window and saw Jim mowing the lawns with his sit-on mower. An idea formed in my head. 'Don't worry, Paul, I have it all figured.' He looked relieved, though, still in an excitable mood, he pounced on me and we rolled around the floor tickling each other trying to get each other to submit. Mum walked in just as I'd managed to pin Paul down and was making him giggle by pretending to bite the end of his nose.

'Mum, guess what's just happened?'

'What have you done now?' she asked resignedly.

We both look at her innocently. 'We've been good. A stone hit the window as the mower went past. It pinged into the window, chipping it!'

I could see Paul looking surprised out of the corner of my eye and I dared not make eye contact with him. Mum walked over to the window and looked. She didn't seem to notice the chip was actually inside.

'For fuck's sake! I'm not paying to replace it. I'll ring them now and they can replace the window,' she said.

We were just about the poorest people on what was already a poor council estate on the outskirts of town, which didn't help our popularity, so the local kids often gave us grief. Occasionally Mum would stick up for us.

Once, on a Saturday she was hosing the front garden when some of the awful kids from up the road started shouting at us.

'Oi, look, the Fuck-it Ducketts live here!' yelled one.

'Yeah, that's where Terrie and Paul the tramps live,' taunted another.

Without hesitation, Mum turned the hose on them.

'Get lost, the lot of you!' she yelled.

They continued yelling abuse.

'Terrie, put the hose in the house; I'm going to give them the fright of their lives.' Mum passed me the hose.

Then to the kids' surprise, not to mention mine, she charged across the road. They legged it up the alleyway opposite the house, and Mum charged after them. I stood, stunned, then quickly threw the hose into the house and gave chase with Paul, not wanting to miss any action.

As I got to the alleyway, Mum was on her way out. 'Buggers ran off too fast.' She puffed.

She walked back to the house and opened the front door.

'Terrie!'

I heard the shout from across the road.

We ran over and I gulped as I saw the flood of water. Arrggh! I'd forgotten to turn off the tap in the excitement. Paul was busy grinning at me while dancing in the pool of water.

* * *

Sometimes it did feel like the three of us against the rest of the world. We started to feel like a proper family. More of Mum's friends came in and out, but one person was there most days when we got home.

'Hello, Terrie.'

Peter was sitting in the kitchen having a cup of coffee as I came bounding in through the door. I'd heard he'd split from Anne and he now worked as a driving instructor for BSM; we'd often spot his red car with the distinctive cone on around the area.

'How was school today?' he asked, swigging back a coffee.

'Oh, okay.' I raised my eyebrow. No one ever bothered to ask how school was.

'I had PE today, but was the last one to be picked as usual.'

'Sorry to hear that. Give it time,' he assured me.

'It's not because I'm rubbish or anything, it's because I'm not liked.'

Peter listened. 'You just need time to make some new friends.' He slurped the dregs noisily out of the bottom of the cup.

'Maybe,' I replied, opening the cupboards looking to get myself something to eat. As usual, I was starving.

'Mum, have we got any peanut butter in?'

'Don't think so,' she called back. 'Have a look at the back of the cupboard just in case Paul put it there.'

Peter was on the sofa the following afternoon, looking relaxed and comfortable. His face broke into a smile as I came in. He brought up the subject of school again.

'I love chemistry, I find maths easy and we get to swim. They even have a pool.'

Peter listened intently. 'Why are you not looking happy then?'

I looked down at my feet. 'Everyone looks down on me. I don't blame them, to be honest. Mum can't afford to get me the equipment I need for school and Dad isn't here to ask.'

The next day when I arrived home Peter was there again.

'When I was growing up as a lad we didn't have much,' he explained, reaching down the side of the sofa. 'So everything I did have I took special care of. Here's my leather briefcase I kept from school.'

Then he clicked it open to reveal a massive collection of felt pens, biros, rulers and even a protractor – everything I didn't have.

'This is for you, Ted.' He smiled. I was a little taken aback. Ted was the nickname Mum used for me.

'Wow, thanks, Peter,' I said. It seemed like such a kind gesture.

The following day I took it to school. I was teased, but I just held my head high. Peter was only trying to help, even if all his old felt pens had dried up.

Chapter 4

'New Beginnings'

Paul

It was about a week after we realised we'd be staying in England. Terrie came into my room with an urgent look on her face.

'Mum needs money for rent. I heard her talking to Cheryl.' She pondered momentarily. 'I've an idea: we could sell our things to raise money.'

I looked about my sparse bedroom. 'What do you suggest we sell? Fresh air?' I pulled my best face at her.

'We could have a jumble sale, just like at school. They always make money.'

Terrie hugged me. 'Brilliant idea; we can go around the neighbourhood and collect unwanted things.'

'And say they're for charity,' I finished.

The following day after school, Terrie made me dress in my oldest clothes – jeans that didn't quite reach my ankles and a threadbare jumper that my arms were too long for. We stood outside the front door and she told me to close my eyes.

'I'm just rubbing a little dirt onto your face.'

I could feel her cold fingers rubbing on my cheeks. 'Why?'

'Well, we want people to feel sorry for us and give us things we can sell.' I peered through my eyelids and saw she was grinning mischievously.

I trusted her and did as she asked. I took a black sack from her and we biked to the estate next to ours.

As we pulled up to the first house, Terrie turned to me and adjusted my clothing.

'Maybe you should pretend you're hungry. Wait until they go and look for something, then moan to me how hungry you're feeling. It might earn us a biscuit.'

It worked! Terrie had told the lady we were collecting for charity and we came away with some clothing, and with my fantastic acting skills I earned us a couple of biscuits.

We did this every night after school for a week. Soon we had seven black plastic sacks filled with goodies.

Saturday morning, Terrie gave me a piece of cardboard and a big pen and told me to write out the sign for our sale. 'Jumble sale, 10p an item. All proceeds to help Mum pay her rent,' I wrote.

We then left the house carrying all of the sacks and walked to our local newsagents. There we neatly laid everything out on the pavement, set up the sign and waited.

A few passers-by stopped to read the sign and I gave them my biggest smile.

'Paul, I think you should be a salesman when you grow up. I can't believe you talked that lady into buying that jumper. It was hideous.' Terrie smiled at me proudly.

I was pretty good; the words just seemed to flow off my tongue.

We had a good day and the time flew by, then all of a sudden I heard Mum's voice.

'C'mon, you two,' she said, picking up the sign and tucking it under her arm so you couldn't read the writing. 'Let's get off home.'

I quickly shoved the unsold jumble back into the sacks as Terrie handed the money we'd made to our very embarrassed-looking mum.

'We did it to help you, Mum,' Terrie said, as we carried the sacks home.

'Thank you,' she sighed, tears springing to her eyes. 'I'm so proud of you both. I just don't know how I'm going to face the neighbours again.'

A few days later, Peter turned up in his red Metro and he and Mum emerged carrying full shopping bags from Tesco.

'Hello, Paul,' he said cheerfully.

I'd never seen so much shopping. Usually we had to get the bus four miles to the supermarket, or walk. I'd have blisters on the back of my heels by the time we got back. But Mum said the bus fare could be put towards more food, which kind of made sense, so I'd stopped moaning.

Now Peter was helping Mum unpack, placing items carefully on the kitchen counter.

'Where does this go?' he asked Mum, holding a jar of peanut butter.

'Wow!' I cried, dashing over to see what else he'd got. I picked up a bottle of 'magic' ice-cream chocolate sauce called 'Ice Magic'.

'Oooh, you'll probably like that,' said Peter. 'You pour it on ice cream and it sets hard like a shell.'

'Really?' I said, my eyes popping out of my head.

Then I realised something. 'Oh, but Peter. We never have ice cream.'

'You do now,' he grinned whilst rummaging around in a bag, producing the largest tub of vanilla ice cream I'd ever seen.

'Oh, brilliant!' I cried.

That evening Peter stayed for dinner, and for once Mum actually didn't burn the chips. We had proper beef burgers, big juicy ones, not like the cardboard discs we were used to. Our plates were full, piled high with chips and peas. I sat back afterwards, feeling stuffed for once.

'That was lovely, Mum,' beamed Terrie. She was as chuffed as I was.

Mum had colour in her cheeks too, as Peter kept glancing over at her as he ate. Afterwards he helped clear the plates and we heard them laughing as Mum washed up.

'I see what you mean about those two eating a lot. I'm surprised they tasted the food, they ate it so fast. I'd barely started by the time they'd finished.' Peter was laughing. 'Maybe you should get them to wash up, as you cooked.'

'He's nice, isn't he?' I whispered to Terrie.

That weekend Peter was back again. He arrived early as we had breakfast.

'Now, kids,' he said. 'Who'd like a trip to Irchester Park?'

We both burst into smiles. 'Yes!' cried Terrie.

Peter whistled as he helped Mum make sandwiches, and even popped a few bags of crisps and chocolate bars into the bags.

'Curly Wurlys are my favourite!' I said, spying them.

'I know,' Peter chuckled, exchanging glances with Mum.

At the park Peter jumped at the chance of a game of hide and seek with us.

'You count, we'll hide!' I yelled.

Off me and Terrie ran into nearby woods. We knew this park like the backs of our hands, but with Peter it was even more fun. Mum or Dad had never played hide and seek with us. We raced off, finding an overgrown bush to hide in. After crouching for ages, we thought there was no way Peter would find us and decided to wander off. As we walked along, chatting, suddenly someone flew out in front of me, yelling from behind a rock.

'ROAAAAAAR!' cried Peter, flailing his arms as he jumped out. 'GOTCHA!'

I fell trembling on the gravelly floor, my heart racing. Peter had frightened the shit out of me.

'Didn't you see me coming, Paul?' he grinned, a glint in his eye.

That evening when we got home, Peter came into my room as I was getting ready for bed. Usually I pulled my PJs on then raced into Terrie's room, sometimes dropping off as we talked. Often I had nightmares, especially about ants and insects crawling up my curtains. Terrie always had to come in and comfort me, explaining I was seeing the black stitching on the orange-coloured curtains, then I'd follow her back into her room. Most of the time, I'd play a game on her bed and then cuddle up and fall asleep in there. My room was tiny, the smallest in the house. It had a single bed and no room to even walk around it, so it made sense to spend more time in hers. I loved her captain's bunk surrounded by all her pop star posters; I didn't know who they were, but they reminded me of my sister so I liked looking at them.

Just as I was about to leave my room that evening, Peter appeared from nowhere at the door.

'Now, Paul, I noticed you don't have many toys,' he said, eyeing my box of well-used, battered second-hand cars. They were my pride and joy. After all, they were now my sole possessions.

I had managed to retrieve them from the bin where my mum had thrown them prior to leaving for South Africa, muttering something about being too heavy and needing the space in the suitcase for some of Dad's stuff.

'I'm okay, I found my cars in the bin,' I managed to say, with as much enthusiasm as I could muster.

'Well,' continued Peter, 'I've got something that I think you'll really like.'

He left the room and came back holding two boxes.

'This is my Meccano set from Germany and my tin toy collection from when I was a little boy,' he said. 'I'd like you to have them.'

My eyes almost popped out of my head. The first thing I noticed about the unexpected windfall was they all looked brand new, even the boxes. Not like my sorry collection of battered cars.

'I didn't have many toys growing up,' he said. 'So I always looked after them and put them back into their boxes when I had finished. You will look after them and keep them in their boxes, won't you?'

'Yes! Thanks!' I shrieked with enthusiasm. However, at the same time I was thinking how on earth I would be able to play with them and keep them looking brand new.

We sat on the bed, pulling out bits as Peter showed me how to screw the metal pieces together. It was awesome, although I was getting annoyed as he kept putting bits back in the box. I preferred getting everything out and surrounding myself so I could see everything. After a couple of minutes I worked out that if I put each unused piece away in the box straight away, Peter would smile and look happy. After satisfying himself that I would treat the new toys with care Peter ruffled my hair and disappeared.

Shortly after I could hear low voices from Terrie's room, so I slipped out of bed to go in and show her my new toys. Peter was sat on the bed chatting to her.

'Back to your bed now, Paul,' he said. 'It's late.'

'But I always come into Terrie's ...' I began.

'Not now, off you go, back to yours ...' he insisted. 'C'mon, Terrie doesn't want to hang around with a little kid all night.'

I frowned. Terrie never seemed to have minded before now. I tried to catch her eye as I normally would, but she didn't look up at me, or say anything, so I went back to mine, new toys under my arm.

Monday morning arrived and as normal I had to force myself from the warmth of my bed and go downstairs for breakfast. Terrie and Mum were already tucking into some toast and were mid-way through a conversation.

'Grab yourself some toast, Paul,' Mum said, pushing a plate towards me. I started to tuck in and Terrie carried on her conversation.

'Is Peter your boyfriend?'

'No!' cried Mum. 'He's just a friend.'

'Then why did I see him leaving in his car at 6 a.m.?' Terrie asked, to Mum's obvious irritation.

Mum paused, then muttered. 'Oh, he probably just had a driving lesson in the area.'

'Bit early for one,' persisted Terrie.

It didn't bother me if Peter was Mum's boyfriend or not, as long as he kept coming around to see us. It was nice to have someone like Peter around who showed a bit of interest and was like an adult version of a friend; of course, the toys and extra food helped too! I liked having the guy around. Mum clearly did too. She'd stopped asking us to fill up her decanter with sherry every evening and rarely fell asleep on the sofa now; instead she sat watching Peter's pirated videos, holding his hand, laughing and generally being nice to everyone. She still had to work all hours, but thanks to Peter life was on the up again and I began to feel more like I felt a happy kid should.

The weekend arrived, bringing with it Peter and the promise of activities and fun; a refreshing change from the normal routine of playing out and fending for ourselves.

'Why don't we go for a "hot picnic"?' Peter suggested. 'It will be an adventure.' It *was* a bit nippy outside and a picnic wasn't at the top of my list of fun things to do, but he made it sound like it would be fun and I was outvoted anyway.

Mum made some jacket potatoes, a hot flask of soup and tea and we set off in his car. It was a real treat sitting in a car; for me this was an adventure in itself.

The day passed as a blur and before I knew it we were back at home watching a pirated copy of a video Peter brought around. I say watched, but I seem to recall seeing more of the pillow I held to my face to hide some of the more gory parts of *An American Werewolf in London*.

No one had to tell me to get ready for bed that night; I was chomping at the bit to hide under the duvet, somehow thinking it would protect me from stray werewolves. I decided to pop in to see Terrie first, though, as I had done every night for as long as I can remember, for a quick chat and to tell her how much the film had scared me (I knew I wouldn't be able to look at Sam, our dog, in the same way again).

I nipped out of my room and ran across the landing to Terrie's. But just as I got there Peter appeared at the door and blocked it.

'Out of here now, Paul, back to your own bed,' he said.

'Aw, but I wanted to see Terrie …' I began.

'No. It's bedtime now, not playtime. You need a good sleep. Back to your bed.'

I stuck my bottom lip out. 'But it's not fair! Me and Terrie always have a game before bed.'

'Life's not fair!' Peter said, his cheeks becoming flushed.

I started to feel a bit upset, as clearly Peter wasn't happy. I didn't want to upset him; I just wanted to sit on my sister's bed like normal.

My eyebrows knotted together as my lip quivered. Peter crouched down to my level and pointed to my bedroom door.

'I'm not telling you again,' he said. 'Hop it.' Then he seemed to take a deep breath as he started smiling again.

'Paul, I'll come and tuck you in. Come on,' he said, more kindly this time.

I followed him and slipped under the duvet. It felt cold and boring in my room compared to Terrie's. Peter sat and chatted about homework and cars and stuff, and then left.

'Night,' he said, flicking off my light. 'Make sure you stay in here now, Paul.'

I did as I was told, but only to please Peter. Inside I thought it was really unfair.

Always being short of money, Mum jumped at any chance given to earn that little bit extra. The carpet shop where she worked had moved premises and was now much bigger, in a better position, and they wanted to bring in more customers. They offered Mum to work an extra day a week – Saturdays – which to her was a godsend. The problem, as always, was me and Terrie. Nan and Pap were not available to look after us and we didn't want to be left home alone yet another day a week.

'Don't worry, Cynthia,' reassured Peter. 'I'll have them on the days their grandparents can't. They're no trouble at all. Are you, kids?'

He winked as he said it, making me smile inside.

True to his word, the following Saturday he arrived in time to wave Mum off and look after us.

'Right!' he said, rubbing his hands as Mum clicked the door shut. 'What do you two fancy doing today?'

'Riding my bike!' I cried.

'Going to the park!' yelled Terrie.

'How about we do both?' said Peter.

Hours later, after all the fresh air, we slumped in front of the TV and Peter came in to join us. He stood near me and gently poked me with his foot. Laughing, I grabbed him by the knees, pulling him until he toppled.

'Hey, Paul, how strong are you?' he cried, a big smile on his face. 'Go on, do the hardest tickle you can!' he said, pretending to play dead.

I leaped on him.

'Oh ha ha!' he cried. 'You're doing it too hard.' Then suddenly he pinned me down.

'Ha ha! Oh no! Ha ha!' I screamed as he tickled.

Terrie spotted us and bundled on top.

'Right, now you're for it,' said Peter, grabbing Terrie this time. 'Let's get her, Paul …'

After a few minutes we were all lying on our backs, flushed, hot and panting. I couldn't believe how much fun Peter was, for an adult.

With Mum working, the next few Saturdays followed the same pattern: a day out with Peter, followed by a sit down in front of the TV. This was then followed by Peter starting another tickle game which turn into a play fight.

'C'mon, Paul, let's get your sister!' Peter yelled.

We grabbed an arm each of Terrie's and pulled her to the floor. I giggled, as I glanced at Peter, glad to have an accomplice. Terrie always seemed so much bigger than me.

'Let's tie Terrie up!' Peter cried.

I nodded eagerly, as Peter grabbed a reel of masking tape from his coat pocket. Rolling and rolling it around her legs; he only stopped at her knees. Terrie tried to squirm but was held fast.

'Oh, c'mon Terrie, don't be a girl,' Peter laughed as he tickled her sides. I could see she was really struggling – she'd turned the colour of a pillar box – but it was all too much fun to stop.

'Peter, stop it!' she screamed.

I was happy to see my big sister getting it for once, but she didn't seem to be enjoying it so I jumped onto Peter's back.

'I'm saving my sister!' I cried, as Peter almost fell backwards.

I expected him to run around like he'd done before, with me as a piggy back, but instead he fell backwards, almost winding me.

'Uggg,' I grimaced, trying to catch my breath.

Peter's dark hair was in my face. It smelt quite strongly of grease, like my hair did when Mum told me it was time to wash it.

'Paul!' cried Terrie. She sounded panicked.

Peter got up off me, and turned to look as I lay on the floor. 'Aw, soldiers never stay down for that long do they, Paul?'

I struggled up, rubbing my sore chest. Peter was much heavier than he looked. Terrie was by my side now, on her knees, still all taped up.

'You okay?' she asked me anxiously.

'Yeah,' I wheezed.

The rest of the year passed quickly, with us all getting used to each other and settling into our routines and what felt like new lives. The new year came and went and Mum and Peter had a house full of friends over to usher in 1982.

We woke up to a bomb site. Empty glasses everywhere, rubbish, streamers from party poppers, dirty plates and empty bottles decorated every surface. Whilst I looked around in stunned silence, Terrie jumped out from the door. 'BOO!' she shouted.

'Hope you haven't got plans for today, Paul. I think you're on clean-up duty with me – Mum and Peter look a bit worse for wear!'

'PAUL, TERRIE!' I heard Mum shout from the kitchen.

'Coming,' we both shouted back in unison.

We went into the kitchen, aka the local council tip, where Peter was buttering his toast and Mum was humming to herself as she poured his coffee, both of them tired with red eyes.

'We have some news,' Mum pronounced as she beamed ear to ear. 'Peter is moving in!'

'Yeeeeeesss!' I said, leaning back in my chair. All that was going through my head at that point was: food, toys, fun, happy. I looked over at Terrie and she looked dead chuffed as well. 'Great!' she said.

'Oh, I'm glad you're happy,' Peter said, holding Mum's hand on the table top – the type of affection we had never seen our Dad demonstrate. 'I'm really looking forward to being part of this family.'

After Mum did the dishes, we all went for a walk around Irchester Park again and then for a quick lunch at the Berni Inn, stopping in at Tesco's on the way home for a quick shop – proof in my mind that Peter moving in with us could only be a good thing.

The following day Peter arrived with boxes and crates, piling our garage high. Along with umpteen cameras, he had all kinds of Territorial Army equipment: flares, ammunition and even a couple of air rifles.

'Wow' I said, watching as he carefully packed them onto shelves and into metal chests.

'Don't touch these, Paul,' he said. 'They are not toys and can be very dangerous.'

I was transfixed. I longed to join the army one day like my dad and Pap.

Chapter 5

'Family Games'

Terrie

I realised Peter was Mum's boyfriend way before she admitted it, but I didn't really mind. Compared to our real dad there was no awkwardness; Peter was always up for a game or a chat.

Soon after Peter moved in, Mum told us Dad was back in Northampton. We saw him every Tuesday after school, but things were tense. We never felt relaxed; we'd have to play strategy games like chess, Risk and Monopoly or sit and complete 30-minute IQ tests, which he'd expect us to pass every time. Dad would even ask questions while cooking up dinner.

'Who knows what herb this is?' he'd ask, holding up a multitude of green leaves. 'What ingredients go into a curry?'

Dad had all of our family photo albums set out on a shelf, but we weren't allowed to look at them, or take any home. Paul and I had barely any pictures of us as kids and it upset me to think Dad wasn't giving them back to Mum just to be mean.

'He's got our memories and I wish he'd give them back,' I said to Paul. It was hurtful.

But Mum was much happier with Peter than Dad, that was for sure, and that's all that mattered. She'd started to rely on Peter for childcare, too; another strain taken off her shoulders. And the fact Peter had time for us meant the world, even if sometimes he took things a bit too far. He always seemed to have bits of rope or tape to hand and he knew how to tie proper knots as well. I often found myself tied up with rope as they both tickled me. Paul loved it, though.

Earlier in the week he'd floored Paul with what he called the 'salt cellar' move, placing two fingers on Paul's neck and pressing hard. When Paul collapsed, he started crying, but Peter laughed at him.

'Oh, you're a bit of a wimp,' he said. 'I thought you were a big strong boy!'

Paul tried to look brave after that, but I could tell behind his smile he was in pain.

Things calmed down by the evening, thankfully, and we cuddled on the sofa as we watched *Escape from New York*, another of Peter's films. Afterwards, Paul asked me if I wanted a game of 'Guess Who?'.

'Sure,' I said. Our version of 'Guess Who?' was much better than the one set out in the instructions. Rather than play with just one card each, we'd often play with two, three or four. It was much more interesting to try and guess multiple people.

As we set up the board, Peter appeared at the door and told Paul to go to his room.

'But Peter,' I said, 'we were just about to play "Guess Who?"'

Peter grinned at me. 'How about you play it tomorrow? Come on, kids need their own beds or they don't sleep properly.'

'I've told you a few times,' Peter said, as he followed Paul to his room. 'I won't tell you again.'

Peter came back into my room afterwards, sitting back on my bed, making himself comfy. 'Little brothers, eh?' he said.

'Yeah,' I laughed. 'I don't mind, though. Paul's fun.'

It was Saturday the next morning, and Mum had already gone to work, leaving Peter to look after us again.

'Hey Terrie, Paul,' he called. 'Come and join me?'

We scrambled into bed with him, just like we did with Mum when she wasn't working, which was rare these days. I snuggled under Mum's brown candlewick bedspread, bought to match the swirly aertex wallpaper coated in beige paint. She said she'd been going through a 'brown phase' when she'd redecorated after Dad left.

As we hunkered down, chatting, Peter glanced playfully down at Paul.

'Oooh, Paul,' he said. 'I bet you don't have any hairs down there yet, do you?'

Paul shook his head.

Peter reached over and pulled down Paul's pyjama bottoms.

'Ha ha,' Peter cried. 'No, you don't, do you?'

I felt a bit sorry for Paul as he pulled up his trousers, but he was smiling shyly so I hoped he didn't feel too bad.

Then Peter turned to me.

'Bet Terrie has got some, though!' he cried.

Before I could react, Peter reached and pulled down my pyjamas too. Quickly I pulled them straight up as Paul giggled.

'Oooh, yes, I saw some hair down there, did you, Paul?' Peter laughed.

I tried to laugh, but my face burned bright red. Next Peter wiggled his hips and pulled down his own pyjamas.

'Look,' said Peter cheerfully. 'I've got a plaster on my willie!'

I glanced down and saw Peter's privates with a big plaster stuck around it. Paul's hand flew to his mouth and he laughed furiously behind it. He looked to me, his eyes wide. I laughed to join in, but inside squirmed. Why on earth was Peter showing us his willy? Peter laughed the hardest, jiggling himself up and down a little as he looked at me. Then he pulled his trousers up again, still chuckling, as if it was the funniest thing he'd ever seen.

47

And then just as quick he changed the subject. 'Right, kids, let's go and get some breakfast. Terrie, go and get some toast on.'

We rushed off to get dressed and quickly munched our way through a pile of Marmite on toast. I didn't think twice about what happened; it had been a bit weird, but Peter was always a joker and I was already looking forward to the day we had planned in the park.

We got home that afternoon exhausted from racing our bikes around the park. Peter started tickling Paul again, but this time Paul ended up running off to his room in tears after he'd crunched his fingers together, squeezing the joints very hard until they cracked. I ran off after him to his bedroom and found him in tears.

'I'm not gonna play with Peter any more,' he sobbed angrily. 'He hurts me every time.'

'I'm sure he doesn't mean to, Paul,' I began. Although, as I was speaking, I could feel the aches in my knees from where Peter had wrapped a rope too tight.

'Maybe it was an accident. You know how we get excited playing "bash up" and we accidentally hurt each other.'

Paul didn't look sure. 'Maybe,' he said hesitantly, 'but you don't accidentally crunch my fingers so hard that they feel like they're broken.'

Mum came home around 6 p.m. and cooked fish fingers and mash for us all. As we ate dinner that night, Peter was rather quiet. He stood up and went to the kitchen cupboard. I thought he was just getting some ketchup but he returned with a jar of peanut butter. He twisted open the lid and slowly moved it around the room so we could all see inside.

'Can you see what's been done to it?' he asked.

'What?' I replied, confused. It looked like a fairly full jar to me, which made sense, as Mum had only been shopping days earlier.

On a closer look, inside there was hardly any peanut butter at all. It had been purposely scraped at such an angle, so it was only left on the glass sides, so it looked full.

Mum's lips tightened into a thin line. 'This isn't on, kids,' she said, exasperated. 'Which greedy little fucker has cleared the jar out? One of you little shits has scraped the jar so it still looks full up. You know how little money we have.'

Knowing it wasn't me, I thought: 'Paul, you little pig!', but then we both started speaking at once.

'It wasn't me,' I gasped.

'Nor me,' frowned Paul.

Mum sighed. 'Well, I didn't do it and I'm pretty sure Peter has got better things to do!' she said. 'I think you should both know better.'

Peter carefully screwed the lid of the jar back on.

'Neither myself nor your mother will accept this kind of devious behaviour,' he said slowly. 'You have three meals a day and helping yourself to things like this is just not acceptable.'

We said okay and slipped off into the living room. The air vent in the kitchen meant you could hear everything in the living room and vice versa. The adults didn't appear to realise this though, and we clearly heard Peter still talking to Mum.

'You can't let them pull stunts like that, Cynth. I mean, money is tight all round, isn't it? There's no need for them to be so greedy and finish off food like that. They need to learn to share.'

We pretended we'd not heard them when they came into the living room.

'Right, who wants to watch a film?' asked Peter. 'And shall we have some ice cream too?'

Paul jumped up on the sofa, kicking his legs high. 'Yeah!'

I rolled my eyes at Paul, he could be so excitable.

After the film I helped Mum clear up as Peter went upstairs to have a bath.

'Cynth, we've run out of soap,' he yelled.

'Ted, would you be a good girl and pop up and take him this new bar?' said Mum, passing some Imperial Leather from under the sink.

I took it from her and ran upstairs. Opening the bathroom door ajar I slid my arm in, holding the soap so Peter could grab it from me.

'Thanks,' he called. But he didn't take it. So I moved my arm in further, twisting my head in the other direction. The last thing I wanted to do was invade Peter's privacy. But he still didn't reach for it.

'Hurry up, I'm shrivelling up,' he laughed.

So I pushed open the door and moved a bit closer in, craning my neck towards the hall so I didn't see anything I shouldn't.

'Don't worry,' said Peter. I wasn't able to hold the position any longer and stepped inside slightly to quickly throw him the soap. As I glanced in Peter hauled himself half out of the bath, his privates for all to see.

Quickly, I slammed the door shut. Peter was chuckling to himself.

'Thanks, Teddo!' he said.

I felt extremely embarrassed. At 13, anything about nudity or sex made me cringe. Mum had already bought me my first bra; Paul had laughed saying my shoulder blades were bigger than my boobs. She'd also shoved a book about birds and bees under my bedroom door. I didn't really understand it, so I tossed it in my bottom drawer out of sight.

We were settled in the lounge, a film just about to start, when Peter pulled out a strange-looking box and plugged it into the back of the TV.

'It's a computer game,' he said. 'Tennis.'

We watched, mesmerised, as he played this game with two straight lines for bats and a flicking blip for a ball.

He handed us a joystick, explaining how it worked.

'This is brilliant,' I said, as I was busy trying to beat Paul.

'I know,' said Peter. 'Good, isn't it?'

Peter was always bringing new equipment into our house. He said he liked all the latest technology as the computer world was changing so fast he had to keep up. We had video cameras, cameras, dark-room equipment and loads and loads of cassette tapes and videos all neatly piled in the garage now. Alongside that was his army stuff too. He also always kept a camera on the dining room table. We assumed it was just in case he saw something fun to film, but I never saw him put it on.

Chapter 6
'Eye of the Storm'
Terrie

*O*ur new routine was the same every night. At eight o'clock I'd get into my nightie, turn off the light, then Peter appeared in the doorway, softly knocking.

'Fancy a little chat, Ted?' he asked when he came in one night.

'Sure!' I said, budging up against my headboard.

He perched in his usual spot, making himself comfy.

'Terrie,' he asked me. 'Can you tell me how you're feeling about growing up?'

I squirmed a bit. What did he mean?

'Have you noticed any changes in your body?' he continued, casually, as if just asking me about the science homework he'd helped with the previous night.

I pulled my covers up a little. Girls in my class talked about sex sometimes in whispers behind their books in lessons, but it seemed strange Peter had brought it up.

'Do you understand what I'm talking about?' Peter persisted.

'No,' I replied.

'Well,' he continued, 'when you become a teenager, hair will grow under your arms and down below. Do you have any hair down there?'

I didn't know what to say, but at the same time I didn't want to lie.

'Yes,' I whispered. Why did Peter need to know, though?

'Can I see it?' he asked.

'No!' I said, my voice rising with fear. I clamped my legs together, my heart racing. What was he on about?

Remaining silent, I watched him push a hand under the bedspread. He slid it up under my nightie and ran his fingers into my pants. I wanted to be sick.

'Your breasts will get bigger too,' he said, softly, moving his other hand up to touch them.

I could feel myself welling up in tears. I wanted to scream and push him off, but I feared upsetting him and this happy new home life we had. Instead my body froze.

A smile curled on his lips as he finally pulled his hand away.

'Goodnight, Ted,' he said, as if nothing had happened.

I buried my head in my pillow, guts churning. Why had Peter done this? Peter was a nice man. Wasn't he? My mind whirred with confusion and horror, as hot tears soaked the sides of my pillow. I squeezed my eyes shut trying to pretend it never happened. Except I knew it had.

The next morning Peter acted like absolutely nothing had gone on. So I pretended it hadn't either. All I could hope was it wouldn't happen again. But that night, just as I was about to turn my light off, his shadow appeared in my door frame again. I slid across to the far side of the bed as he reached up to my captain's bunk. In silence he lifted up the covers and swiftly pushed a finger inside of me.

'When you become a woman,' he said, his eyes half closed, 'a man can slide things inside you.'

I was so tense with horror I could barely speak.

'Stop!' I managed to say.

'Do you like it?' he asked.

'No!' I hissed, rigid with fear.

He ignored me, and carried on.

'I'm going to tell Mum,' I gasped, tears streaming down my cheeks. 'She won't like you doing this.'

'Ah, Terrie,' Peter said, keeping his hand down below. His eyes opened wide now. 'That's not a good idea. You know how much your mother struggles with money. If she loses me she'll more than likely lose your home. And then you'll be separated from Paul and your mum and probably be put into care.'

I started sobbing as he suddenly pulled his hand away.

Paul wasn't allowed in my room, Peter had put a stop to that within six weeks of moving in, so his visits were uninterrupted and my head hurt with confusion as he appeared the next night and the next. I so badly wanted to scream and stop him, but I felt too ashamed. He was always gentle with me, like it was a perfectly normal thing to do. None of it made sense at all.

Each time I lay awake for ages afterwards not knowing what to do. I couldn't tell Mum. What if she didn't believe me? Plus she'd never been happier.

The feeling of helplessness on the fourth night of his visits made a rage I'd never experienced before bubble up inside me. I tried and tried to stop him. After he'd left my room tears flowed as I opened my mouth, barely recognising the sound of my own voice as it boomed into the gloom of my bedroom.

'I hate Peter!' I shrieked. 'I. HAAAAATE. YOOOUUUU. PEEEEEEEETER!'

Repeatedly I screamed until exhaustion took over.

I half expected someone to come rushing or at least yell upstairs to see what was wrong. But no one did. No one heard my cries and nobody asked me what was wrong.

Over breakfast now, I saw Peter in a different light. The way he combed his greasy hair to the side reminded me of Hitler, and his pungent BO and stale coffee breath turned my stomach. His teeth were a funny brown colour, stained and rarely brushed properly.

I'd never noticed these things before, even during the play fights, but since his bedroom visits, touching me, he made me feel nauseous.

I had art first thing that Friday morning – my favourite subject – but I couldn't find my homework anywhere. After a quick scout around, I was starting to panic.

'Oh, where is it?' I sighed, hunting under some old newspapers.

Paul was playing with his cars on the table and Mum was looking for her door keys.

'I'll be home late tonight, kids,' she said, swigging down her coffee.

Peter was sitting very still at the table like an eye in the whirlwind of our family life. He'd been quiet all morning.

'Mum,' cried Paul suddenly. 'Have you seen my PE kit?'

Mum looked harassed as she glanced at her watch.

'I'm going to be late now,' she sighed.

'Right,' said Peter, suddenly. 'The mornings are a bit of a mess, aren't they, kids? There's no structure. We need to work out a routine.'

Mum nodded. 'That's a good idea, Peter,' she agreed.

I could tell Mum had had enough of telling us off and nagging us. We often ignored her, as kids do.

'How about we set a timetable?' suggested Peter. 'So we all know where we are?'

I shrugged, and looked at Paul; he was busy looking for his PE kit.

'Well, I think it could work,' agreed Mum. 'And Paul, your PE kit is still in the washing machine, so we'll have to wash it later.'

Terrie Duckett and Paul Duckett

I didn't think anything more of Peter's idea until we got home. I opened the front door, chucked my bag on the floor and then flopped on the sofa as usual. I was knackered. I'd spent my lunch hour evading a group of spiteful girls and then I'd had to run all the way home as I'd been held up by a teacher talking about homework.

To take my mind off it all, I flicked on a cartoon. Then the door opened, and it was Paul, who kicked off his shoes and plonked himself next to me on the sofa.

'Want one?' he said, offering me one of his gobstoppers.

'Nah, it's okay, I've got some Black Jacks left.'

We often spent our pocket money from Nan and Pap on sweets. I pulled one out of my pocket and started chewing on that instead.

We heard a key in the lock. It was Peter. Sam started whining by his lead as he came through the door.

'Anyone taken the dog for a walk?' Peter said, as Sam's big eyes gazed up at him.

'No,' we said in unison. 'Mum usually just opens the back gate for Sam to have a run around.'

Peter rolled his eyes and then laid out pieces of paper and pens neatly on the table. 'Turn the TV off and come out to the kitchen.'

'Right,' he said, once we were both sitting at the kitchen table. 'I want you both to organise a routine. Write down a time when you'll be up, when you'll get showered, then when you'll be dressed, what time breakfast is, etc.'

It seemed almost fun, so I wrote down my list.

7 a.m.: Wake up
7.15 a.m.: Have a shower
7.40 a.m.: Get dressed
7.50 a.m.: Have breakfast

7.55 a.m.: Clean teeth
8 a.m.: Get school bag sorted
8.10 a.m.: Leave for school

That looked about right to me. Paul could get up after me and then we'd both have time for a shower and plenty of time to walk to school.

Obviously, we wouldn't stick to an exact rota every day, but it was a good idea to work out who could get in the shower first. I usually annoyed Paul by jumping in ahead of him. I held it up for Peter to look, but as his eyes scanned my words he shook his head vigorously.

'No, no, Terrie,' he tutted. 'You've only put approximate times. You can shower quicker than that. It doesn't take five minutes to brush your teeth. No, this is all wrong. I want something more like this.' He picked up the pen and started writing furiously.

6.45 a.m.: Up
6.47 a.m.: Bathroom to shower
6.50 a.m.: Exit shower and immediately clean teeth
6.51 a.m.: Go to bedroom and put on clothes; tidy room
7 a.m.: Make breakfast

'After your breakfast, you will immediately clear away the dishes and do the washing up. Paul, you can get up at 7 a.m. and follow the same timetable. As Terrie washes up you can dry,' he said, his words firing like a machine gun. 'Following this, you can do the hoovering, and clean the floors so I'm not walking through your crumbs all day.

'One of you can walk the dog and the other can make coffees for myself and your mum and bring them to our room. Is this understood?'

At the bottom he also wrote a list of chores we each had to do.

'It's only fair,' he said. 'Takes the pressure off your mum.'

I felt uneasy, as he tapped his pen on the pad. He looked very pleased with himself, but it just made me feel more uncomfortable.

'This is a proper timetable,' he said thoughtfully. 'Minute by minute. Every second counts. No time is wasted.'

I opened my mouth to speak, but no words came out. Inside all I could think was: What the hell?

Still wanting to please Peter, we nodded, but in the lounge as we were playing a game of Mouse Trap we spoke honestly.

'What the fuck's all that about?' I said angrily to Paul.

Paul was furious too. 'I don't like it either, Terrie.'

But we both knew we'd have to go along with it. There was something about the way Peter had spoken that made us know we weren't to complain.

I overheard Mum talking to Peter through the air vent as she made him a coffee.

'Look,' she said. 'I know you're doing your best, and I appreciate it so much. But try not to be so hard on them. They've been through a lot the past year.'

Peter sighed. 'Of course, Cynth. I'm just learning as I go along.'

A little later, as I was walking out of the bathroom, Peter appeared in front of me.

I stepped back as he reached out with both hands to tickle me. He was smiling, but there was a gleam in his eye that I didn't like.

'Stop it,' I snapped. As he brushed the sides of my breasts, I just wanted him to leave me alone, but he seemed determined to make me join in. At that moment, Paul appeared, but just as quickly he glanced over and disappeared. He no longer took part in Peter's tickling games; I wished he would. I hated Peter being anywhere near me, especially when I was on my own.

I wasn't looking forward to Monday morning and the start of our new schedule, but Mum seemed to support Peter's idea.

'They might not make it to the very second, Peter,' she said. 'But thank you for helping.'

'No problem,' said Peter. 'You just focus on getting ready for work in the mornings and I'll deal with the kids wherever possible.'

'That is good of you,' Mum said, looking relieved.

That Monday, Paul and I raced around, bumping into each other on the landing as our paths crossed as we cleaned our teeth and showered. But we were up and out of the house fast and things were a bit more organised even if we did have to rush.

Back home that afternoon we had our jobs as Peter had assigned. I was to do the hoovering and washing up, while Paul had to walk Sam. Peter had left a pile of plates and stained coffee cups from his day at home.

But nobody was home when we got back so we decided to relax for a bit.

'Guess as long as we get the jobs done by the time he gets home it's fine,' I said to Paul. He nodded, heading off to the kitchen to get a drink. I was famished, so I made a beeline for the kitchen too, raiding the cupboards. Then Paul and I had a bit of a chat as we looked at the schedule.

'Best get on with this then,' I said, munching. By the time Peter was back, the dog had been walked, the cleaning was done, and we'd started our homework.

'How did your schedule go?' Peter asked, as soon as he came in.

'Fine, thanks,' I nodded.

That week, we felt things ran like clockwork, apart from Peter complaining about our cleaning. We both really hated how fussy he was: he'd carefully examine every item that had been washed up and he would put the whole lot back in the sink if he found anything with a speck on. He'd also wander around, his finger lightly dragging over surfaces searching for dust. We'd have to restart the jobs if they weren't to his satisfaction. By the end of the week we were relieved it was Friday. Time to relax at last.

As I washed up, Paul dried. It was the last thing on our schedule for the week, thank goodness. Paul couldn't resist having a mess around as we finished the last plates, flicking the tea towel around. I yelled at him to stop, but threw some bubbles from the sink at him when he didn't.

'Terrie! Paul!' cried Mum. 'Will you quieten down.'

'Sorry,' I laughed, as I dodged an incoming flick from Paul.

Then Peter appeared at the door, a frown on his face.

'How did the schedule work out this week?' he asked. 'Did you stick to it?'

Paul and I dutifully nodded.

'Really?' pressed Peter.

'Yes!' we said, nodding in unison.

'Can you please come into the living room?' he said. 'You too, Cynth.'

Puzzled, we all followed him. Paul and I exchanged confused looks.

We sat dutifully on the sofa facing the TV.

'What's this about, Peter?' asked Mum.

'Now, kids,' started Peter, smoothing his moustache. 'Did you stick to your specific timetable?'

'Yes,' I said. Though in my head I was thinking, not quite the way you wanted me to.

'What about you, Paul?' he asked.

'Erm, yeah, me too,' said Paul, glancing nervously at me. 'We followed it exactly.'

'Exactly, hmm,' said Peter. 'So you got home on Monday, came straight in and did the hoovering and dusting, did you, Terrie?'

My heart beat a little faster. I felt a bit nervous now; something wasn't right.

'Yes, of course!' I said, shifting uncomfortably on a cushion.

'Okay,' smiled Peter. 'Let's see, shall we?'

He picked up the remote and pressed 'play', his eyes not leaving my face.

We all turned and watched the TV as an image of me walking into the kitchen flickered onto the screen.

I gasped audibly, as I realised what Peter had done. The video camera that always sat in the same position in the dining room wasn't just there collecting dust. It had been carefully positioned for a reason – for Peter to secretly film us.

'Oh for goodness sake, Peter,' Mum said, laughing nervously. 'How utterly ridiculous.'

'Just wait,' said Peter, holding up his hand, his eyes still fixed on me.

There I was on the screen: I slung my bag on the floor and dashed to the kitchen cupboard. Flinging it open, I pulled out two slices of bread, crumbs flying everywhere. Then he forwarded to me smearing on ketchup and brown sauce, my favourite sarnie when no one was in. I knew Peter didn't draw a line on either of these bottles, so I could help myself. Next I was browsing through a book, looking carefree, like I had all the time in the world.

As this all unfolded in front of us, I sat with my hand over my mouth. I kept glancing at Paul. I could see the fear in his wide eyes.

'So,' said Peter, pausing the tape. 'You're lying, aren't you?'

I nodded imperceptibly, my mind racing. Why on earth was this man filming us in our own homes? I felt violated, I felt sick.

Next up, Peter turned to an uneasy-looking Paul.

'And what about you, Paul? Did you take the dog straight for a walk?'

Paul looked panicked.

'Yes, I did walk Sam!' he tried to protest.

'Right,' said Peter officiously. 'Let's see what Paul actually does, shall we?'

Peter pressed play and we watched as Paul rushed in from school, raced to the sink to get a glass of water to drink, grab a slice of bread from the bread bag and flop onto a chair before disappearing upstairs. Peter fast-forwarded the next few minutes, until finally Paul picked up the dog lead.

By now I was incensed. How dare he secretly film and humiliate us like this? My guts churned just like they did when he'd visited my bedroom at night. It felt like there was no escape.

But that wasn't the end of it.

'Shall we look at Tuesday's rota now?' he snapped. 'Terrie, what was it you did when you got in from school?'

'I can't remember,' I said. I didn't want to be accused of lying again.

'Think harder then,' said Peter.

'Erm, I might have made myself another sandwich?' I offered. I'd no idea what I'd done.

'Is that on your routine?' Peter demanded, waving it in my face.

'No,' I almost whispered.

Peter went through each day methodically, looking at the schedule we'd drawn up and fast-forwarding to the relevant days. Other scenes showed me and Paul using dining room chairs to peer into cupboards in case Mum had hidden treats at the back. Then we opened the two doors leading from the living to the dining room and ran around madly, playing chase with each other.

We were, by all accounts, just acting like ordinary kids. But suddenly, thanks to Peter, our every movement looked like we were being naughty.

I couldn't stand it any longer.

'That's an invasion of our privacy!' I cried, standing up.

'Well, obviously you need it invaded when you can't be trusted to do as you're told!' Peter yelled back.

'What?' I gasped. 'We still got the jobs done. We still did as we were told.'

'Now you're just being argumentative,' Peter snapped.

Paul and I just stared at him. It was both awkward and surreal. This was mind games, beyond anything we'd experienced before. I looked at Mum, pleading with my eyes for her help. Thankfully, she threw her hands in the air and stood up.

'Okay, Peter,' she said. 'That's enough. You've made your point. Kids, you will try harder now?'

Paul said he would, but I couldn't bring myself to respond. Instead I just glared at Peter.

That night he came upstairs again and touched me. After he left, I lay there again in tears. I was angry, I was scared, and I was full of rage.

'I HATE PETER!' I screamed. 'I HATE PETER! I HAAAAATE PETER! I HAAATE PEEEEEETEEEEER!'

But afterwards all I got was the same response: complete and utter silence.

Chapter 7

'A Dog's Life'

Paul

The memories of being happy when Mum told me and Terrie that Peter was moving in were fading fast. The feeling of being in a family where I could live the life of an eight-year-old, carefree, loved and having fun, was also disappearing. Every night now for the last few weeks Terrie had screamed, shouted and cried. I felt for her but didn't want to go in just in case Peter had a go at me and I ended up being the one screaming and crying. It felt selfish and I did feel guilty, but Terrie was bigger and older than me, so I thought she'd be able to take whatever it was better than me.

It seemed to really wind Peter up if I went into Terrie's bedroom, not just in the evenings, but even during the day at weekends. I didn't get it, though. The less time I spent with Terrie in her room, the more Peter did. A few months before I would have felt upset, but now I was actually beginning to be happy. It came down to a simple equation: the more time spent with Peter the more you were likely to be in pain and crying; the less time, the happier you were.

Mum said it was hard for us to accept having a new father figure in our lives, and it was normal to be a bit overwhelmed and rebel against the rules, but it didn't feel like that. We just couldn't do anything we wanted any more. She said we'd get used to it soon, but I think she missed the point – we didn't want to get used to it.

I'd often come home to find Terrie and Peter having play fights. I didn't join in any more as Peter was a lot rougher with me than when we first played games and I'd inevitably end up getting hurt from an extra hard pinch, a foot in the stomach or a stray fist. I assumed Terrie still found it fun, though.

Peter's secret camera stunt really upset us; now we had to look over our shoulders and follow a strict routine every day of every week of every month. We already felt like servants and, while we had an ever-growing list of jobs to do, Peter just lay on the sofa watching films and eating.

For the next few days I kept checking to see if the camera was back but it had disappeared and I hoped that him recording us had been a one-off. Instead of worrying about it I focused on remembering what jobs I needed to do so I could catch up with TV after. If I was this busy at the age of nine I didn't want to be 10!

The next day I took Sam for a walk, but as I returned Peter was waiting for me with a now familiar disapproving look behind his glasses.

'Paul, that wasn't a long walk,' he said gruffly. 'Come with me.' He grabbed his coat and keys. 'I'll show you exactly where you need to walk Sam every day.'

He walked down the long alley that started across the road from the house and then around the corner of another one until we reached an oval of grass on the estate.

'Now,' he said, pointing around the area. 'I want you to walk Sam around the perimeter of grass three times, and only then can you come home.'

He tapped his watch. 'That should take at least 12 minutes. Go.'

It was so precise and exact. You freaky twat, I thought to myself. The next thing he'll be doing is marching me around, 'Left, Right, Left, Right, Left, Right, Left.'

The following evening Peter looked a bit grim-faced as we ate our beef burgers and mash.

'Paul,' he said. 'Did you remember to walk the dog?'

'Yes!' I beamed. 'I did!' I had ensured I had followed the route exactly and even delayed going home by 30 seconds to make the walk 12 minutes exactly.

'Brilliant,' said Peter, although he didn't look too thrilled.

We carried on cutting up our food. I noticed Terrie was quieter than usual.

'Did you also hoover the sitting room?' Peter asked.

'Oh,' I replied, stabbing my fork into my burger. 'No, I forgot about that.' I was desperately thinking of when he had told me to do it, but for the life of me I couldn't actually remember him telling me to hoover.

'Hmm, okay,' smiled Peter. 'Tomorrow you'll need to do the hoovering and, to make up for forgetting today, dust the living room too.'

'Okay,' I said, glancing at Terrie. But her eyes were looking straight at her plate.

'And don't forget to walk the dog and do your homework,' he added.

I stared momentarily at the ceiling. Hoovering, dusting, dog walk, homework, I recited to myself. No time in there to watch TV or play with my toys.

'Yep, got it,' I said.

The next afternoon I raced home knowing I'd be busy; I wanted to get the jobs done as fast as possible so Peter would have nothing to moan about. I worked though my rota, did the hoovering, ensuring I moved everything to get underneath and even put the soft brush on so I could get the cobwebs off the top of the walls. Exhausted, I flopped down at the kitchen table and did my homework.

Over dinner later that evening, I expected Mum and Peter to be chuffed. But instead, Peter looked at me as if I'd done something else wrong.

'Did you do all your jobs?' he asked.

'Yep!' I replied without hesitation.

'No you didn't,' he said, punching the air with his index finger. 'What happened to the dusting?'

I smacked my head with my hand.

'Oh no!' I said. 'I forgot again.'

'Oh no!' Peter mocked. 'Yes, you forgot, didn't you? That's the second time now, Paul. I think you're forgetting on purpose because you're too lazy to help around the house.'

The following day I had my 'normal' rota – this list already had over 20 items on and at the end of the rota was a new line: *Check with Peter if there are any other things he wants you to do*.

Great. That last line means we can never technically finish our jobs.

With extra determination, I did everything on the list, paying particular care to get each and every job right. I didn't want him to have any excuse to keep adding to it!

Tea time arrived and the four of us assembled around the table. But before I'd even managed to fully sit down, Peter blurted out: 'You didn't do the washing up. You didn't put the rubbish out. And you didn't check with me to see if there were any other jobs that needed doing.'

I just stared at my plate. Now I knew I had done the washing up and I couldn't ask about other jobs because he had only been in the house 10 minutes.

Putting the rubbish out – eh, what the fuck? That's not on my list and he hadn't told me to do it, I thought furiously.

'I did the washing up. I put a tick by it,' I said, pulling the rota from my pocket and passing it over for him to look. 'I don't remember you mentioning putting the rubbish out and you weren't here to ask if there were any other jobs,' I offered, feebly, already knowing the outcome.

'You missed my coffee cup that I left in the bedroom,' Peter informed me happily. 'And you're using an outdated rota. The correct one is stuck on the fridge. It includes the rubbish, and you could have asked about additional jobs before you sat down to eat.'

I glanced at the fridge and a new rota had appeared – it wasn't there 10 minutes ago. It felt like he was doing things just to make it look like I was lazy, forgetful or just useless. I'll just have to be more careful and try and stay one step ahead of him, I thought to myself.

I started lifting the first forkful of food to my mouth when Peter started again: 'Right, Paul, here's a notepad and pen for you. You need to write down the tasks that I ask. Then we'll both know where we are, won't we?'

I stared at the notebook. I couldn't be bothered with this on top of the rota, but I had no choice.

'Okay,' I sighed, taking it from him.

'Aw, Paul,' said Mum. 'If you didn't keep forgetting you wouldn't need it. Why don't you just listen a bit more?'

'I'll try harder, Mum,' I promised, but inside I was thinking, am I the only person that can see Peter is making stuff up to make me look bad?

Terrie was given a notebook too. They were pocket-sized, so, Peter said, we could keep it on us at all times. As we would find out later, forgetting to have the pocket book on us would carry its own punishment.

Days later, my notebook was filled with tasks. Peter was constantly coming up with things. He said the bathroom windows needed cleaning, the skirting boards dusting and the kitchen cupboards wiping – chores I'd never thought about before. I was sure Mum didn't even do them. But by the third day I'd forgotten to clean the bath, another job suddenly added.

'Right,' said Peter to Terrie and myself before Mum got home. 'Every ACTION has a REACTION, remember that. So in this instance you are both going to do some lines.'

'Lines?' I gasped. Lines? This wasn't school.

But Peter already had a pen and paper to hand and placed them in front of us, the pen at a precise horizontal angle to the paper.

'I want 500 lines,' he said, politely. 'I must do what Peter tells me because Peter is always right.'

I looked at him, swallowing hard. This sounded mental. But he looked quite calm, like it was the most usual request in the world.

'It's for your own benefit,' he said. 'Help you both to remember that if I say something then it needs doing.'

I sat down and started writing them. I was keen to get back in his good books again just to minimise further punishments.

I looked at Terrie; she looked furious. 'Stinky German twat,' she mouthed, mock-saluting behind Peter's back.

It made me giggle.

After about 50 lines, my hand started aching. So I decided to write the words down in columns instead. All the 'I's first, then the 'must's and so on. Terrie saw what I was doing and decided to do the same.

'Finished!' I said, almost proudly. Terrie finished a few moments later.

Peter picked them up and ripped up the paper in half, glaring at us over his glasses.

'I said write lines, not columns. Do not disobey me. Who's idea was this?'

'Mine,' I said.

'Write them again, but this time 600 times,' he ordered. 'I must write lines not columns when I'm asked to write lines.'

Sobbing, I picked up the pencil. Terrie protested and Peter ordered her upstairs.

My hand was killing me, my eyes ached, and by the time I'd finished I felt exhausted.

As I went upstairs to bed, I heard Mum cry out; she'd found the sheet with the lines on.

'Peter!' she snapped. 'Do you really need to hand out strings of punishments like this?'

'Do you want them to learn or not?' Peter replied.

The new notebook and schedule system were a pain, but we managed to scoot around doing our jobs as fast as possible, or we'd get in first and relax for a bit and then do them. Thankfully, there was no sign of the camera again. Then, one Saturday evening, as we were watching *Blockbusters*, Peter had another suggestion:

'Now then,' he said, wiping his moustache with his fingers. 'As part of the new routine, we're going to have a weekly accounts review.'

'Accounts what?' Terrie asked, scowling.

'A review, so we all know where we are,' Peter said.

'Eh?' I said. I'd no idea what he was on about.

'Every single penny you have, I want to know about it. So no money is wasted.'

'But we hardly have any money anyway!' I cried.

'I want to know what you have in your piggy banks, what pocket money and birthday money has to be accounted for too. And if you spend anything it needs to be noted down.'

He drew lines on a piece of paper to show us how he wanted his system to be operated. We had to keep track of exactly what money we had and what we spent, and then every Friday Peter would carry out a review.

'But I only ever buy the odd magazine or 10p mix,' Terrie said.

'Okay, well then, that's all that will be in the book,' said Peter.

'What about birthday money?' Terrie asked. We were always allowed to spend our birthday money on whatever we liked.

'Half of it goes in the bank, the other half can be spent,' Peter continued.

'But we don't have bank accounts,' I said.

'Well, you can open one at the weekend,' Peter retorted. 'I want you to count out a pound from your piggy banks. That's all you need to open an account. You need to learn how to save.'

That Saturday we went down to a branch of Midland and I felt quite grown up as they asked for my signature. I was also thrilled with my free Midland Bank green money box, which sorted out the change when you slotted the coins in the top of it.

'It's a good idea of Peter's,' Mum said on the way home. 'Saving from a young age makes sense.'

But one bank account wasn't enough. Peter made us each open a second as well, insisting we needed it, but never fully explaining why.

He warned us in the sternest terms about keeping track of the passbook for each account. 'I need them to audit your accounts,' he said. 'If I see anything that doesn't add up there will be consequences. You must keep them safe and have them available at all times when I ask for them.'

Mum came home from work and Terrie told her what Peter was planning.

'It does seem a bit over the top, Peter,' she said, quietly.

'Over the top that the children save and open bank accounts?' he asked. 'And learn how to manage their money?'

Mum looked worn out and sighed. 'Yes, I guess,' she said.

'Cynthia, I'd have thought you'd be more grateful. Few stepparents would take as much interest as me.'

I tried hard to make sure I knew what I'd spent, but sometimes I couldn't quite remember whether I'd bought five- or ten-penny sweets or how much the comic I'd lent my friend Mark had cost.

Very soon, things didn't add up. Just a week later, Peter was sat counting out the coppers I'd placed on the kitchen table.

'You are out by 13p, Paul,' he said, sternly. 'Why is that?'

I shrugged. I had counted everything myself, and just assumed it must be because I had got some sweets I'd forgotten about.

Peter sighed, looking at Mum. 'Now, it seems like we'll need to ask for receipts. Yes, that's what we'll do. Right, Terrie, Paul, I want a receipt for everything you buy.'

'Everything?' gasped Terrie.

'Yes, everything,' he said. 'That way we'll all know where we are, won't we?'

The following morning, I was home from school before anyone else so I sat on the doorstep waiting for Terrie, reading my book. Terrie was the only one with a spare key, but Peter arrived first.

'What are you doing?' he asked.

'Reading,' I shrugged, turning back to my book.

'But where did you get that from?' he persisted.

'From the house,' I said.

I often took a book to school to read at lunchtimes, in case the other boys didn't let me join in football. There was nothing better than burying my head in a book to escape.

'Right,' said Peter as he turned the key. 'New rule. You are NOT to remove anything from the house without permission.'

'Eh?' I was confused.

'And I am going to check your bag before and after school every day,' he said. 'Just in case.'

I wondered what he was on about, but didn't bother to ask. I just did my jobs fast that evening and kept out of his way and then went to my room.

Next morning, just after Terrie had set off for the day, Peter put his arm out across the front door and stopped me from following.

'Pockets,' he said. 'And bag please.'

I slowly turned out my pockets and unzipped my bag.

Peter grabbed my tiny Warhammer figures, some sweets, a book and a half-eaten bag of my favourite crisps, Spicy Nik Naks.

'This is all confiscated,' he said grimly. 'Now hands up.'

He forced me to hold my arms up like a passenger in airport security as he patted me down.

'Good,' he nodded. 'Now lower your trousers and your pants.'

'What?' I gasped. 'Urgh no.' This can't be normal, I thought to myself.

'Do it now or get punished for disobeying me,' he ordered, glaring at me.

I was going to be late if I didn't leave soon. The last thing I wanted was detention. So I whipped down my trousers. Peter pulled down my underwear and then spread my buttocks.

'What do you think I've got?' I asked. 'A pencil stuck up there?'

'Don't be so fucking cheeky,' Peter barked, putting his face an inch from mine, the smell of his stagnant breath washing over me.

I pulled my pants up again, burning with humiliation.

I went to school with nothing in my bag except for my text-books and pens. Anything that would provide me with any pleasure or entertainment had been confiscated. All the way to school, my heart was beating wildly, as I thought of what Peter had done. It seemed so unfair, but he made it seem so normal. My head was spinning by the time I got to school. I sat down in the classroom, feeling so depressed as I opened my almost empty bag. Looking inside, I wondered what else Peter could take away from me.

Over dinner that night, Peter started telling Mum he had more ideas to improve behaviour within the household.

'I've noticed sweets can spoil dinners,' he said, peering at us over his glasses. 'I think the kids shouldn't eat anything before dinner. Or before bed, as all that sugar prevents proper sleep … do you agree, Cynth?'

Mum nodded. 'I guess so, Peter.'

'Ah yes, well, don't you agree Terrie and Paul are better behaved now?' he beamed. 'I mean, since we started the sched-ule. It's a real turnaround, isn't it?'

Mum looked at us and smiled. Mum was much happier now with Peter to mete out the punishments and hand out the chores. She could relax when she got home from work, all the housework completed and two children who acted like robots to meet her and Peter's every need.

The perfect children: quiet, invisible, helpful and obedient.

'Yes, Peter,' she agreed.

'Oh, and I cancelled the subscriptions at the corner shop for the *Beano* and Terrie's girls mag. It's much more productive for kids to read proper books.'

'But they like those comics,' Mum said.

'Yes, but you'd prefer them to do well at school, wouldn't you?' Peter replied immediately.

After dinner he asked me to make him a cup of coffee. So I made him my newly invented 'Paul's Froth-a-chino'. I poured in the milk, spat in it and then frothed it up with spoon.

'There you go,' I said, bringing it through to him with a grin. 'Made just the way you like it.'

It sounds pathetic, I know, but I needed to do something, anything, to get back at him. It felt like a tiny victory, but a victory nonetheless. I got enormous satisfaction as I watched him take a slurp.

Just before bedtime, I walked into my bedroom to find Peter pacing back and forth.

'Paul!' he snapped. 'Look what I found. Did you think you could get away with this?'

He was holding a fluff-covered penny sweet in his hand, pointing at it.

'I … I …' I spluttered, trying to work out where it was from. It must've been an old one, lost in a jacket pocket.

'Every ACTION has a REACTION, Paul,' he spat. Then, raising his hand, he whacked me hard on the backside.

'Arghhh!' I screamed, as he stood over me.

'You deserved that, you devious little shit,' he screeched. 'Don't defy me again!' Then he stormed out of the room.

For minutes I just lay there crying, clutching my backside. He'd walloped me as hard as he could and I had a perfect replica of Peter's handprint to prove it. Then I scrambled to my feet and went and laid on my bed, sobbing. For some reason, knowing that Peter had been through my wardrobe to find that sweet made things even worse. He wanted to catch me out.

Wiping my eyes, I thought back over what had happened over the past week. Peter seemed like a different man. The schedule, the pay review, the body checks, and now he had physically punished me. Was there no end to this? How much worse could it get?

Later that night I overheard Peter continue his rant as I slipped out of bed to use the loo.

'Cynth, I know you're doing your best as a mum but clearly there are problems with the kids. They're a pair of compulsive liars. Both of them have lied about their doing their chores and the amount of food that's going missing … for Christ's sake, that's where all your money is going. They need a firmer hand.'

As he went on and on, Mum just listened.

Chapter 8

'Hidden Hurt'

Terrie

Since Mum had delegated all of the responsibility of punishments and chores to Peter, she seemed more relaxed. Paul and I both had our notebooks keeping careful track of all of our jobs and accounts, and the house was running a lot smoother, it was true. But it felt like a constant grind and we were exhausted. By the time we'd done jobs and homework and eaten, it was almost time for bed.

I was feeling resentful towards Mum for allowing Peter to have total control of our lives. I got back from school feeling really tired, it had been a really hard day, to find Peter lounging on the sofa, with his feet up on the table.

'Finally! You're late, Terrie. I'm hungry.' he said, not once taking his eyes off the TV screen. 'Make me scrambled eggs on toast with coffee!'

I was annoyed. I was sure he'd been here all day. Lazy bastard should try cooking it for himself, I thought. I had enough to do. I'd never seen him make so much as a coffee for anyone else.

But I liked cooking, so to keep the peace I reluctantly followed his orders.

I heated up a frying pan, made eggs the way Mum had shown me and took the steaming plate through to the living room. But Peter grimaced when he peered at it.

77

'I can't eat that,' he said. 'They're overcooked. You need to serve them so they are sloppy, not rubbery. You'll have to do them again. And if you get it wrong again you can sit and write out "I don't know how to cook perfect scrambled eggs" fifty times.' He turned his gaze back to the TV.

I was furious. I wanted to smash the bloody eggs on his head. I expected him to be more grateful than that. I made a new batch, accidently dropping his toast on the floor and standing on it. The eggs looked disgusting. I slopped them over the trampled toast. His face lit up as he took the plate through, as if I was a waitress.

'Thanks, Ted,' he said, tucking in.

'Fuck off,' I thought, feeling incensed.

I wandered off to start my homework, when Peter stopped chewing and looked up. 'Where do you think you're going?' he asked. 'You're not doing anything until all of your jobs are done.'

Paul joined me upstairs as we cleaned the bathroom. It was an old white one, fitted in the 1970s, and Mum had glued brown lino to the walls and floor. She always kept it spotless before, but now, under Peter's regime, the lino had to be shiny. I leaned over the bath, polishing, as Paul scrubbed the sink with Jif.

'I only did this two days ago,' Paul grumbled. 'It's not like it even needs doing again. He is treating us like slaves. I feel like we're in prison.'

'Hmm,' I said thoughtfully. 'I'm sure they use a special piece of equipment to clean bathrooms in prison.'

Paul realised what I meant straight away and watched as I grabbed Peter's toothbrush and started scrubbing all around the pipework and floor.

'This can be Peter's way of helping out,' Paul said gleefully.

Smiling inwardly, we both finished off cleaning the bathroom.

'You two seem cheerful,' Mum said, as she served up our favourite for tea – Findus crispy minced beef pancakes and mash.

I looked up at her and smiled. I'd noticed she was looking more worn out than ever.

'Did you have a good day?' she asked, as I was scraping up the last of the mash on my plate.

I shrugged. 'It was all right, Mum, same as usual,' I lied. I actually couldn't remember when I'd had a good day. The only fun Paul and myself seemed to have now was to make each other laugh by secretly fighting back against Peter. I could see she wasn't really in a mood to talk, though, so I just fell silent.

As Paul and I stood up to get on with washing up, Peter raised his hand. 'Paul, Terrie, what route do you usually walk to school?' he asked.

We looked at each other. I usually walked the same way, unless I spotted a friend or was late, then I'd cut through the park. Occasionally me and Paul would walk back home together; it all depended what mood we were in and if I'd walked fast enough to catch him coming across his school field.

But Peter spoke over us before we could answer. 'Right, well, I have worked out the quickest route,' he said, marching up and down the room, 'and there is to be no deviating, and no discussion about it.'

Then he laid out a map of the area. He had actually high-lighted in red pen where we needed to walk. I frowned, so much effort had been put into it.

'I will be following you sometimes to make sure you adhere to the route,' he said, prodding the highlighted areas.

79

I laughed uneasily. 'What? You're kidding? I'm not five!'

Paul looked apprehensive and was biting his lip.

'You heard me,' said Peter. 'I'm going to all this effort because I'm trying to help your mum.'

'He's not doing this to help Mum!' Paul whispered, as we did the washing up that night.

'He's fucking controlling,' I hissed back quietly. 'Just make sure you have a good look around on the way home. He'll be there.'

The next afternoon, after the bell went, I took off from my class to make my way home. Peter wanted us back at 3.50 p.m. on the dot. It meant speed walking all the way. If I had a lesson on the other side of the school I knew I'd have to leg it past everyone in order to make it on time. Of course I knew it would make me look even weirder than my classmates already thought I was.

As I made my way home, a familiar red-coloured car caught the corner of my eye. I carried on as normal, keeping my eyes facing forward. My heart started thudding like a drum. I could see clearly now. It was Peter's car, and he'd taken the cone off, I assumed to make it less obvious it was him. A wave of sickness washed over me as I looked into his eyes, glaring intensely through the windscreen, directly at me. He didn't smile, or wave, he just glared. Like a predator eyeing up his prey.

For fuck's sake, I thought in anger. I wanted to show him my middle finger, but I kept my hand firmly in my pocket. Quickly I looked at the pavement, pretending I hadn't seen him, and walked faster, my feet moving in time to my heartbeat. Knowing Peter was serious in his threat to stalk us made me feel scared and angry. Nothing was mentioned when I got home and I carried on with my routine as normal. I told Paul what had happened and we arranged to walk home together the next day.

As I was walking up to Paul's school playing field, I met one of our neighbours walking to meet her daughter.

'Hi, Mrs Roberts.' I smiled.

'Hello, Terrie. You're going to think this strange, but I'm sure I just saw your stepdad standing behind the large bush at the top of the hill.' She looked concerned.

'Oh, it's okay.' I thought quickly. 'He arranged to meet us. I guess he's hiding as a joke.'

She smiled at me. 'What a good man. I hope you realise how lucky you are?' She carried on walking to meet her daughter.

Lucky? I thought to myself. He's a creepy bastard. I saw Paul and called out to him. He waited as I ran up to him. Breathless, I blurted out the conversation I'd just had with Debbie's mum.

Paul's eyes widened. 'I just don't believe it. Why the hell would he want to stand in a bush?'

'Just keep your eyes in front and don't let him catch you looking around you.'

We walked quickly, aware we'd not long before we had to be home. There didn't appear to be anyone around. Then a flash of light reflected from two circular pieces of glass caught my eye. There, squatting among the shrubbery, his face framed with leaves, was Peter, staring intently in our direction. Gazing ahead, I whispered quietly, 'Peter is crouching in that bush. Don't look.'

The look on Paul's face said it all. 'Why the hell is he doing this?'

'He's just a bloody weirdo with nothing better to do.' Paul looked genuinely freaked out. Exactly how I felt.

Over dinner that night Peter started quizzing us over who we'd spoken to or seen en route.

'Terrie,' he barked, another evening after dinner. 'Which way did you walk this morning?'

I looked at him, worried. I'd walked the usual way. 'The usual,' I began. 'The way you told me to.'

'Who was in front of you?' he asked.

I gulped. Thinking back to that morning felt impossible. I'd no idea who was walking in front of me. Was this a trick question? I decided to make something feasible up. 'Um, a girl, I think. A sixth former.'

'You're lying!' he spat.

I frowned. I really couldn't remember. I'd been too busy thinking about events at home.

'Maybe you didn't follow the route after all!' he said.

'I did!' I protested.

'I don't believe you,' he replied. 'For liars in this house there has to be a punishment.'

Paul and I looked at each other, as Peter got up and walked to the kitchen drawer.

'Why should I have to hurt my hand in order to make you behave?' he barked. 'I'm not the one who's done anything wrong.'

He pulled out Mum's metal spatula. She was at work still, but I wished more than anything she was home now. 'Come here,' Peter snapped. 'And bend over this chair.'

'Do you think I'm bloody stupid? I'm not bending over so you can hit me!'

The veins in his neck were throbbing. I could see the anger rising in his face. 'COME HERE!' he demanded, pointing at the chair, taking one step closer to me.

'I've done nothing wrong. I will not stand still while you beat me with that thing.'

He looked enraged. 'Paul, you go first, bend over, and then I'll deal with your sister.'

I stepped in front of Paul, who by this point was standing. 'We are not going to stand and let you smack us with that thing.' I felt strong and wanted to protect Paul.

All of a sudden Peter snapped and strode towards us, the spatula held high. We cowered into balls huddled up to each other. 'This. Is. What. Happens. When. You. Lie. And. Disobey. Me,' he shrieked manically, bashing us with each word.

We both cried out, scared he wasn't going to stop. Our saving grace was that the spatula was bending so much he couldn't get a good whack. Eventually he stopped and told us to go to bed, booting us both as we left the room. My sense of defiance was still strong.

'You didn't even hurt me, you fucking twat,' I sobbed as I ran upstairs.

But when I looked into my mirror and stared into my eyes, all I saw was sadness staring back. What was he going to do next? How long would we have to put up with Peter? Surely things couldn't get any worse?

I walked home from school with Paul again later that week. Peter didn't trust him to have a house key, so he'd often have to sit outside and wait for me to get home, sometimes for a few minutes, other times if I'd got detention he'd have to wait an hour or so. We hung up our coats, just as Peter liked, on the hooks in the hall. I went upstairs to do my homework. But it was only a few minutes before Paul called me down again.

'What's up?' I asked. He was looking pale.

'Don't look up,' he whispered. 'I've found Peter's camera.'

My mouth fell open. 'What do you mean "found"?'

Paul grabbed my arm and indicated to peer around the doorframe. There on the fake mahogany TV cabinet was a big dark brick-like object covered in a piece of net curtain. I stood in the hallway, momentarily frozen.

'Whatever you do, make sure you don't look at it when you're cleaning,' Paul whispered.

As I hoovered and dusted, I looked everywhere, everywhere except at the camera. Then it occurred to me that it looked obvious if I also wasn't looking at it. I didn't know what to do. I couldn't win.

As we ate our scheduled breakfast the next morning, Peter quizzed us on our jobs. 'How long did you spend dusting and hoovering?' he asked.

'Erm,' I thought back quickly to the previous day. I'd no idea. I could hardly remember what I'd had for lunch. 'About 10 minutes?' I hazarded a guess.

'It was 12 actually,' Peter smirked. 'But I asked for 15. That means you're going to go without pudding this evening.'

Are you for real? I was thinking to myself, fingernails digging into my palms in anger.

Mum looked up as she packed her bag for work.

'They are lying again, Cynth,' he said simply. 'I can show you the footage as proof later after *Coronation Street*.'

My heart sank. Something told me he knew we knew we were being filmed; he wouldn't have come out with this otherwise. But neither of us was going to say anything about it.

I began clock watching at school, dreading going home. Wasn't home meant to be somewhere you could relax away from the stresses of the day? I marched home as usual. Paul nodded at me after he had a quick scout around.

'He's positioned it so he can see the front door and the lounge this time,' Paul whispered. 'Clever, huh?'

I shuddered. 'I really, really don't like this, Paul.'

We looked at each other. I could feel tears starting to spring into my eyes. How could things have got to this? It made me feel physically sick.

'I know,' said Paul. 'He won't win though, Terrie. We can find a way to beat him. Let's make ourselves a promise. We just have to keep one step ahead.'

I looked at my little brother. He was growing up so fast. I felt proud of him.

Later, after we'd been sent to the kitchen to wash up, we could hear Mum and Peter talking. 'You might think filming is over the top, Cynth,' he said. 'But actually it's proof they're a pair of compulsive liars. Watch this.'

Mum remained silent as Peter rewound another one of his tapes.

'See?' he went on. 'Not only is Paul eating a bag of sweets when he's been asked not to, he's even brought a friend home without our permission.'

I thought back quickly. Paul had brought a friend home on Tuesday, but just for a few minutes after school so he could lend him a book. And I didn't understand how Peter had it on film. We'd scouted around for cameras as soon as we'd got in, and found them before we'd allowed ourselves to be seen. I decided he must have had another one hidden somewhere.

Then the next day Paul found it. 'He's only hidden a camera on the bottom of a shelf in the hallway,' he said. 'So he can catch us coming in and out of the house!'

I would use the word 'game', but that's pushing it too far, but each day after school we did have a competition to see who could spot the camera first. It was usually Paul. But then I became good at it too. I came home and spotted my bedroom cupboard ajar slightly. Instantly I knew what it was. Quickly, I slammed the door shut with my hip, not looking at it. 'No spy holes for you this evening, Pervy Peter,' I thought grimly.

Peter's keenness to punish had us permanently on edge. Then, just a few days later, he called us down to the living room on a Saturday morning. We knew he must be angry about something as he was up before us. 'Right, you two,' he said, waving a headless porcelain Shire horse that normally lived on our windowsill. 'Who broke this?'

I looked at Paul and he looked at me. I could already sense he was as baffled as me. 'Um,' I began. 'Wasn't me.' I assumed it must've been Paul.

'It wasn't me either!' Paul said quickly. Usually I could tell if he was fibbing, and I didn't think he was.

'Right, stand up straight to attention, arms by your sides,' Peter commanded. 'And you can stay like that until one of you decides to own up.'

We stood up straight and stared ahead. This was insane.

'No, Terrie, arms straight by your side. And Paul, chin up higher,'

'C'mon, Paul!' I thought to myself. 'Just own up!'

But, as the minutes passed, we started to sway a little and Peter told us off. 'C'mon, one of you must have done this!' he yelled.

'Oh kids,' Mum said, more gently. 'Come on, own up, and then this can all stop.'

I started to cry. It was so hard to stay in the position, my joints had already begun to ache. But as time passed I grew to realise neither of us had done it, and that could only mean one thing. The thought was too awful.

Peter told us to stand in the living room, facing away from the TV. Minutes turned to an hour. My back and feet ached. Paul started crying, but I just felt so stubborn. How dare Peter treat us like this? An hour turned into another hour. When Paul slouched Peter slapped his face hard. 'Stand straighter!' Peter commanded.

'Right, that's enough!' Mum cried. 'Peter, they can go now. I think you've made the point. They won't break anything again.'

Our shoulders sagged and we ran upstairs to our rooms crying.

As time passed, though, something changed in Mum. I saw

it happen, but I didn't know what the cause was. Within a few months of Peter moving in, she'd gone from being much happier to gradually less. Mum often complained about his stale BO. 'Peter, please go and have a shower,' was her mantra before bedtime. Sometimes she'd wrinkle her nose, and push him away if he breathed too close to her on the sofa. 'Can't you clean your teeth?' she snapped.

She was on edge as well with all of Peter's punishments. 'If you just did your jobs then Peter wouldn't have to complain,' she sighed when he told us off.

Occasionally she told him to stop handing out 'strings of punishments' but Peter always quickly pointed out the first punishment hadn't worked. Whenever he argued, he always seemed to make perfect sense.

But while he made sense sometimes, strange things also started happening. One Saturday we were all looking forward to a family trip to the local swimming pool when I couldn't find my costume.

'What are you doing up there, Terrie?' Mum called upstairs. 'We're leaving in a minute.'

I pulled everything out the top drawer and then rifled through the next one, and the next one. Then I pulled out all of the drawers to check it hadn't slipped behind.

'Come on, Terrie!' Peter yelled.

'Coming!' I replied, looking under my bed. Where was it? I knew it must be somewhere. In vain I had to scour through my wardrobe. I didn't expect to find it in there and indeed it wasn't. 'Muuuum!' I cried. 'I can't find my swim suit.'

Instead of Mum, Peter appeared at the door. 'What's wrong, Terrie?' he sighed. 'We're all ready and waiting at the front door.'

'I can't find my costume,' I said. 'I'm sure I put it back in my top drawer.'

Mum stuck her head around the door. 'Ted,' she said. 'What's keeping you?' She joined in the search as I explained.

By now, Paul came upstairs too. He was ready, swinging his swimming bag impatiently.

'Right then,' said Peter. 'Looks like Terrie has lost her costume, doesn't it?' He glared at me as he spoke. 'So we won't be able to go,' said Peter, slowly and deliberately.

Tears pricked at my eyes.

'You really should look after your things better,' Mum said, sighing as she went back downstairs.

Paul started complaining, but was sent to his room.

Miserably, I sat on my bed. It was so unfair. I knew it was my fault, but I really had no idea where it had gone.

I woke feeling tired the following morning. As I pulled open my top drawer, my black swimming costume was there in the top of my drawer, neatly folded up on top of my knickers. I felt my head spin a little; I knew exactly who must have put it there.

Peter had us standing to attention that afternoon for an hour for not washing up properly. He said he'd found two dirty dishes and a chipped glass in the cupboards. This time he got a metal spatula out to smack us if we started to move. 'Why should I leap up and down off the sofa to make sure you're doing it properly?' he snapped.

Mum was upstairs having a bath as he whacked us. He did it a few times and Paul started crying. I was waiting for Mum to stop him, but this time when she came down she just looked at us sadly and went into the kitchen. My guts churned with a new feeling. Betrayal. How could she let him do this? I wasn't surprised. For weeks now Mum had started to take on extra hours at work and I'd heard her arguing with Peter a few weeks before about money. 'You never bring any in,' she'd cried. 'I'm paying for everything. It's not fair, Peter.'

'You're a stupid cow,' he snapped back. 'I do my bit and, God, what I've done for those kids as well.' The following day Peter didn't appear at breakfast.

'Where's Peter?' I asked in the morning.

'In bed sulking,' Mum replied.

He stayed there all day and was still there when we got back after school. It was brilliant. The house was peaceful and we just quietly got our jobs done. That evening he was still in bed, and the following morning too. So when we got home from school, we did our chores as normal and then I flicked on the TV with Paul.

'*Scooby Doo* is on,' I called out. It was Paul's favourite.

Suddenly we heard footsteps on the stairs. Peter marched across the room and ripped the plug off the TV. 'Get on with your jobs!' he yelled. 'You're making too much noise!' Then he grabbed Paul and walloped him a few times around his head and torso.

'Stop!' I cried. But then he turned to me, and slapped me hard around the face.

We waited for him to go back upstairs and slam the bedroom door. Paul poked the two wires that were sticking out into the holes in the wall and used another plug to secure them there. He turned the TV back on and I turned the sound as low as I could. We sat on the floor and finished watching our cartoon.

Chapter 9

'Fighting Back'

Paul

*A*bout six months after Peter had moved in, I caught sight of my body in the mirror as I took my clothes off to have a bath. I had bruises all over, covering my arms, my legs, my chest and my back. Various shapes, sizes and colours. I looked absolutely battered. Peter had used the metal spatula on me several times, but he'd also started clouting me around the head or punching me in the chest. It had happened so often I'd lost count.

As I stared at my reflection that morning before school hot tears emerged. 'It's not fair!' had become a running cry of Terrie and mine; for the first few months we'd screamed it at Peter whenever he'd punished us for something. Little good it did; it just seemed to make to make him enjoy punishing us all the more.

'Life isn't fair,' Peter would shout back with a grimace on his face.

Depending on what mood he was in, answering back would result in anything from a slap or a punch to a beating. I'd learned to adapt and would just bite my tongue, somehow containing the growing rage inside myself.

That morning, I shivered and hugged myself as I wondered what to do. There was no way I could continue like this, and God only knows how Terrie felt, but I knew it couldn't be much different.

Nothing I could do or say to Peter seemed to have any effect other than to encourage him to do more bad things or dream up new punishments. Telling Mum how I felt wouldn't work as Peter had her thinking we were bad kids and he was just keeping us in line to make her life easier. I knew anything I said to her would just be repeated to Peter.

Then an idea formed. What if I just marched into my head teacher's office and showed him my bruised and battered body? He would do something. Surely that was all the proof I'd need? Then, whatever Peter said, the authorities would have to listen.

'Paul, what the hell are you doing in there?' Peter's voice bellowed from downstairs. 'You've already had your allocated three minutes.'

'Coming!' I called back.

My anger rose again, just at the sound of his voice. Yes, tomorrow, I was going to do something, something that would save us from Peter and his regime once and for all.

The next morning, I completed all my jobs, made sure my uniform was correctly tucked in and checked my school bag. I had taken to thoroughly checking it myself for non-school items as on a couple of occasions Peter had 'found' something tucked in there so he could prove to Mum how I was still being disobedient and needed searching.

I didn't mind the body search or the long cold walk to school because, today, everything would change. It would be Peter's turn to realise every ACTION had a REACTION. He needed to know that what he was doing to me and Terrie was not okay, not even remotely near the region of okay.

But the long walk to school didn't help – it gave me too long to think about what I was about to do. It went past butterflies in the tummy; I felt like I had a war raging inside me. You see, by this point in time I had adapted to having two different mes: there was the compliant, quiet and obedient me who would say, 'Yes, Peter', and scurry around, then there was the fiery, clever, devious and hot-tempered me that existed inside.

The inner me was forcing me, step by step, closer to school, urging me to go in and get it over with. But the compliant me didn't want to say anything, in case it went wrong, scared of the punishments. That part of me couldn't help thinking that I was overreacting and maybe I deserved the punishments. As I walked to school that day, I felt like an observer, watching and listening to the two sides putting their arguments across, fighting with each other to be the dominant voice.

Somehow I ended up outside reception. I took a deep breath, then walked up the steps and through the double doors. 'Can I see the Head please?' I asked the school secretary.

She looked at me and gave me a smile. 'Hello, Paul. What would you like to see him about?'

'I've got a family problem,' I blurted out before I could change my mind.

With the rubber at the end of her pencil she pointed at a seat. 'Sit down. I'll go and see if he's free.'

I sat swinging my legs on the chair, looking at the walls adorned with calm paintings of fruit and plants, wondering what the headmaster would say and how Peter would respond. I imagined we'd have to go to the police station afterwards. Mum might be a bit upset at first, but she'd have to agree this was not on and the bruises on my battered body would back me up. That was the other trouble, though: Peter rarely did it in front of her and made sure that the bruises were in places covered by clothes. For some reason I never got bruises on my tummy, which is where he hit and sometimes kicked me really hard. All that aside, the one thing I knew I could rely on was my sister Terrie. She would back me up.

I'd not been to the Head's office for a long time but it still smelled the same: old furniture and stale coffee, a bit like Peter in fact. I shuddered. I couldn't wait to have him out of my life.

Finally, the secretary's phone rang. 'You can go in now, Paul,' she said. 'The Head's busy, but the Deputy Head will see you instead.'

'Good morning,' I said, standing awkwardly in front of her desk. I was determined not to cry, but it was hard. I was really nervous and beginning to have second thoughts.

'Morning, Paul. It's been a while, hasn't it? I think the last time was when I presented you with a certificate for running, if my memory serves. Anyway, what can I do for you today?'

'It's my mum's boyfriend,' I stammered. 'He keeps hitting me.' I rolled up my sleeves and showed the purple bruises on my arms. They were the shape and size of Peter's fingers.

The Deputy Head leaned forward in her chair. I was relieved at how concerned she looked. Encouraged, I pulled up my school shirt. More blackish bruises where Peter had punched me hard in the chest and ribs.

'Oh dear God,' she said, looking visibly shocked.

'There's more,' I said, twisting my back around. As I struggled with my shirt, I ended up just pulling it off. Then I tried to pull up my trouser legs to show her my shins where Peter had kicked me a few nights before – the bruises there were raised. My trousers were always too small for me and I couldn't squeeze them up any further on my leg, so I just pulled them off completely. I thought it was important she got the full picture.

'I just want him to stop,' I said simply, sniffing a bit as my eyes filled up.

Standing there in my brown Y-fronts, the Deputy Head turned me gently to the left and right as her eyes scoured my pale body, blackened with bruises like a leopard. 'Okay, Paul, put your clothes on,' she said. 'I'll sort this situation out.'

She seemed a little shaken, and I was glad. I didn't know if she'd call 999 or the police station or my mum – whatever she did I hoped it would be quick because I felt like bolting. I buttoned up my shirt, slid on my trousers and sat back outside. As I waited, the secretary kept glancing up at me. I wanted to tell her what had happened, but I daren't. I thought it was best it was made official when Peter was arrested.

Ten minutes later, I looked up and my heart almost seized up in my ribcage. It wasn't a police officer who'd arrived. It was Peter, standing with his hands on his hips. I blinked, thinking I was imagining it. This had to be a mistake.

'I've come to pick you up,' Peter said, jangling his car keys. His piggy eyes flashed as he took me by the crook of my elbow. 'Your mum asked me to come and get you after the school called her at work. Apparently there's a bit of a problem.'

I started to tremble as my mind raced, imagining Mum at work, busy, harassed with her clients. Then suddenly the realisation hit me. Of course Mum would ring Peter to collect me. He was at home doing nothing. She might not believe my story. After all, Peter rarely hit me that hard when she was around.

With that he disappeared into the Deputy Head's office for five very long minutes. The next thing I saw was Peter stepping out of the office smiling his biggest, broadest smile, shaking hands with the Deputy Head and thanking her for her understanding and promising to get me help to stop my lying. How the hell did he talk his way out of that? I thought.

Then Peter grabbed me and frog-marched me to his car, his fingers pinching the skin on my arm. As soon as the car door clicked shut, he turned on me, swinging his clenched fist as hard as he could into my chest. 'You fucking little bastard!

What did you think that would achieve exactly?' he cried, spittle flying out of his mouth, his nose virtually touching mine.

The overwhelming feeling of dread and powerlessness was awful, as he twisted the ignition key.

'I mean, Paul, really, what were you hoping would happen?' he snapped. As he changed gear, he raised his arm and swung his clenched fist into my chest again. I gasped, and fell forward as if I'd been shot.

'Did you REALLY think anyone would believe YOU?' he continued. Whack. He thumped me again, this time a bit lower down. I groaned, cowering in my seat with nowhere to hide.

All the way home, at each set of lights, at each gear change, he thumped me as hard as he could. By the time we got home, I felt physically sick and had numerous new lumps, bruises and aches. I fell out of the car sobbing.

'Fuck off to bed,' Peter screamed. 'And don't think you'll be getting any dinner either, you devious wanker!'

The following day, Peter was at the breakfast table earlier than usual, sat there quietly with Mum. 'Today your mother is going to take you to see your GP,' he said calmly.

'Why?' I asked, wondering why the hell would Peter *want* me to go to the doctors. I would have thought it was the last place he would want me to go.

'Because you've got psychological problems,' he snarled. 'Lying to your teachers, making things up, doing things to yourself to get bruises and cuts. This needs to be nipped in the bud!'

I couldn't believe what was happening as Mum took me to our surgery that morning on the bus. 'Mum, I didn't lie,' I sobbed.

She just sighed. 'Look, Paul,' she said gently, 'I don't know why you want to cause Peter so much trouble. I mean he's very precise about how he likes things but you don't need to turn against him like you are. Things are much better with him around and I'm really happy. Do you not want me to be happy? Do I not deserve it?'

The last two things my mum had said echoed my own thoughts but I had to try and show her I wasn't making it all up about Peter. I pulled up my top to show her some bruises. 'But Mum, how did I get these?' I wailed.

'Peter told me about how you fell out of that tree,' Mum said. 'And that you were likely to lie about it. You tear around everywhere, you're always climbing trees and being, well, a boy!'

I wanted to scream. How could she not believe me? Or worse still, why did she not care? In tears, I followed Mum into our doctor's office. If my own Deputy Head wouldn't believe me then what was a doctor going to do?

The GP didn't even look at me. He just nodded as Mum filled him in on how I caused problems by not doing my jobs at home, how I kept trying to make out Peter was a bad person and how I lied about things. The doctor was concerned that I harmed myself and tried to blame it on other people and confided in my mum that everything would be okay and he was going to get me professional help. He gave her a letter to give to the school to explain what was happening and told her she would be contacted by post about my referral.

Two weeks later the promised letter arrived: I had been referred to a family therapy centre, a place that offered 'family guidance' for 'troubled children'. The first session was booked for a week later and we were to go as a family.

Peter made a big thing out of it. 'Look how your behaviour is putting everyone out,' he said. 'How do you think your mum's going to hold her head up when this gets out?' All of this was said in front of other people for full effect and to extract sympathy for himself.

What did I do? Nothing. By this point anything I said would be considered a lie, with Peter's words now considered gospel. Instead, on the inside, I let the fiery me take more control. I had a new agenda: to maximise the problems I could cause Peter. And the devious me set about this task with relish, while the outwardly obedient me kept up the façade of compliance.

The first session arrived. The journey there was awkward, everyone sitting in silence. As we drew near in the car, Peter gave the final warning 'not to lie', which of course meant 'don't tell the truth'. With that, we entered the door to a very big old building with high ceilings and wooden panels.

After Mum said a few things to a receptionist we were ushered into a large open room to wait. A few minutes later a middle-aged lady in a cream dress invited us into another room.

As we sat in a circle, the counsellor began: 'Hello, so you're the Duckett family. We're here to try and work through some family problems that you're having, that's right, isn't it?' she continued, in a sweet sing-song voice.

Peter glared at me; I stared at the floor. I wished it would open up and swallow us all, or, better still, just Peter.

'Okay,' the lady continued. 'My name's Sally and I'm going to be leading your session today. What I'd like to do first is ask you all to be as honest as possible. This is very important if we are to find a way forward as a happy family unit.'

I glanced at Terrie and knew she'd be thinking exactly the same as me. If we said anything close to the truth we'd end up being killed outside the room. And family unit? Peter was just the enemy within. So when Sally turned to me, asking for my opinion, I just shrugged.

Peter had plenty to say when it was his turn, though. 'Well, where do I start, eh, Paul?' he said, pushing his glasses up his nose. He spoke more gently than usual with genuine concern. He deserved an Oscar.

'We just can't cope,' he sighed, puffing out his cheeks. 'Goodness knows how we've tried.' He looked at Mum and squeezed her hand.

He never holds Mum's hand any more, I thought, as he continued.

'There does get to a point though when it has to stop, doesn't there? We can't take much more. The lying, the manipulation, the disrespect. He doesn't do his chores or help his mum.' He allowed his voice to trail off as he looked at the posters about self-harm on the walls.

'We just need your help, Sally,' he pleaded. 'And it's my duty to try and ensure our lad here gets it.'

Sally nodded, impressed by Peter's little outburst, jotting down notes, ticking boxes. I just sat there, the obedient and compliant me looking awkward. Inside I was raging: 'LIAR! WHAT A LOAD OF SHITE, AND THE OSCAR FOR BEST ACTOR GOES TO … PETER.'

The session lasted 60 minutes and by the end of the afternoon the verdict had been given: Paul Duckett was now officially branded a 'delinquent who needed regular sessions of psychological support at the centre to help improve his behaviour'.

Peter and Mum went to speak to the counsellor alone for a few minutes, leaving me and Terrie in the room.

'Idiots,' said Terrie. 'They really do believe him, don't they?'

I nodded, sadly. We may as well have been invisible.

Afterwards, Peter came back clutching a form. 'Right, all sorted now,' he said.

Sally asked Peter and Mum when a suitable time would be for my visits. 'We have after school or weekend sessions,' she said. 'They're usually most popular, so as not to disrupt lessons, or we can do during the day. Whatever is most convenient.'

'I think during the day is just fine,' Peter said, his eyes narrowing at me. 'Paul will just have to leave his class. We will let all his teachers know the situation. It's best they are aware of his behavioural problems from the very start, don't you think?'

'Absolutely,' agreed Sally. 'The more help Paul has in overcoming his issues the brighter his future will be.' She smiled at me but I just glared back at her. I couldn't believe how stupid she was.

We drove home in silence, until we turned the corner of Churchill Avenue. 'I'm very glad we've got the help needed for Paul now,' Peter sighed. 'This will improve his behaviour in ways even I can't, and now he knows he can't go to people at school and lie about his situation he might have to actually change.'

Mum nodded. She turned back and looked at me in the car seat. 'Paul, it's all for the best,' she said, actually believing all the shit Peter had been feeding her.

Resigned to the fact it was now just me and Terrie against the world, I went straight to my room and fell asleep, lost in thought.

That week passed quickly and Peter actually seemed to back off a bit during the week leading up to my first appointment with the counsellor. I suppose in his head he had won a major battle and he could do pretty much what he liked now and have professionals back him up in blaming me.

All of my teachers had been told and already I'd noticed a change in their attitude towards me. Some shouted at me more, others moved me to the front of the class automatically. Now I'd been firmly labelled as the 'troubled' kid, I was blamed for everything, both at home and at school.

I walked out of the classroom eyes glued to the worn carpet, signed out at reception and made my way to the waiting taxi.

The sessions in the centre were not as bad as I'd expected, though. We had a huge outdoor area, lots of games to play, and we were allowed to cook and then eat the food we'd made, which was fantastic. I immediately recognised another girl there. She was the daughter of one of Dad's army friends. 'What you here for?' she asked me suspiciously.

'For lying, being disobedient and general bad behaviour,' I reeled off. 'But really I just told the truth about my mum's boyfriend beating me up. What about you?'

'Lying, being disobedient and bad behaviour,' she repeated. 'My dad beats me and my mum up.'

Soon I realised what the truth behind most of the kids' bad behaviour was. We were all from homes where violence was normal, but instead of our parents being punished, we were. During each session, I told my therapist what Peter had been doing. She ummed and ahhed and made notes, but she never brought it up during the 'family' sessions.

Then during the next session she listened intently as Peter talked at length about my bad behaviour, listing example after example. 'He can't be trusted,' Peter said. 'This centre is the best place for him.'

Chapter 10

'Tipping Point'
Terrie

Soon after Paul was referred to the family therapy centre, Peter made a private appointment to see my Head of Year. I had no idea what it was about, but afterwards I was called out of my lesson. 'Your stepfather told us we're to look at your behaviour as you've had some problems with lying at home,' she explained.

I opened my mouth to protest, but she carried on scribbling notes, barely looking at me.

'You're going on report and I've asked your form tutor to keep an eye on your progress. I've already had reports you're often missing lessons.'

I sunk lower in my seat, knowing exactly what was happening. Peter was determined to pre-empt any complaints I might have about him too. He was weaving a web, making sure I had nowhere to turn, no one to ask for help. Yes, I did often wag lessons, but only because I couldn't concentrate. I knew there was no point arguing – the way she looked at me made my heart sink. It was then that I realised just how alone I was.

I was actually relieved to get home that day, but Peter was in a mood when I got in, so I disappeared straight upstairs to my bedroom. It was freezing that afternoon – Mum couldn't afford to have the heating on often, so we'd got used to just putting extra layers on. I reached for my favourite jumper but it was missing from my chest of drawers. I remembered that I must have left it out somewhere and I started to panic. Peter had a new rule about anything they got left out or on the floor – if he saw it, he confiscated it. It was really cold, though, so I plucked up my courage and went back downstairs to ask Peter if he'd seen it.

'Yes indeed I have,' he said. 'If I find things on the floor they get taken away. You know the rules. If you don't ask for it within a week it's in the bin. You're going to have to write 200 lines: "I must not leave my jumper on the floor otherwise it will be confiscated" before you stand a chance of getting it back.'

I sat for two hours writing out the lines, as I really wanted that jumper back. Then Paul came downstairs, sobbing. 'What's happened?' I asked, concerned.

'Cars! My ... c-cars!' he cried.

I dashed into his room as he pointed to the floor. For years and years he'd had a precious box of 30 toy cars that he'd salvaged from the bin.

'He didn't, did he?' I cried, knowing the answer already.

That evening Paul had to write 200 lines as well: 'I must not leave my toys on the floor or I'll never see them again.'

The threat of violence hung in the air at all times, but thankfully Peter had stopped visiting my bedroom at night. I was relieved about that, and just wanted to forget it'd ever happened. But sadly my relief wasn't to last.

The next afternoon after school, I opened the front door to find Peter waiting in the hallway, a furious look in his eyes. Paul was at his mate Mark's house for tea and Mum was at work. Instantly my heart started racing.

'You're a greedy little bitch,' he snarled. 'Think I've not noticed? You've been eating all that magic chocolate sauce, haven't you, eh?'

My mind raced as I tried to work out what he was talking about. Paul and Mum loved magic sauce, but usually I avoided the stuff. 'But I don't even like it,' I began.

His face red with fury, he grabbed at my arm and yanked me towards the stairs, shoving me up them. 'Greedy cow, we know it was you,' he screamed. 'Your mum has told me to punish you for it.'

He shoved open the bathroom door and pushed me into it. 'Take off all your clothes,' he screamed, staring at me icily.

I looked at him in shock. 'No!' I began, sobbing. Why was he doing this? Crying hard, I took off everything but my underwear. No way did I want to take that off.

'And the rest,' he snarled.

I shook my head, sobbing loudly now. 'No!' I said defiantly, my arms wrapped around my chest.

Then he reached into his back pocket and took out a pair of scissors. Slowly, and deliberately, he scraped them down the skin on my arms. I flinched, imagining him plunging them into me. Then he opened the scissors. He roughly cut at the seams of my knickers, catching my skin with the scissors, then he snipped the straps of my bra and yanked it off. I felt exposed as he tore them from my body. 'Go and stand in the bath,' he commanded.

I was confused as to what was happening. It was all happening so fast and for no apparent reason. He slapped me hard, making me wince as he raised his hand. 'Hands down by your sides,' he growled. 'If you dare move you'll be sorry.'

I eyed the scissors in his back pocket, glinting at me. I was terrified, more than I'd ever been in my life.

He raised his hand out again and I flinched, automatically moving my hands up for protection.

'Put your hands down!' he yelled, slapping me around the face hard.

I put my arms tight to my side, my nails digging hard into my flesh. Then he pulled out a bottle of magic chocolate sauce from his other back pocket, flicked open the lid and held it up high over my head. 'If you like chocolate sauce so much,' he gloated, 'you can have this whole bottle to yourself!'

And then he squeezed it, a trail of gloopy brown cold sticky sauce dripping down my hair, face and body. He kept squeezing, a look of satisfaction on his face, as I scrunched my eyes tightly shut, sobbing. I'd never felt so humiliated and disgusted. The empty bottle made a whistling sound as he squeezed out the last drop. Then he rolled up his sleeves and rubbed his hands all over my body, sliding them over my breasts, back, thighs and legs, until every single part of me was shining with it. Then he reached between my legs, forcing two fingers inside of me hard.

'Urghhh!' I screamed. It was so painful I caught my breath, crying loudly.

He yanked out his fingers and grabbed the roots of my hair, pulling my head sideways. He then pressed the open scissors to my neck. I let out the loudest scream I could, just hoping someone, anyone, would hear. I was terrified. I was about to die.

'Next time,' he spat, 'it will hurt even more.'

He shoved my head back hard, and I fell backwards, hitting my head against the wall. I slipped down into the bath.

He looked down at me with total disgust. 'Clean yourself up,' he snapped, and walked off to wash his own hands thoroughly in the sink.

I stood up, pulled the shower curtain closed and turned on the shower. I was sobbing, horrified at what had just happened. The shower curtain yanked back. 'You're taking too long,' Peter screamed.

He grabbed my hair again, as I cowered into a ball at the bottom of the bath. He picked up the showerhead and held it close to my face so the water was choking me. I couldn't breathe, I pushed his arm away and he began to whack me across my head and body with the showerhead. Breathing hard, he put it back in its holder, and turned the temperature to freezing. 'You've five minutes to clean yourself and the bathroom up,' he said, matter-of-factly. 'And don't even think about changing that to warm.'

Then he went downstairs. As fast as I could, I cleaned myself in the freezing water and dried myself with a hand towel he'd left on the floor. My entire body ached and felt bruised. A strange mix of terror and total humiliation was coursing through my veins. I dressed myself again, picked up the pieces of cut underwear and blotted the wet floor and walls with the towel. I couldn't believe what had just happened. Just what kind of monster had wheedled his way into our lives? That was the only word for Peter: a monster.

Then I tiptoed quietly to my room where I lay on my bed shaking and crying, trying to absorb the horror of what Peter had just done.

Paul and Mum got home later, but I just stayed upstairs until I was called for dinner. Mum didn't seem upset about anything, or mention the magic sauce. She didn't notice my swollen eyes from crying either. Maybe she thought I'd learned my lesson. I was afraid to bring up the subject so I tried to act normal.

After dinner everyone went to watch *Magnum* on TV.

'Hey, Terrie,' said Peter, nice as pie. 'I really fancy a bowl of ice cream with some magic sauce.'

'Oooh, yes, me too,' said Mum.

'Oh great,' said Peter. 'Go and get some for your mum, me and Paul please.'

My scalp and temples throbbed from the beating earlier as a rising anger welled up inside. I swallowed hard, breathing in deeply. 'Sure, Peter!' I replied, desperate to control the terror in my voice.

I went to the freezer and dished up four bowls of ice cream. The last thing I wanted was some myself, but at the same time I didn't want Mum or Paul to ask me why I wasn't eating it. Sam had followed me into the kitchen and watched me as I scooped into the bowls. It was then I had an idea. 'Sam!' I said, quietly, his ears pricking up. He rose to his feet as I knelt to offer him one of the bowls. Then I watched as he wrapped his tongue around some of the scoops in Peter's bowl. Quickly I poured over the chocolate sauce and handed it to Peter.

'Thanks,' he smiled.

Now Peter had proven to me he was capable of extreme violence, I did nothing but worry about when it would happen next. The stress of not knowing made things worse. I never knew when Peter would appear in my room, or what he'd accuse us of doing. But I couldn't have even imagined what would happen next.

It was just a week after the shower attack when I was met in the hallway by Peter again. 'In the front room,' he ordered this time.

There was a camera set up on a tripod facing the sofa. I frowned, not understanding what was happening. 'Take off your clothes,' Peter commanded.

'What?' I gasped. I clutched my school cardigan around me. 'No!'

'Do as you are told,' he snarled. 'Comply. With. My. Wishes.'

I started trembling; already he was very angry. Before I could react he grabbed my neck and threw me up against the wall. Then he held me in a vice-like grip, his fingers pressing hard on my throat.

'Urggghhhuh,' I gasped.

I tried to struggle, but he raised his hand and slapped me a few times. 'Comply with my wishes,' he screamed in my face. 'Do as you're told, you little bitch.'

Instinctively I tried to twist my head, to release his grip. My chest was burning as I desperately tried to take a breath. Then, as the seconds flew by, my vision began to distort. Everything started to go black at the edges. I began to fade.

'I'm going to die ...' I thought, suddenly, clearly.

Just as I began to be convinced it was the end, he let go. I dropped to my knees, spluttering and gasping, rubbing my throat. But there was no time to recover as he pulled me to my feet again. 'You'll do as I say or wake up one day to find Mum and Paul dead,' he shouted. 'Now take your clothes off.'

Slowly, sobbing loudly, I pulled off my shirt and skirt until I was standing in my underwear. But he pointed at that too. I felt sick, and so badly wanted someone to come home – anyone, just to save me.

I took everything off and sat shivering on the sofa, eyeing the camera with suspicion. I was so terrified I could hardly breathe, and felt so embarrassed I could feel my face flush red. This was disgusting. Peter also got undressed. The sight of his hairy, pale, spongy body made me shudder. Already I could see he was aroused. It made me want to scream with horror. The smell of him alone made me want to gag.

'Put these on,' he ordered, chucking me a pile of horrible, pink, frilly, silky underwear.

'What?' I asked. But the look on his face told me not to ask again. I quickly put it on, actually relieved to be able to cover myself up.

Peter turned the camera on and stood behind it as told me what to do. 'There,' he smiled. 'You look so pretty. Doesn't that make you happy?'

I stared at my hands, shaking slightly, wondering how he could even think such a thing.

Peter turned the camera on and stood behind it as he told me what to do. 'I want you to do some poses,' he said. 'First I want you to spread your legs and put your arm up against the back of the sofa.'

I started crying, as I tried to do as he said. It was all so humiliating. Wrong. Evil.

'Relax,' he ordered. 'Look as if you're enjoying yourself, for god's sake.' But my legs had turned to jelly and my arms felt stiff.

'Why are you filming me?' I sobbed.

'Don't ask questions,' he snapped. 'Just do it.'

Still not happy with my positions, he roughly grabbed my arm and forced it above my head and then kicked my legs further apart. He took a few more shots and then, looking satisfied at the results, he showed me them. All I saw was the fear in my eyes as he forced me to look. I turned my head away. I just thought I looked ridiculous.

'Now get up and dance,' he said, pressing 'play' on the stereo. The room filled with the sound of 'Holiday' by Madonna.

'What?' I gasped.

He pulled me roughly to my feet. 'I. SAID. DANCE!' he screamed.

'Holidaaaaaay … Celebraaaaaate,' Madonna sweetly sung as I stepped two and fro, trying to move my arms in synch.

Sobbing, I hated every second of it. 'You bastard,' I thought, as Peter laughed as he checked through the viewfinder. Finally the song was over. Afterwards, he shoved me roughly to the floor and jumped on top of me. He started rubbing himself up and down on my stomach, groaning like an animal as I twisted my head away from his revolting breath. The bristle of his pubic hair made me sore. Then he made a horrible noise, and got off. I swallowed hard to stop myself from throwing up. 'Get up and get washed,' he commanded, turning to get dressed again.

I ran upstairs, sobbing. It felt like I was caught in a nightmare I'd no escape from.

Chapter 11

'Down not out'

Paul

*P*eter was always dreaming up new punishments and ways in which he could blame us for things. About a month after being referred to the family centre I learned just how far he would push his punishments. I'd had a good day at school that day, came home, scouted for the camera, did my jobs and felt relieved – for once I didn't appear to be in trouble for anything. Then Peter and Mum came home from work, Peter with a packet of tobacco in his hand. 'Can you tell me where this is from, Paul?' he asked me, in a low voice.

'What?' I said. 'No idea.' I didn't smoke. I hated the smell. I knew a few boys at school who did, but it didn't appeal to me in the slightest. I was only nine, after all.

Peter opened it, laying it all out on the dining table in front of me. It was virtually empty, and I'd never seen it before in my life. 'I found this in the alley you walk down to school,' he barked. 'I picked it up after you'd been down there.'

'Me and half the neighbourhood!' I wanted to yell. But I thought better of it.

'So where did you get it from?' Peter demanded.

'It's not mine!' I cried, rising frustration in my voice from the unfairness of it all.

Then he pulled me to my feet. 'Cynth, we can't have this lying,' he said to Mum. 'Do you really want your nine-year-old smoking?'

Mum looked visibly shocked. 'Are you really, Paul?' she asked, eyeing me suspiciously.

'Look, I'll deal with this,' Peter replied. 'You go and make us a coffee. I'll have it sorted in a few minutes.' With that, he grabbed me by the arm and dragged me into the living room. 'You will stand to attention until you admit this is yours,' he said.

Sobbing, I placed my arms by my sides and looked straight ahead, just like he'd told me to. Then Peter settled down in front of the TV, flicking on the highlights of *Hit Man and Her* he'd recorded. An hour passed, Peter reaching to whack me now and then. 'Straighter,' he barked.

Then he moved closer to the TV, as he grew absorbed in the show. 'Cor, look at the tits on that, Paul,' he chuckled, pointing at the TV presenter Michaela Strachan.

I didn't dare as I knew if I did he'd probably slap me, and to be fair I wasn't really into girls and didn't know what all the fuss was about. Clearly Peter *was* into girls as all he ever seemed to watch were the highlights from shows he had taped which nearly always contained either naked/semi-naked women or women with clothes so small an elastic band would have offered more protection.

The adverts would come on and he would hit fast forward. To pass the time he would start on me again. 'Is it yours? Where did you get it? Where did the money come from?'

'No, it's not mine, I have no money other than that in my accounts,' I replied out loud, while my inner me carried on, 'and the £2.50 under the bed, the 50p in the sole of my shoe and the £2 buried around the side of the house.'

'Admit it!'

'IT'S NOT MINE,' I said, with perhaps too much steel in my voice.

Slap. 'Well, you'll stand there some more, then!'

I watched as the digital clock on the video flicked around, until three hours had passed. My back, knees and feet were aching badly. I started to cry. I couldn't take any more. A piece of snot dangled like an icicle from my nose, but I daren't wipe it.

'What does communication mean?' Peter suddenly demanded, breaking the silence.

'Errm … talking,' I offered.

'Communication is a two-way flow of information. TWO-WAY! I ask you a question, you reply with an answer. Do you understand?'

'Yes,' I said, wondering what was coming next.

'It's very frustrating when I ask questions and you ignore them and don't answer. In fact, it's rude, disobedient and I won't have it. I WILL beat the disobedience out of you. Let's try again, shall we?'

It was more of a statement than a question.

Pretending to be helpful, Peter said, 'All you've got to do is tell me this tobacco is yours when I ask.' He took a deep breath, 'Whose tobacco is this?' he asked again, waving the sorry-looking packet in my face.

I couldn't bring myself to answer.

'COMMUNICATION IS A TWO-WAY FLOW OF INFORMATION,' he shouted.

More tears spilled down my cheeks, and as I started to move from one leg to another he reached out and slapped me.

'Okay! Okay!' I cried. 'The tobacco is mine. I'm sorry!'

Peter sat down, a sly smile curling under his moustache. 'Well, finally,' he grinned. Then he grabbed me by my collar. Wallop, wallop, wallop. The strikes came in quick succession. 'You fucking little wanker, you deserve this for lying!' he yelled.

* * *

The pressure inside Churchill Avenue was mounting, with punishments happening every day now. If it wasn't lines, it was a beating with the spatula, and if not that then it was standing to attention. Sometimes when Terrie had to stand with me, we'd wait until Peter disappeared to the loo before jumping manically up and down on the sofa for a few seconds – anything to relieve the unbearable tension from standing on one spot for hours on end. Terrie always kept a look out and nodded at me to stop so we could get back and find the exact spot on the carpet where our feet had been. 'Shhhh,' she'd say, making sure I was ready.

I knew Terrie hated watching Peter beat me, just as I hated her being beaten. So when, a week after the tobacco incident, Peter told us over breakfast that he'd planned a family holiday, our hearts sank. To make it worse, he'd hired a barge. Straight away all I could think about was how cooped up we'd be – a full week with absolutely no escape. On the plus side, there would be no rota, no accounts, no bag and body searches. Peter was over the moon. He pulled out a map and showed us his carefully planned route. 'We're going to travel from Northampton to Market Harborough and back again,' he said, looking pleased with himself.

I glanced at Terrie's face. She didn't look happy. 'Can I bring a friend, Mum?' she asked.

Not wanting to lose out, I asked too.

'Okay,' Mum replied. 'If that's okay with you, Peter?'

I'd noticed that Mum always ran things past Peter recently. She said it was because he made things work more easily at home, but there was something about her tone that was unsettling.

Peter didn't look thrilled at the idea of Terrie and me bringing friends with us, but Mum had already said yes, so what could he do? 'Okay, as long as they pay £30 each,' he replied.

I'm guessing he was secretly hoping none of our friends could raise the necessary funds.

Much to both Terrie and my surprise both of our best friends, Mark and Lisa, managed to cajole their parents into parting with what was a large sum of money and letting them come. So, entrance fee paid, bags packed, routes planned, checked and agreed, we set off on a family holiday.

We all set off squashed in the back of Peter's car to make the journey to the canal, an hour away. We'd not had a holiday since the South Africa trip, so we were excited to get away, and with our friends there Peter would have to be nice. The barge was small and cosy on board, with just two small sections for bunks, where we'd sleep, a living area and tiny kitchen; it quickly felt claustrophobic with Peter prowling around. But at least he and Mum were sleeping up near the front of the barge.

As soon as we got on board, I leaped up the steps through the hatch to the top of the boat to get away from Peter as he inspected how clean it was inside. For someone so obsessed with cleanliness, I'd yet to see him so much as wipe a top down yet. I was only up there for a few minutes before he was behind me.

'Paul, you're not to walk down the edges of the boat,' he said, pointing at the area with grips and a handrail.

'Why?' I asked. It seemed strange, as obviously it was a place designed to be walked across.

'Because I said so,' he spat back at me, 'and that is reason enough for you.'

I pulled a face behind his back. 'Tosser,' I shouted in my head.

'But it's designed to be walked on,' I protested later that evening.

Peter glared at me. 'Yes, Paul. But if you slipped you would go straight over the side, wouldn't you?'

'It's for your own good, Paul,' Mum chipped in.

'But what about everyone else?' I retorted. 'How come they can walk along there?' Deep down I knew why he'd done it. He just wanted to exert some kind of control over me. After all, he couldn't put a finger on us with Mark and Lisa there.

So I watched miserably as Lisa, Terrie and Mark all clambered along the side, chasing each other around the boat, or just hanging on for a different view. Instead, I had to walk through the middle, up and down the ladder, through the wooden hatch, often past Peter; something that was hard to do quickly.

On the first day, after 12 long hours squashed on the boat with nothing to do for entertainment or fun, we arrived in Leicester. Peter announced we were going to see his friend Roger and his family. Roger was also in the TA. 'He's got kids too, so make sure you're on your best behaviour if you play together,' he warned.

As soon as we arrived at Roger's house, we went straight outside to the garden with his two sons. They had a big algae-filled pond and we all went to have a look in it and poke around it with a small net on a stick.

One of the sons started yelling. 'Dad, someone's chucked our toy frog to the bottom of the pond! Dad, quick!'

However, it wasn't Roger who appeared outside first, it was Peter, rushing out as if the house was on fire. 'What toy?' he snapped curtly. If there was ever a chance of 'catching' any trouble, Peter was straight on the case.

Roger's sons pointed to the bottom of the pond. It was a green toy frog with a pump attached which made it 'jump' when you squeezed it.

'Who did it?' asked Roger, now by Peter's side. 'Own up!' he shouted, looking at me first, then Mark, Lisa and Terrie too.

Both Roger's sons looked up and shook their heads. 'Not me,' they said in unison, looking far too guilty for anyone to ever believe them.

Peter grabbed my arm, shaking me until I rattled. 'Oh, don't worry, it'll be him,' he spat.

'It's not a problem, Peter,' Roger said as he quickly fished it out.

'Well, it is a problem because this little wanker does this stuff all the time and lies about it,' he said, squeezing my elbow hard. 'Honestly, we can't take him anywhere.' He gave me a look to say there'd be a punishment later. Then he marched back indoors and relayed the whole event to Mum.

All I could see was her shaking her head in disappointment as he gesticulated at me. I'd only been outside for two minutes. I hadn't even seen the frog, let alone touched it, and there were two very red-faced, guilty-looking children, who may as well have had a big sign above them saying 'WE DID IT'.

That evening, we said goodbye to Roger and headed back to the boat for an early dinner. After the meal, Peter glared at me. 'For lying today and showing both your mum and me up you're going to bed now,' he ordered.

'What?' shouted Terrie. 'But it's our holiday, and our friends are here too. It's only 7 o'clock and we all know Paul didn't touch that frog – it was Roger's kids.'

'And for your insolence you can go to bed now too,' Peter replied.

There was no point in arguing, so at 7 o'clock, with it still light outside, we both escaped downstairs. Mum and Peter stayed up with Mark and Lisa playing snakes and ladders together while we were in bed.

I lay, unable to sleep, for hours that night, thoughts whizzing around my mind. I bet Peter wanted to isolate us from our friends as a punishment for bringing them along in the first place, I thought. Plus he wants them to think badly of us, just like everyone else.

'We can't keep accepting this behaviour, Cynth,' I heard Peter saying to Mum. 'If they insist on lying or being rude there will be repercussions.' I heard the rattle of the dice, and then Peter cheer, as he found himself at the bottom of a ladder. With the sound of everyone else having fun I drifted off to sleep, cramped into the tiny top bunk.

The next morning Peter was upset at the way we'd done the drying up. 'They are putting the plates back completely soaked,' he complained to Mum. 'I think another early night is on the cards.'

For the first three nights, Peter managed to scrape together enough reasons to punish us and send us to bed before dark. Each night we lay there listening to our friends play with Mum and Peter.

On the fourth day, Peter stepped off the boat onto the side of the canal. As always, he had his camera with him, filming the day as it unfolded. But, as he disappeared off the boat I jumped at the chance to join the others along the sides. I carefully held the handrail and walked slowly, behind the others, wondering what Peter's problem had been with me doing this in the first place.

Then, suddenly, his voice bellowed across the water. 'Paul! What did I tell you?' he yelled, his voice echoing off the walls. He came storming across a nearby bridge, just a few metres away. The others laughed and all ducked under the hatch, except for Terrie, who loitered near the entrance. I could tell she was worried for me. She knew what he was capable of.

I froze as Peter bounded over, his camera swinging on his shoulder. 'What did I tell you?' he cried, through gritted teeth. He was keeping his tone down a bit – maybe he didn't want the others to hear – but I could see his fury bubbling.

'I … I was just … just,' but already he was next to me, his face inches from mine. I winced as foul coffee breath hit my nostrils.

'You. Just. WHAT?' he hissed.

He looked over my shoulder briefly, straight at Terrie, and then picked me up in one movement by my throat. I scrambled for a foothold, my legs turning madly like Wile E. Coyote, mid-air over a ravine before a fall, but there was nothing I could do. He held me there, static for a moment, then with a shove threw me down the hatch with all his might – it was about a five-foot drop. However, instead of throwing me through the gap, he threw me at an angle, so my head hit the thick wood hatch itself with a sickening crunch and then I bounced all the way down, landing past the stepladder, unconscious.

Opening my eyes, Mum was the first person I saw, her face all fuzzy. I'd never felt so unwell in my life, so I closed my eyes again.

I didn't wake again until nine hours later, this time in the top bunk of the cabin Mark and I were sharing. Mark was laughing below me. 'Urgh gross! Paul! You sicko,' he yelled.

Lisa rushed in to see what had happened and started giggling. 'Paul's been sick all down the bed and onto Mark's pillow,' she cried to Mum. 'He could have eaten it!'

They both fell about laughing, as Mum and Terrie stood over me. 'Oh God, you must have concussion,' Mum cried. 'See, Peter, we do need to take him! This could be something serious.'

'We're not wasting hospital time,' Peter shouted from his own bed. 'All he's had is a bash on his head.'

'Peter did it,' I managed to whisper to Mum, as she felt the back of my head softly.

'Shhhh, I know love, I've already been through all that with Terrie,' she soothed. 'It was just an accident. He wouldn't throw you through the hatch on purpose, Paul.'

I felt too weak to argue.

'Peter was doing his best to save you,' she sighed. 'If you'd fallen in the water you'd have ended up under the propeller and, my goodness, it's not worth thinking about the state you'd be in then. Peter explained it all to me, Paul. You're really very lucky he was there.'

As I dropped off to sleep again, I wondered just what fairy tale Peter had dreamt up this time to explain nearly killing me.

The next day I kept dozing off, in between throwing up. By the third day I still couldn't get out of bed and had the king of headaches.

'C'mon, Paul, up,' hissed Peter, as Mum was on the top of the boat. 'You've dragged this on for long enough. There's nothing wrong with you, get up.'

'I can't,' I groaned, clutching my bruised and lumpy head. I was still seeing double.

'Get. Up,' Peter hissed, his face next to my ear. 'If you'd done as you were told this wouldn't have happened. Get up, NOW!'

I moaned as I tried to sit up.

'He's just putting it on,' he said to Mum, who appeared at the hatch. 'I'm sure I heard him laughing with Mark earlier.'

I spend the rest of the day quietly sitting on the side. My vision was still blurry, my head ached terribly and I had a bruise and accompanying lump on my head to match. But thanks to Peter, everyone seemed to believe I was okay. Everyone, except for Terrie, who saw what Peter did. He looked Terrie straight in the eye as he threw me, probably a warning if she said anything she'd be next.

'You okay, Paul?' she kept whispering every time she saw me wince. I looked at her. We both knew I wasn't, but what could we do? She was only thirteen still. But I was so grateful she cared. She'd seen what he'd done. She knew the truth.

Chapter 12

'Into an Abyss'

Terrie

'Hey, Terrie, I heard your barge holiday was rubbish,' one of the girls at school said to me on the first day back after the holidays. Lisa was sat in the corner with a group of girls. None of them liked me. As they spotted me come in their giggling grew louder.

'Yeah, what happened?' cried another. 'Sent to beddie-byes early every night, were we?'

Bloody Lisa! I wanted to kill her for telling all those bitches. It wasn't my fault Peter ruined it. He ruined everything. My one relief was that Lisa hadn't spotted the other things he tried to do to me; at least she hadn't seen him trying to touch me up. I thought having a friend on board would mean Peter would leave me be; that was why I asked if Lisa could come.

On the third day of the trip, Peter had ordered me to steer the boat. I agreed, but beforehand pulled a jumper over my swimming costume, to make sure I was covered up while I was on my own around him. Meanwhile, the others were playing on the other side of the boat, about five metres away.

To begin with, I rather enjoyed the feeling of the gentle wind in my hair, the sound of the water lapping at the edges. It was the first time in ages I could appreciate peace. I recognised his smell before seeing him. Greasy sweat mixed with Brut and coffee – unmistakable. Then I felt a hand on my shoulder.

'Terrie,' Peter murmured, snaking his arm around my waist, his hands reaching up under my jumper to touch my boob.

'Get the fuck away from me,' I'd snapped, shrugging my shoulder. I did not want him pawing at me, but at this moment I was most worried that Lisa might spot him doing it. What would she think? She'd be disgusted. She'd think it was my fault.

Peter took a step back. 'Don't defy me,' he warned. 'Otherwise you know what I'll do to your precious family.'

It was just 24 hours later that he picked Paul up by the throat, caught my eye and then threw him down the hatch. I knew then what Peter was saying. In that nanosecond I completely understood how much power Peter had over me. He knew how much I loved Paul and he couldn't care less; he would go to any lengths, he was prepared to toy with his life for his own disgusting ends.

Watching Peter throw Paul was one of the worst moments of my life. I had come to cope with the horrific physical abuse, the control, I thought I could even deal with his perverted behaviour, but this was my little brother – sweet Paul who wouldn't hurt anyone. As Peter lifted Paul's feet off the floor, he sailed through the air for a split second, before landing with the most sickening crunch I'd ever heard. I was amazed his poor skull hadn't smashed to smithereens with the force of the blow. Then I saw Mum standing over him, pale as a sheet. I assumed she'd take action: how could she watch Peter treat her son like this? But it was Peter who didn't stop talking … persuading her he was fine, that he had saved Paul from something much worse.

She was taken in by his every word and it made me feel sick inside. I tried to speak to her later as well, but she didn't believe me.

I was dreading going home after that holiday. I knew that wouldn't be the end of it. What Peter did to Paul was scary – he wasn't right for weeks after that, but I knew that wasn't the end. Peter would punish me further for not letting him touch me.

The evening after we got home, I heard Mum and Peter arguing in bed. 'You're not working enough, Peter,' Mum cried. 'You've not paid a penny towards the house for almost a year now. And that other credit card bill I found is not going to make things easier. You already owe the tax man money. How will we manage?'

'Oh, we'll manage somehow,' Peter said. 'Look, you've got your hands full with those kids and I'm helping manage them. Plus, let's face it. Who'd want you now? You're a fat stupid cow whose kids are delinquent liars. You're lucky I'm even here.'

I heard Mum sobbing as he berated her a bit more. 'I will try and help you pay the cards off,' Mum said quietly later.

I was stunned to hear how beaten down she sounded. Broken. Peter wasn't only affecting us now; he'd wheedled his way into Mum's mind too. Peter controlled everything.

Every day, I dreaded putting the key into the front door. I'd never know what would be waiting there. Would Paul be home, laughing and joking with me, running around doing his jobs? Or would Peter be there, roughly frog-marching me into the living room to do his pervy filming? There was no way of knowing what lay behind it – that was the worst.

It was about a week later that I got home and spotted Peter's red car out front. My heart sank. As I turned my key in the lock, my guts tied into a knot. I'd barely crossed the doormat when Peter was by my elbow.

'Living room. Now,' he ordered. I was having my period and more than ever didn't want to get undressed. I started sobbing as I spotted Peter's camera all set up.

'Please, no,' I said, begged. 'I have my period. Please, not now.'

Peter paused. 'Okay,' he said. Then he went out of the room and returned with his diary. In it he'd written all the dates and times of our school term and where we were supposed to be and when. 'Terrie's period,' he scribbled on that day's date. 'Right, I have a note of that now, so I'll know for next time,' he said. 'But you're putting this underwear on anyway.'

He chucked me some black silk this time. Sobbing, I slowly started to get changed. 'Hurry up!' he snapped, smacking me a few times on the head. 'Before your mum comes home.'

He was already undressed, fiddling with his camera. Then he shoved my limbs into position for the 'poses'. Afterwards, he laid down a bathroom towel on the living room carpet. 'We don't want you messing up the floor with your filth,' he growled. Then he started rubbing himself over me as tears streamed down my face. He forced me to my knees and undid his trousers, pulling himself out into my face.

'Please, Peter, no,' I sobbed, as he grabbed the back of my head.

He pushed himself into my mouth; as I choked, he did it harder. 'Do it! Just do it!' he screamed, slapping the sides of my head. 'You little bitch.'

Panic rose in my tummy, along with my lunch, and I started to gag, throwing up as he jumped backwards.

'You disgusting bitch, clear that up now,' he screamed at me.

I ran upstairs, spitting into the sink. I grabbed my toothbrush and scrubbed my teeth until my gums bled. I just wanted the taste of him out of me. Feeling filthy, I turned on the shower and jumped inside, scrubbing myself with the nail-brush, but however much I scrubbed I still didn't feel clean. Exhausted, I went downstairs for dinner, as Mum was home now. She'd spotted I'd had an early shower.

'Oh you're being very organised today, Terrie,' she said. I said nothing, as I sat down to our egg and chips.

A day or two later, we had a repeat performance. This time Peter used gaffer tape to tie my wrists up as he took pictures of me down below.

'You're a pervert!' I shrieked. 'Fuck off, I hate you!' I didn't want to stop fighting. I knew he could physically overpower me but somehow I wanted him to know he couldn't mentally.

'Ha! Ha!' he laughed. 'Say whatever you like.'

After he'd finished relieving himself, he sank his teeth into my neck like Dracula. Sucking at my skin hard, he gasped as he pulled himself away. Then he sniggered, pointing at the mark on my neck. 'Explain that away at school tomorrow,' he laughed and quickly cleared away the camera equipment as he glanced at the clock. He was always very efficient in packing things away before anyone got home. I'd no idea where he hid it all, although I suspected it was in the attic or the garage. 'Now get dressed before Mum gets back,' he barked.

As I tied my hair up for school the next morning, I spotted a livid reddish mark on my neck. Gingerly I traced my fingers over it, wincing a little. I wanted to heave in the sink, but had no time. After all, the clock was ticking and I didn't want a slap for being behind my schedule as well. I pulled up my shirt collar higher, hoping nobody would notice. It only took until second period in maths before someone did.

'Oooh, Terrie,' cried a girl. 'Is that a hickey?' Suddenly it felt like everyone turned to see the evidence.

I tried to pull my collar up, but it was too late. I didn't even have the hair either to hide behind. Closing my eyes, to the sounds of more laughter, I wanted to curl up and die. I wasn't the least bit interested in boys. The thought of even kissing one, let alone letting someone bite my neck, was repulsive to me. Peter had seen to that.

But that wasn't all. Back home Mum also spotted it over dinner while Peter was out at the TA. 'Terrie!' she gasped. 'What the hell is that on your neck? It's not a love bite, is it?'

I shuddered, lightly touching my skin.

'Where is it from?' Mum demanded as I stared at my plate.

Shame burned my cheeks. I wanted to scream the truth – 'Peter! That Bastard!' – but I knew it was pointless. 'I let a boy in my class do it at lunchtime,' I whispered, quietly.

Mum shook her head. 'Oh, Terrie. I thought you'd have more respect for yourself.'

It was the ultimate betrayal. I felt tears smart in my eyes as a feeling lurched in my tummy. I hated the idea Mum thought that of me, but I couldn't help thinking that if she knew what Peter had made me do she might think even worse.

I'd no idea how Peter managed to orchestrate Mum and Paul being out together at the same time so often, but he did. And with no real friends from school to visit, and little money, I'd no choice but to go straight home after school. Then, one day in class, an obvious plan to buy more time hit me.

In English that day, a lesson I usually loved, I purposefully turned and started talking to the girl next to me after our teacher told us to be quiet and, according to plan, I got given a detention. It was perfect. It would foil any plans for Peter and be enough time for Paul to be home too.

The only other respite I got was when I went to Nan and Pap's. I loved visiting them, but I could never bring myself to tell them what Peter was doing to me. It was a mix of fear and shame that stopped me, I think. I just wanted to forget about Peter and enjoy my break with them. Besides, they'd already decided any changes in me were down to my hormones.

'You'll never be too old for a cuddle,' Nan said, grabbing me tight. 'Already, I barely hear a peek out of you these days at the table, and you've gone all moody on us.' I shrugged. She was right; I was much quieter, and I always wore baggy dark clothes. 'It's normal. Your mum was just the same,' she continued, giving my arm a squeeze.

I shrugged. Little did she know I just wanted to hide my body and pretend it wasn't there to stop Peter perving at me.

Within months of Peter moving in, we'd grown used to walking on eggshells. His temper was less than wafer thin at the best of times. Sometimes he was just totally incapable of controlling himself. I'd just finished vacuuming our brown tiled carpet one morning in April, for the second time (Peter said he could still see white fluff in places), when he called us into the kitchen.

'Now then,' he started. 'I want to know who broke the egg timer?'

I knew neither me nor Paul ever used the thing, so I shook my head, as did Paul. 'Cynthia,' Peter started. 'Did you break the egg timer?'

'No, Peter.'

'Sam, did you break the timer?' Sam just whined.

'It must have been ME,' he announced. Then, like a little imp, Peter started leaping around the kitchen, hitting himself with the spatula, telling us what a naughty boy he was: 'Naughty Peter, naughty Peter, breaking the egg timer. Naughty Peter.' I caught Paul's eye and we both just laughed as hard as we could.

That evening, Paul re-enacted the scene. We were both in stitches. 'I know,' I laughed. Then we both fell silent.

'You know, Paul,' I said, 'I don't like watching you get hurt.' It wasn't like us to be soft. In many ways, we couldn't afford to be too sympathetic. I often feared if I started crying I'd never stop. But I needed him to know. He was my little brother. I should have been able to protect him. He needed to know I cared at least.

'We can take it in turns,' said Paul. 'You admit to the next thing and take the beating, I'll take another one. We'll just try and make it even.'

I grinned uneasily. 'It's a deal.'

Looking across at his lovely cheeky grin and the splatter of freckles across his nose, I felt a surge of pride for him in that moment. Like me, he was a survivor. 'I never want you to get as hurt as I've been,' I murmured. But Paul had already zoned out. Unable to sit and chat in an emotional way for long, he was busy digging around under his bed to show me his secret sweet stash, so I dropped it.

A week later, Mum was out visiting relatives and Paul was at his mate Mark's house. It was the first time Peter and I had been alone in the house for a while, and Peter had clearly noticed. As soon as I turned the key in the lock, I could see he was keen to make up for lost time.

'Right, Terrie,' he said, stripping off, and making sure the camera was focused. 'You're doing something different today.'

I started trembling. 'Fuck off, you disgusting pervert. I don't want to do this!' I hated him so much. Even though I knew my words would just make him angrier, I had to try to fight back. He handed me a long thin piece of plastic, a bit bigger than a lipstick.

'What's this?' I asked.

He gave a horrible smirk. 'A vibrator. I want it inside of you.'

My stomach knotted as I started crying again. 'I can't,' I sobbed. I'd no idea why he wanted me to do such a thing. It didn't make sense.

'You can, and you will,' he said.

I put the cold hard object near me, feeling so violated and nauseous. I just didn't know what to do with it. Peter did, however, barking instructions as he filmed. When the session was over, I just lay on the bed and sobbed. I felt trapped.

The following afternoon Peter appeared in my room with a bigger vibrator. I started sobbing as soon as I saw it.

'Please, no, please,' I begged. But he just snarled, ordering me downstairs.

He had his equipment all laid out as usual, neatly on a towel, and the camera set up on a tripod with the light on red for record. My chest heaved with sobs as he bent down to force it into me. I screamed in pain. And the flashing red light on the camera caught every second.

Life became an unbearable struggle. The only way I could cope was to completely switch off during the torture and sex sessions. I hated my life, I hated school and I hated being home. I was feeling more and more isolated. All that raced through my mind was what I'd face next at home. I lived in dread of what was coming next.

It was only a couple of months later I'd find out.

It was a Wednesday in June and I had just got home from school. Within minutes of me getting in Peter marched me into their bedroom, or Mum's room as I still thought of it. He forced me to take my clothes off and told me to lie on my back on their bed.

'Spread your legs,' he ordered.

129

I twisted my head, eyes closed, feeling so exposed and vulnerable.

'I won't hurt you,' he said, in a strange, softer voice.

I glanced up and already he'd taken off his clothes. I just wanted to throw up and bit my lower lip. 'I don't want …' I began, sobs heaving my chest. I knew what he was planning.

'Just keep still and let it slide in,' he said, climbing over me. He reached to the side of the bed and pulled out a piece of foil. Then he unwrapped a condom very carefully.

Then he raped me. His greasy smell filled my nostrils as he panted with each moment. It turned my stomach. 'Can you feel it?' he gasped. 'Do you like it?'

I just turned to face the familiar swirly aertex wallpaper, staring at the beige paint Mum had loved so much, wondering how the hell this was happening.

Done, he flopped to one side. As he clambered off, I clutched Mum's brown bedspread with tight fists, a rage filling me, replacing the terror.

'You're disgusting!' I screamed. 'I hate you! You're a filthy pervert and I'm going to tell my dad what you're doing! He will come round and kill you! You're NEVER going to do this again!'

Then Peter moved, suddenly, pinning me down by the throat. 'I will have you … how I like … when I like and do WHATEVER I LIKE,' he screamed, a vein bulging on his forehead.

My bravado withered as I struggled for each breath. 'Now clean yourself up, you little bitch,' he said, letting go.

I lay there crying for a moment as he went to the bathroom. I was almost 14 years old and had just been raped. My virginity was stolen. And the truth was I'd never tell Dad what was happening. I couldn't. Not only would he probably not believe me, I didn't trust him to care. I felt that nobody could save me but myself.

Escape plans flitted through my mind at every moment. I often turned over and over in my head who I could talk to. Nobody ever spoke of sex, unless they were laughing about it at school. How was anyone going to believe what was happening? A troublesome girl that no one liked.

'It's for children who desperately need someone to talk to when they have nobody else,' I heard Esther Rantzen explaining on *That's Life*. She was talking about a new charity she was setting up: Childline. 'All you have to do is ring this number.' I made a mental note of it. Maybe that was my way out.

As I lay in bed that night, I imagined running down to the phone box at the end of the street and making the call. But in reality I knew I'd never go through with it. Peter could sweet-talk the stars from the sky. I just felt like there was no hope. He'd probably just tell the police how 'troubled' I was, how I wouldn't accept him as my stepdad. And then what? He'd probably kill Paul. And it would be my fault.

I'd convinced myself that Childline probably wouldn't even believe what I'd told them. No, it was a risk not worth taking, I reasoned. But I had to do something – I couldn't take any more. So, the next day, instead of going to school, I ran all the way to Nan and Pap's. It was four miles and took me over 30 minutes at full pelt. I was out of breath by the time I'd got there. The sight of Nan's smiling face as she opened the door made me want to weep, but I bit my lip. I didn't know where to begin.

'Oh Terrie!' she said. 'What are you doing? Aren't you supposed to be at school?'

I nodded, then walked in. Nan looked worried as she called Pap. 'Pap, Terrie is here.' Then, turning to me, 'How did you get here?'

'I walked,' I said, miserably. 'I have no money.'

I looked at Nan's gentle smiling face as Pap came downstairs and I so desperately wanted to blurt out the truth of what was happening. I wanted to scream out the words. But where could I start?

'Peter is raping me. Peter is touching me. Peter forces things inside of me.' These were not words I could say to my lovely Nan. I knew she'd be mortified. She might not understand. In their old-fashioned world of values and standards and morals and cooking, could they even comprehend the depth of Peter's sickness? And how could I admit I was part of his disgusting world?

Miserably I pushed the thought of saying anything to the back of my mind. I just wanted them to let me stay. 'Nan,' I said finally. 'Please can you let me stay here? Can I stay in your spare room?'

Pap laughed gently. 'Oh Terrie, Peter has told us how you're changing into a big girl now with your own ideas and opinions. Don't worry, it's just part of growing up. Your hormones are raging. We all feel frustrated sometimes.'

I started to panic, as Nan nodded along, smiling away at me in her usual loving way. Then Pap reached into his pocket. 'Look, Terrie, here's 50p to get the bus to school. Come on, love, you don't want to be late.'

'You know we love having you. You can come any time,' Nan added. 'But you have a home already.'

I looked at the coin in Pap's hand, my heart and stomach sinking. Of course this wouldn't work. Nothing was going to work. Peter was in control of everything. I took the 50p, swallowing hard. 'Thank you, Pap,' I said. 'And sorry.'

'Don't be sorry,' Nan smiled, waving me off. 'We'll see you soon, okay?'

With that I turned, from their cosy house, with its familiar smell of lavender and cooking, back to a world I'd no escape from.

Chapter 13

'An Eye for an Eye'

Paul

$\mathcal{B}$y the age of 10, I'd honed my ability to think on my feet and think fast. I had developed the knack of being able to look at a situation and almost instantly analyse all the possible outcomes and select the one with minimum consequences and maximum gain.

Peter was always looking to catch me and Terrie out or blame us for something. The 'two-way flow of communication' he demanded meant I had little time to decide what to do. Should I own up even if I hadn't done it or hold out and risk standing to attention for hours on end or writing endless numbers of lines? Often that was better than owning up and getting beaten.

When he started spying on us and following us around, we had to act fast. If I saw his car cruising past after school, I'd leap in between my two mates, Mark and Elouise, or I'd borrow a hat or coat from someone to disguise myself. After all, I wasn't allowed to walk home with friends. Elouise was a bit of a life-saver really. We got really close at school and for many years she became an extra set of eyes and ears, a co-conspirator and someone that I could trust and rely on. Every time I managed to outwit Peter it made me feel better. It didn't matter that they were tiny victories, it was still a gain.

A week or so after we returned from the barge trip Terrie did the goose-step in front of Peter, and the Heil Hitler sign. I tried so hard not to laugh as my head still hurt from the concussion, biting down on my tongue to stop myself. She got whacked with the metal spatula after, but I did admire her for it.

'Wow, what's got into you?' I whispered quietly afterwards in the kitchen. I eyed the air vent, conscious of the fact Peter had recently learned that you could hear people talking in the other room through it, a fact we later played on to great effect.

'I'm just sick of that disgusting bastard,' she said. It wasn't like her to swear. I'd noticed she was more angry around him than ever, but like Nan had said, Terrie was at upper school now and was growing up fast. I just looked at her, raised my eyebrow and walked away.

Some of what Peter did went past unfair or even malicious. It bordered on being plain nasty and evil for pleasure's sake. I had taken an interest in science, nature in particular, and spent many an hour studying onion skins, fly wings and pretty much anything I could get my hands on under a battered old microscope Peter's mum had given me.

I think Peter realised I enjoyed it and it was a bit of an escape for me, and he resented that. He bided his time and waited for my birthday. I never really had much at birthdays, but this time Mum had bought me a microscope that projected the slide on to the wall. The best present ever!

I began to unwrap it excitedly when Peter blurted out, 'Have you taken the dog out?'

'No,' I replied, 'not yet.'

He grabbed the microscope, which wasn't even completely out of the box yet, and threw it against the wall, then stamped on it over and over.

I burst into tears – my dream present destroyed. When Terrie came to see what was up, he grabbed her pride and joy

– a Timex watch – off her wrist and stamped on that too. 'Fuck off, both of you,' he spat venomously.

As we ran upstairs, Terrie tried to cheer me up. 'Well, there goes his rule about wearing a watch at all times.'

It didn't help.

But the more Peter did bad things to us, the more me and Terrie worked together. We swapped ideas, discussed different routes home, worked on helping each other avoid getting caught by him. Anything that would help us scupper his plans.

'Wow, Paul, how did you get those past Peter?' Terrie asked one afternoon when she saw me walking home after school with some Panini football stickers.

I had chucked them out of my bedroom window the night before and then picked them up in the morning on my way to school. 'Works like a dream,' I said, grinning mischievously. Of course I still needed occasionally to let him 'find' something I shouldn't be taking to school in my bag, otherwise he'd get suspicious. But the grass outside our house in the back wasn't exactly a cricket lawn, so there was plenty of growth to hide things. Peter still searched me regularly as I left the house, but the truth was, as a young boy, with not many friends, I needed to take toys and things, just to fit in. I didn't want to be the kid who could never join in with the games, and Panini stickers were great for learning the art of bartering. I had a natural knack for bartering.

Terrie was impressed. She decided to go one step further and actually buried things in the patches of dirt outside our house, until one of the neighbours asked her if she was hiding something she'd stolen.

This was really the start of me and Terrie turning Peter's own systems against him. The trick we would learn was always staying one step ahead by letting him feel he was still in control.

And so my devious side set to work figuring out how I could get some money 'off the books'. My Pap used to say, 'A man with money in his pocket can do what he likes.' Well, clearly I wasn't a man yet, but I would like some money. I wasn't looking to make myself a millionaire, but a few spare pennies would be nice – I'd work up to the bigger money.

Each week where we lived the Corona lorry used to come around, laden with big bottles of fizzy pop. We used to have maybe one or two bottles a month, which was always a treat, but the bigger prize was the bottle top. If you took it back to any newsagents (complete with the bottle) you would get 10p back.

I considered knocking on people's doors and offering to take their bottles back for a 1p or 2p commission, but I couldn't work out how to get around Peter seeing me or avoid the chance that someone might mention it to Mum.

Then, DING! I had a light-bulb moment. The wall of the local newsagents had been badly damaged in a storm, and sitting in the yard were crates upon crates of empty bottles. What if I could sneak in and grab a couple, then take them in to get the return money? I felt bad for a moment, as this was stealing, but I convinced myself I needed the money more and it would allow me a bit of freedom. It took eight weeks for the wall to be repaired; in that time I acquired 24 bottles, three a week. I promised myself I would repay the newsagents at some point; a promise I kept many years later.

I kept a careful eye on Peter's diary too, always sneaking a look when I could to check when he was working, when he definitely wouldn't be home and when he had days off, information Terrie and I put to good use. He was monitoring our every step, so to keep up we had to keep tabs on him too.

We were always on the lookout for the latest hiding places for cameras as well. Normally they would be positioned under the unit in the living room, under the nest of three tables, under the rack of books, in the hall under the shoe rack, or in my, Terrie or Mum's room. The position always changed, but the little red LED light would always be covered in the same way with a big piece of black tape. Once we even found it up in the attic.

We often hid up there – it was warm and peaceful, and it was normally a safe haven without Peter's prying eyes – but then Peter found an empty box of Poppet chocolates that Terrie left behind and went mad.

The secret to camera-hunting was to walk in the house as normal as possible and then to walk around, pretending to look for the dog, or the source of the bad smell where Sam, our dog, had had an accident. It gave the perfect excuse to go everywhere. And if we spotted a camera, we would never look at it. Instead we would sweep our eyes past it, and pretend to continue looking for a while longer.

One drizzly Thursday afternoon in the middle of winter I came home from school, my tummy rumbling painfully as usual, and was overjoyed to see Peter wasn't home yet. After searching all the regular spots, I was relieved to see there was no sign of a camera either. Phew! I knew I had to do my jobs – Sam needed walking, I had the bath to clean, the kitchen cupboards, outside and inside, and the hoovering. But all I could think about was food, so I made a quick bread and butter sandwich, and flopped on the sofa in the living room to eat it.

As I sat, munching away, I glanced up and saw the over-head light reflecting something on the bookcase: a camera lens. How had I not spotted it? 'Oh bugger!' I thought. 'There is a camera after all.'

I'd no idea how I'd missed it that day, but my mind was now in overdrive – I'd already been caught on camera, eating food I was not allowed and not taking the dog out immediately as I was meant to. I could feel the fear building in my belly as I started to imagine the punishment Peter would think up. I had to think … and fast.

Pacing the room and rubbing my head, my heart was thumping. All of a sudden I realised he'd be watching that too. Instinctively I reached forward, round the back of the big blocky video recorder, and hit 'stop'. Now I knew I'd have to come up with a plan or he'd kill me. Not only had I found his camera, but I had the gall to touch it and switch it off.

It was probably the pressure, the total and utter terror, but suddenly I had a bright idea. My mind still spinning, I ran to the hallway. Trembling with excitement, I grabbed a chair from the kitchen, dragged it through the corridor to the porch, under the fuse box, and climbed up to get a closer look. Running my fingers over the buttons, I felt like a man who'd cracked a secret code. 'Paul, you are a genius!' I giggled to myself. How had we never thought of this before?

I ran back to the lounge and rewound the tape. Sitting back on the sofa, I watched myself come in, flop on the sofa, eat my sandwich, and then look up and spot the camera. You bastard, I thought, as I imagined Peter watching this scene that evening. There was no doubt he would have used it as more 'proof' to Mum that I was an evil lying little boy.

When you pressed 'record' the camera took a good few seconds before it actually started recording pictures – vital seconds I needed to reset the camera and then dash out of the room. 'Take that, Peter,' I chuckled to myself, as I left the camera filming an empty room, recording over the footage of me coming home. Then I dashed back to the hallway, out of shot still, and, after a few silent minutes, jumped on the chair and tripped the fuse. Instantly the house fell silent as the lights went off, clocks turned to zero and the fridge stopped humming.

'Yesss!' I laughed, punching the air as Sam barked. 'Yes, boy! It's good news,' I cried, patting his head.

Now the power was off, so was Peter's horrible little spying game. The footage he had had no trace of my earlier behaviour, and now I could do whatever the hell I liked. So, still starving, I dashed to the fridge and pulled out a pint of milk to glug and some jam for toast. As I bit down on the bread, I heard the door, and suddenly I wondered if it was Peter. Thankfully, though, it was Terrie.

'What's going on?' she asked, cautiously wandering into the silence of our house.

'If you want some time to yourself, just cause a power cut,' I laughed. 'Peter'll never know.'

That evening Peter and Mum were annoyed at the power cut. Peter more so as he couldn't check on us. 'I wonder how many neighbours had been affected?' Mum sighed. But it worked! Peter had no idea what I'd been up to and no one suspected anything.

The power-cut technique was so effective I couldn't resist using it again … and again. Then a couple of weeks later I came home to find the camera positioned in the hall, facing the white fuse box. And this time it wasn't plugged into the wall. It looked like it was powered by a battery. 'Right,' I thought. 'Peter's on to me, so what do I do next?'

I racked my brains as the house was empty, and I so badly wanted some time off again. Then I had a Eureka moment. I grabbed a pair of metal scissors and turned them over in my hands while looking at a plug socket in my bedroom. 'That'll do it,' I thought.

It sounds crazy looking back on it, but I was desperate – willing to do anything for a moment of freedom – so, without any further concern for my safety, I shoved the scissors into the plug.

The noise and shock were instant, as the scissors flew out of my hand, mangled, and my arm painfully buzzed as I was thrown across my room to the wall a few feet away. 'Argh!' I yelped. I picked myself up, my head vibrating still, but looked at the light. Everything was in darkness and quiet.

'Ha! Ha!' I laughed, almost hysterical. I did it! The pain in my arm didn't matter – I'd found a way around Peter's regime. I quickly cleaned the brown burn stain on the plug as best I could and then chucked the burned scissors in the bin (they'd been seared in half by the surge).

Next I walked downstairs looking calm and quickly started about my jobs for the evening; all the while the camera in the hallway whirred away, filming the untouched white box. After I'd finished I thought I'd make the most of my free time, so I ran upstairs and jumped like a maniac on Mum's bed, hitting the ceiling with my hands. Then I went and made another sandwich and ate it in my room while I counted my football stickers I'd sneaked in.

Once again, Mum and Peter came home that evening, annoyed that all the electricity was off, but, as Peter's camera proved, I'd had nothing to do with it. I'd got away with it again and learned a priceless lesson: never use the same technique more than a few times.

So then, every so often, I started letting Peter catch me doing things I shouldn't. Sometimes I'd get home from school and deliberately flop in front of some cartoons for ten minutes before taking Sam out for a walk. I knew the camera was filming me, but I figured that way Peter would think his tactics were still effective and wouldn't change his spying to something I wasn't prepared for. His face always lit up as he quizzed me on these comings and goings I'd slipped up on. It was worth a beating or two to know I was still one step ahead.

But for every small win I was able to achieve through my tricks and games, there was another beating I couldn't avoid. I went downstairs quite late one evening to get a drink of water. Out of the window at the front of the house I spotted Peter, hunched over and lugging our electricity meter to the car. Mum had saved for months to pay for that meter and we were always scrabbling around for coins to fill it up.

'What are you doing up?' Peter screamed, running through the door, grabbing my arm and yanking me back down the stairs.

I opened my mouth to reply, but before I could he slapped my face, hard. Then he punched me in the stomach and told me to 'fuck off back to bed' and 'mind your own business'. We didn't bother to scrabble around for coins for the meter after that. And when the electricity meter reading man came we all had to hide behind the sofa. Peter had clearly been up to no good that night.

But despite how much Peter clearly despised me and Terrie, he still insisted we spent time together as a family. One Saturday Peter took us all to Overstone Park swimming pool. Peter drove and on the way Terrie nudged me as she revealed a tiny piece of tuna in a tissue she'd saved from the tuna pasta bake we'd had for dinner last night.

'It's a little treat for Peter,' she whispered.

'What's that?' snapped Peter, overhearing her despite the sound of the fan heater and car radio.

'Just saying how we're looking forward to swimming,' Terrie replied, loudly. Quickly she took the tuna out of the tissue and stuck it between the back seats.

I still couldn't swim as we couldn't afford lessons and Mum said she couldn't teach me, but I was excited to go to the baths and, despite everything, I suppose I half-hoped Peter might have some tips. 'It's about time you learned,' Peter said, as we walked out of the men's changing room.

'I really want to,' I began, trying to keep up with him.

'Yeah, well, it's not difficult,' he snapped, leading me down the side of the pool near the deep end. Then, quick as a flash, without a second glance, he grabbed me and threw me into the deep end.

Panic gripped me as I went under, then, cycling my legs wildly, I gradually worked my way back to the surface, panting like a dog and gasping for breath. As I finally reached the side, spluttering, I looked up and saw Peter grinning. 'You'd better learn how to swim quick,' was all he said.

Nobody moved; not even the lifeguards seemed to notice. Somehow I pulled and clambered my way to the ladder, where I dragged myself out, trembling. All the while, Peter was just standing, glaring at me, as much as he could without his glasses on, his piggy eyes all unfocused now. 'Manage it, then, Paul?' he said.

'No, Master,' I replied.

'Don't call me Master,' he replied. 'I've changed my mind. I want you to call me God!'

I wanted to laugh, but the look on his face told me not to. And that's who Peter was in our house now: a little god. One who had control over everything: what we ate, what we drank, where we went, how much money we spent, what we did from the moment we woke up to the moment we closed our eyes. God. He might as well have been.

In the car on the way home Mum handed us both ham sandwiches she'd made for lunch. I nudged Terrie as I popped a piece of the ham into the pocket on the back of Peter's seat. I hoped the meat and tuna would rot together for a long while and stink his car out.

Causing a stink seemed a good tactic – Mum was starting to get really annoyed, and it was driving a bit of a wedge between her and Peter. The number of times we heard her nagging him about having a shower … The day after our trip to the swimming baths, I took one of Mum's kippers from the bin and shoved it into the 'dog hole', the place where Sam slept near the heating vent system. It worked a treat, and within minutes the whole house reeked to high heaven of fish. It was disgusting, but worth it to watch the rows unfold.

'Oh my God, Peter!' Mum cried when she got home from work. 'What is that stench? Have you had a bath today?'

Terrie and I both listened through the vent in the kitchen, doing our jobs, trying not to laugh.

'It's not me,' insisted Peter.

'Well, I went to get the map from your car and that bloody stinks too,' Mum continued. 'And you're the only one who's been in it all day!'

It was funny to watch, until Peter started getting his own back on Mum. He seemed unaffected by her criticisms, but he'd retort by telling her she was fat and ugly. Mum would break down in tears. He would pick at her constantly, crushing her self-esteem.

Peter's accusations about our bad behaviour steadily became more and more bizarre, too. 'Who threw a Lego brick down the toilet?' he demanded one day after school. It was such a ridiculous thing to ask. I certainly hadn't done it, and was pretty sure Terrie hadn't either, but Peter wouldn't let it go. 'Right, someone needs to own up!' he yelled, 'or you'll both be writing lines.'

'Not me!' I insisted.

'Nor me!' said Terrie. 'What would I want with a Lego brick?'

'Well, one of you must've!' Peter shouted. 'I'll give you five minutes to own up!'

Terrie and I went into the dining room, while Peter went through to the living room to watch something with Mum.

We knew Peter would listen in, as you could hear everything through the air vent, so we used it to our advantage. But on this occasion neither of us wanted to take the blame. We knew Peter must have planted it and I guess we'd both had enough of the beatings that week. Plus, sometimes it worked if we both refused to admit something. Either we'd get off with no punishments or we'd both get it in the neck.

'I promise I didn't do it,' Terrie protested loudly.

'I didn't either,' I said.

After five minutes, Peter came back and turned to Terrie: 'So, have we got a confession yet?' he asked.

But I could see in Terrie's eyes she'd had enough. She jumped up. 'I hate you!' she screamed and ran upstairs to lock herself in the loo.

But Peter ran up after her, dragging me with him. Outside the door, he gave me a sly grin. In a loud voice, so Terrie could hear, he said: 'I knew it wasn't you, Paul.'

My eyes widened. I'd never heard him say that before. What was he doing? Playing us off against each other? Then he continued: 'Have you been a good boy this week?'

It sounded a bit like the old Peter, the nice Peter, the one we knew when he'd very first moved in, something that felt like decades ago now. 'Yes, Peter,' I said, trying to understand what was happening.

'No,' said Peter. 'It's not "Yes, Peter." It's "Yes, Boss!"'

'Yes, Boss,' I said, feeling embarrassed. Surely he didn't expect us to call him that now?

'Now,' he continued. 'What do you think we should do to your sister? Let's work it out. She lied and then tried to blame you. Now, if that had been you, what punishment would you expect?'

I shrugged. I hated the idea of Terrie being punished. I didn't want to gang up against her. This didn't feel right. I could picture her sobbing on the other side of the door. But Peter's eyes were boring into me over his glasses, expectantly. 'I s'ppose I'd expect a slapped bum,' I shrugged.

'Ah!' said Peter. 'I s'ppose you're right. But she lied twice, didn't she? She lied about the Lego, and then she lied again to get you into trouble. So she deserves a slap for that as well, surely, eh?'

I shrugged again and fell silent. I didn't want to be involved in plotting what was going to happen next. Terrie was my sister, I loved her.

It was an hour before Terrie emerged, but Peter waited silently outside the bathroom door the whole time, and as soon as she did he grabbed her, pulling her downstairs and forcing her to bend over the chair for a good whack, not stopping until she screamed with pain.

I went to see her afterwards. She was just lying on her bed, her eyes all blotchy from crying. 'Yes, Boss! No, Boss!' she teased, her eyes flashing, as soon as she saw. I bit my lip; somehow I felt I deserved that. I was so angry with Peter. Not only had he beaten Terrie, he'd managed to drive a wedge between us.

Chapter 14

Holiday Hell

Terrie

*W*hen, two years after he'd moved in, Peter announced we were all going to go away to Torremolinos in Spain for a holiday, my heart sank. After the barge horror, I couldn't think of anything worse. He'd almost killed Paul on that holiday and completely got away with it, so what on earth could happen this time?

My spirits lifted when I realised we'd be staying in a self-catering apartment with Peter's friends Jim and Sandra and their kids. It meant security in numbers. Surely, with that many people around Peter wouldn't be able to lay a finger on me all week? What bliss.

Peter had arranged for us to get a coach all the way to Spain as it was much cheaper than flying, so we all piled into his car to set off for the pick-up point. But as he turned the key in the ignition, the car made a terrible sound, a popping bang that made us all, except for Paul, jump off our seats.

'What the …?' Peter gasped, leaping out of the car.

He went to look at the exhaust and picked up the remains of a frazzled potato someone had stuffed in there.

'The little wankers!' he cried, his eyes roaming along Churchill Avenue.

I glanced at Paul, who looked like he was about to burst a blood vessel, in desperation not to laugh. It didn't take a genius to work out he was involved. I loved my little brother all the more for fighting back. Little jokes like this kept us going. Watching Peter erupt with annoyance, or irritation at little things in life, from a shoe lace that snapped or a cuff of his shirt dropping off as he pushed his hand through (sabotaged by us) to a smell in the house he couldn't stand was our way of taking back a bit of control, making his life difficult. For every tiny act of defiance we got some strength from somewhere. With Peter swearing and cursing we set off to the motorway service, the first leg of our journey to Spain.

Exhausted, and with pins and needles, we finally arrived and Peter showed us to the apartments. Paul and I were sharing a room with two single beds, Mum and Peter were in another. It was lovely. We even had a swimming pool on the roof.

Quickly we settled into a routine of getting up late, having a leisurely breakfast and going for a swim. I wore a string vest over my swimsuit the whole time. It was fashionable at that time, but I wasn't wearing it to look cool. I was just desperate to cover up my body. I hated the way Peter looked at me, running his eyes up and down even with others there, like I was a piece of meat, or something that belonged to him and him alone.

One afternoon we all went off to watch a bootlegged showing of *ET* in the cinema. But there was a torrential downpour as we left, so we dived into a couple of local shops to get out of the rain. Paul and I were browsing when he picked up a pack of cards and started giggling. 'Eurgh, look,' he said, waggling one in my face. 'Why are these men putting their willies in women's mouths?'

I felt bile rising in my throat as I thought of Peter forcing my head in between his legs, his hands twisted in my hair. 'Stop it, Paul. I don't want to see that, thanks,' I snapped.

Then Mum caught Paul and snatched them away. 'Paul!' she said. 'That's not nice. Don't look at those.'

'If only you knew,' I thought grimly, pushing my sense of shame even deeper inside of me.

Peter heard the commotion and took the cards himself. 'Paul, you little wanker,' he spat, before he slowly browsed through them. 'No, you really shouldn't be looking at these. This is not suitable, not at all. Especially for underage kids.'

I walked off in disgust.

'What's up, Terrie?' Paul asked.

'Nothing,' I said. I never ever wanted Paul to know about this. He was still such a kid, an innocent little boy. My instinct was still to protect him.

Peter's irritation at Paul was apparent all the time. The poor kid was excited to be abroad, always jumping up and down, asking where we were going next. But Peter just kept glaring at him, giving him warning looks.

'Will you keep quiet in public?' he growled. I could see his hands itching to give him a whack.

The next morning I was sat by the side of the pool, reading, as Peter leered at me. 'Oooh, Terrie's boobs are getting bigger now, aren't they?' he quipped.

I shuddered, folding my arms, doing everything I could to cover my breasts, the ones he'd bitten and pinched until I screamed with pain.

'Oh, leave her alone,' Mum laughed.

Peter had bought another new camera for this trip and he took it everywhere with him. That evening we went to a local bar for a dance, and as we boogied on the dance floor Peter kept taking snapshots, his flash blinding other holidaymakers as they danced nearby.

'Oi!' one yelled. 'Stop it!'

Peter skulked off when he spotted a pretty blonde woman. Then, without her permission, he started taking shots of her too. 'She looks like Debbie Harry,' he shouted with glee above the music. I cringed, wondering what Mum was thinking, but she just ignored him.

The following night we all went out to a taverna for tapas and beer. I'd been allowed a glass too, although Peter kept trying to top it up.

'No thanks,' I said. 'It's too bitter.'

Quickly I felt tired and longed to go back. Paul had already gone alone about an hour earlier and I just wanted to join him. 'I'm off, Mum,' I said. It was only 10 minutes away so I knew I'd be okay walking on my own.

'Okay,' she said.

Peter put down his beer and stood up. 'I'll come with you,' he said. 'Make sure you're safe.'

'No, it's fine,' I insisted.

'No, really,' he pressed, giving me the hint of a smirk. 'Look, I've just finished my drink.' He picked up his glass, gulping the dregs.

'Go on,' said Mum. 'Let him walk with you.'

I pulled a face, and shrugged. At least Paul was in the room, so Peter couldn't try anything.

Peter was a bit drunk, staggering slightly as he walked with me. He tried to make conversation but I just stayed silent; even walking in public with him made my skin crawl. When we finally arrived, I raced the short distance to the door, anxious to wave goodbye quickly. But he caught up, reaching it at the same time as me. Quickly I opened it and almost ran to my bedroom. 'Goodnight!' I called over my shoulder, hoping he'd disappear. But he followed like a shadow. As I reached my bed, he pressed himself against my back.

'Paul's here,' I hissed, turning around. 'Don't wake him!'

The look on Peter's face told me he didn't care and he wasn't going anywhere. He started fumbling at his flies.

'Stop, no,' I whispered hoarsely. 'Fuck off!'

He walloped me round the face. 'Just shut it and lie down,' he snapped. 'It will only take a minute.'

'No!' I half yelled, pent up fury erupting, pure anger that this man had the audacity to even try and rape me while my poor little brother lay next to me. Paul knew nothing of this sick evil, and I wanted to keep it that way. A 10-year-old boy wouldn't understand what rape was.

'You stupid bitch,' Peter spat. 'Just be still and get it over with.' He'd managed to pull himself out of his pants and started ripping at my top.

'Fuck off! FUCK OFF!' I screamed. I glanced over at Paul. All I could see was a body-shaped lump in the gloom.

Peter slapped my head a few times, then grabbed my hair by the roots. He started pushing me into the mattress, then pulled the pillow over to cover my face as he fumbled at my pants. He'd managed to just get his penis in, as I wildly kicked out at him. 'You fucking bitch,' he yelled.

I gasped for air, as the pillow squashed my nose against my face, making me sweat with panic. I could barely breathe. He punched me hard in the stomach. Now I was winded as well as breathless. It was agony. Then something inside told me to go limp. With all my strength of mind I forced my body to be still. 'Pretend you're dead,' I repeated to myself, allowing my arms and legs to go floppy.

Within seconds he let go. I heard his flies zip up and the buckle of his belt jangle closed. Then rapid footsteps and a door slam. I waited a few seconds, then peeled the pillow, the material wet with tears and sweat, off my face.

The bastard thought he'd killed me but hadn't even

bothered to check. Immediately I looked across the room. Paul hadn't moved. I guessed by now he must be awake. A dead person couldn't have slept through all of that. But I couldn't bring myself to ask. I didn't want to know what he thought. I just couldn't bear to talk about it. And if he didn't ask any questions I wouldn't have to tell him what Peter had tried to do.

The next morning Peter barely looked at me. He avoided me after breakfast and went off for a walk on his own. Thankfully for the rest of the holiday he didn't bother me. I stayed away on the other side of the pool from him and his camera and ignored him over dinner. I liked to think even he'd been shocked at his actions, but I didn't hold my breath.

We always holidayed out of season as it was the only way to afford it, but I was glad to be away from school as it was as miserable as ever when we returned. I woke the Monday morning after our holiday and I just couldn't face going to school. Home life with Peter was tough and there were days I just couldn't concentrate. Paul had informed me that Peter was working all day, so I sneaked out a butter knife to open Paul's window later.

I called for Lisa as usual and we walked to the park and waited until we knew it would be safe to return to my house. We climbed over the back fence, then up onto the shed roof. I took out the butter knife and slid it between the panes. The window opened and I turned and signalled to Lisa to join me. We clambered in, feeling pleased at the easy entry.

'What do you fancy doing?' I asked Lisa. We decided to get out a few magazines she'd bought and have a read over them. I loved *Smash Hits* and *Just 17*. I wanted to put on my new Blondie LP but didn't dare just in case the neighbours heard or Peter came home unexpectedly. After chatting on my bed for an hour or so, we got out a game of cards, when I heard a sound. It was Mary, our lovely neighbour. Mum had given her a key to let Sam out into the garden if she and Peter were at work.

'Sam!' she said. 'Oooh, what a horrible smelly poo! You naughty boy, Cindy won't be pleased with you!'

I covered my mouth as Lisa and I listened in, giggling at the sound of Mary talking to Sam.

'Oooh, it smells so bad!' she continued. 'It's a stinky one.' We kept laughing, muffling our mouths.

Then we heard her leave, laughing at the fact she'd no idea we were upstairs, merrily playing our game. It felt so good to have some fun.

About 20 minutes later, I glanced out of the corner of my eye through the frosted part of my bedroom window to spot a red blur. But this time my smile immediately disappeared. Red only meant one thing: Peter's car.

'Quick!' I hissed at Lisa. 'It's Peter! We need to hide.' I shoved the cards under the mattress and did a quick scan of my room, making sure everything looked the same. My heart raced as I grabbed Lisa's arm. We'd no time to get back out through Paul's bedroom as Peter's key was already chinking in the lock, so I pointed to the wardrobe. 'We'll have to hide in there,' I whispered urgently. I shoved Lisa in as she giggled, thinking it was the best game. Huddled next to her, I pulled the doors shut as quietly as possible.

Lisa was trying hard not to giggle. 'Shut up,' I hissed between gritted teeth. 'Please! We really do have to be totally silent.'

Lisa's face fell a little. 'Are you really that scared of him?' she asked.

'Yes,' I replied. 'He'll kill me.'

How little did she know how true this was.

We fell silent, listening to his footsteps already on the stairs. Hugging my knees, covered with coats and cardigans, I rested my head on my arms. My heart was pounding so loudly I was sure he'd hear it. My whole body was trembling with fear. The padding of his shoes was now by my bedroom door. We heard him enter the toilet, which was opposite my room. The sound of his pee hitting the toilet bowl was thunderous in the quietness of the house. I seriously wondered if he'd hear my heart as I slowed breaths, trying not to panic.

We listened, as the toilet flushed. We heard soft footsteps. Then he was *in* my room, shuffling around. He was rummaging through my underwear drawers. One. Then another. Then the bottom one. Then he opened another again, I assumed the top one, and paused. The thought of him touching my underwear made me squirm. How dare he?

Then after a few minutes and more footsteps, the door hinges squeaked as he closed it. The front door slammed and the car revved up.

I flopped out of the wardrobe door, exhaling loudly on the carpet, Lisa piling out after me.

'Wow,' she said. 'What was he doing?'

'I dunno,' I said, shrugging it off. 'He was probably just looking for something.' But I knew it was weird, my stepdad rooting through my bedroom. I also had proof now Peter did go through my things, and I hated him all the more for it.

Peter later returned home and found me alone in my room. He showed me some pictures of a girl with horrible satin underwear on like the stuff he made me wear. She had big sad brown eyes and looked very upset. 'Will you pose for pictures for my friend Stephen?' he asked.

'No way!' I gasped.

'Why not?' he said. 'It's good money and a proper studio.'

'Over my dead body!' I snapped, walking away so I could get on with my jobs. I was amazed he'd bothered to ask me. Part of me was scared that he could force me to.

It wasn't only me and Paul who were frustrated by the number of tasks we had to do, Nan and Pap had also started to notice just how 'busy' we were being kept, at all times, even when they came to visit. Occasionally they would come over on a Sunday for dinner. I'd help Mum cook a lovely roast, usually a chicken or turkey, with lots of vegetables and roast potatoes.

After dinner, Nan and Pap sat down on the sofa to let their food 'go down' while Peter pulled out his film collection. 'Do you fancy watching a *Carry On* film?' he asked.

'Go on then,' said Nan. I could tell she wasn't keen on Peter still. As polite as ever in front of him, she often gave Pap a withering look if Peter's back was turned. Peter popped the video into the machine as Paul and I perched on the sofa arms, wondering if we'd get to join in. But, like always, relaxing in front of the TV for us was vetoed. Just as the film started, Peter peered at me over the top of his glasses. 'You tidied your room, Terrie?' he asked.

'Yes,' I replied.

'Really?' he said.

'Yes,' I said.

'Go and check,' he said.

I went upstairs, and while I was up there he followed me. 'Call this tidy?' he said, pulling out some clothes from under my bed. 'Fold them all up.'

I returned a few moments later. But as soon as I sat down, Peter glanced at me. 'Can you help Paul finish the washing up?' he ordered.

I sighed and got up again. When we'd both finished, we went back to try and catch up on the film and have a chat with

Nan and Pap. But as soon as we both snuggled up next to them, Peter glared at us. 'You two,' he said. 'Did you dry the sink?' Paul looked at me. 'No, I thought as much,' said Peter. 'Right, back out there. And wipe all the tops down and clean the floor while you're in there.'

By the time we'd finished, so had the film.

The following Sunday, Pap started pulling a face as he watched me rushing to and fro, dusting the mantelpiece and even the top of the TV as they watched it. 'Terrie, love, why don't you sit down and relax?' he urged, after I'd given it a polish, removing all the ornaments one by one as Peter liked.

I looked at him. I daren't say anything against Peter. Not while he was within earshot in the kitchen. 'It's fine, Pap,' I mumbled.

Pap started huffing as he realised I wasn't going to stop. He kept shifting in his seat, looking for Peter to come in again. When Peter appeared Pap could no longer contain himself. 'Right, that's enough, Peter!' he said, as Peter started barking orders at Paul to tidy his toy box. 'We hardly see the kids when we come over. They're given that many jobs. We're here to spend some time with them, not watch films by ourselves,' Pap ranted.

Peter sighed. 'Yes, George,' he replied calmly. 'But you see if they'd done all the jobs they were supposed to do before you came this wouldn't have to be like this. I'm just trying to teach them.'

I listened to Peter as everything that poured out of his mouth sounded so normal, reasonable. Like, really, he only ever had our best interests at heart. I wanted to scream. He was so manipulative, so good at making it out it was our fault.

Once Nan and Pap had left around 8.30 p.m., Peter turned on us, his face glowering. 'If you dare question my authority,' he said, in a low voice, 'you'll pay for it.'

Instead of making me pay, he picked on Paul after they'd gone. He ran to the kitchen drawer, but the spatula was missing. Occasionally Paul hid it if he suspected a beating was on the horizon. 'Where the hell is it?' he screamed, grabbing at knives and spoons. He pulled open the drawer below and then whipped something else out instead.

His eyes flashed as he grabbed Paul's neck, pushing him over the chair. Above his head he brandished a new weapon for us all to see: a meat tenderiser.

'No!' screamed Paul, as Peter pushed his head down so he had to bend over.

'You little bastard,' said Peter. 'Thinking your sister can question me!'

Afterwards Paul lay sobbing in his room. He had a livid pattern of pin-pricks in a square shape over his arms as he'd tried to defend himself.

I tried to make him see the funny side. 'At least you'll be popular at school. I bet no one else has a bruise that shape. It looks like a grid.'

Somehow, bless him, Paul managed to smile.

While Peter's choice of implements to hit Paul with was growing more vicious our rape sessions in front of the camera were also becoming more regular and now happened at least several times a week. Most weeks he would engineer us being alone, even just for half an hour.

Peter always managed to organise the time perfectly. He'd lay out what he was planning to use on me or force me to wear in the lounge, abuse me on film and then tidy everything up before anyone got home.

Then one evening Mum told us how she was going away for two nights to a carpet seminar. 'I have to stay in a hotel,' she said, 'so Peter will be holding the fort.'

Peter grinned at me behind her back. I knew exactly what this meant. He'd have a whole two days and nights to do whatever he liked with me. Just hours later I heard him tell Paul to arrange a night away at Mark's house. I felt sick.

As the weekend approached, a rising sense of desperation gripped me, but, aside from running away, it felt impossible to keep this man away from me. In a last-ditch bid to try and put Peter off, I decided to stop washing completely and stop cleaning my teeth. I figured if I smelt that bad it might put him off.

Quickly my hair turned greasy and after just two days my breath started to smell. I felt horrible, uncomfortable and grim, worse than I did already, but it was worth a go. Every night for about four days I went upstairs to run a bath in the evening or put the shower on in the morning, but I didn't wash anything.

But it was pointless. As soon as the house was empty, Peter pounced on me. And if I expected him to say something, I was wrong. As he pulled my top off, I could smell my own armpits, but he didn't say a word about it. His breath and body odour were so bad anyway it nearly overpowered mine. This time he pulled me into Mum's bedroom and raped me on the floor. I lay there all night afterwards, as Peter wouldn't let me go to my own bed, shivering and crying inconsolably. How could I take much more of this?

Chapter 15

'Timed Torment'

Paul

*H*earing Terrie and Peter in that bed in Spain stayed with me for a long time after we got home. I'd no idea what he was doing but hated hearing my sister cry like that. He'd hit her a few times but he seemed to be standing over her breathing hard as well. I closed my eyes and pretended to be asleep as I knew I'd get the beating of my life if I said anything. Terrie didn't say anything at all afterwards. We both dropped off. I think there was an unspoken bond between us that we both felt relieved if one of us was being beaten it meant the other one wasn't.

We'd missed a week of school to go away to Spain but then the real summer holidays arrived. Now we faced having Peter at home most of the day and we were dreading it. But Peter had plans for us. 'You're to be out all day long when Mum's at work,' he said simply. 'And woe betide if I catch you sneaking back in.'

Sneak back in? I thought. No chance of that. I intended to stay as far away from him as I possibly could.

He opened the front door just after Mum left and we weren't to come home again until after she got home. There was no mention of food or money. Mum had none for us anyway. The money situation was worse than ever. As more cameras and other gadgets filled our house, more credit card

159

bills piled on the doormat and Mum worked longer and longer hours.

Peter also loved to send us off to bed without dinner as punishment. We were constantly hungry and knew of every single orchard and bush within a two-mile radius of our house. We ate blackberries, apples, pears, cherries, plums and walnuts and if really desperate crab apples that made your mouth instantly dry; our diet was truly organic. But after a few days of this, fruit wasn't always enough to fill us up – we needed something not fruity. We were starving most days.

But by now Peter's eagle eye was accounting for virtually everything, so we had to be careful. We looked so hard at the cupboards to see what angles the tins were and how many there were, to try and outwit Peter's seemingly photographic memory. He'd even marked with a pen where the liquid came up to in the bottles of squash or pop to monitor what we drank. That was easy enough to get around – we simply topped things up with water.

One day Peter's car was sat outside all day long, with him inside watching TV and drinking coffee so we couldn't access the house at all. Neither of us could bear to wait until dinner for something to eat so Terrie nicked a Mars bar from the corner shop, but she was caught and Mr Oakley told Mum the next time she went down there for milk. She came back fuming and told Peter, who didn't hesitate to hand out a proper beating with the spatula.

'I am sorry, Cynth,' he said afterwards as Terrie wailed in pain. 'Can't you see how off the rails Terrie is now? She's a little thief.'

The next day, as we sat under a tree in the park, I had an idea. 'Let's time ourselves to see how long exactly it takes to get in and out of the house via my bedroom window. I'll keep a lookout for Peter and you slip into the kitchen and grab some food.'

'Wicked,' Terrie replied.

I checked Peter's diary (he'd left it on the bookshelf) to see when he'd be working next, and that evening Terrie timed Peter to see how long it took for him to walk from his car to the front door. It was exactly 21 seconds.

Next we timed the whole manoeuvre of getting in and out of the house, with me acting as a lookout in the top bedroom for signs of Peter while Terrie grabbed food. 'Two minutes and 53 seconds,' I said, proudly.

Just before we left Terrie took a tin of potatoes, choosing something from the back of the cupboard and moving everything else forward so Peter wouldn't notice anything amiss. Every label had to be facing forward in the way he'd left it. Then quickly we climbed out again and back down to the shed, pulling the window shut behind us. We practised it again until the whole exercise took 1 minute 45 seconds.

But we had one more issue to deal with. We needed to know precisely when Peter would be home in the coming days. He always kept his diary by the computer so I decided to sneak a peek when he wasn't looking. I made a quick mental note and then jotted down the times and dates for the week in my bedroom. It felt brilliant to know we now had the option to go home and help ourselves to food without anyone noticing a thing.

Over the next couple of days we sneaked back and forth, taking extra slices of bread and a few tins, then eating them outside. However, it wasn't long before eagle-eyed Peter noticed something amiss. A few nights later he looked at me sternly over his glasses. 'Has anyone had a can of meatballs?' he asked. 'I noticed one has gone missing.'

I looked as innocent as possible. We both loved Princes meatballs, even eaten out of the can cold with a spoon. 'Yes!' Terrie said brightly. 'I cooked some for you, remember?' She smiled. 'A week ago last Tuesday.'

I exhaled with relief as he looked puzzled and then his face relaxed. I knew if he did notice things missing we'd have to think on our feet.

The following night I was mixing some dog food and biscuits for Sam as was on my rota. 'Mmmmm, this smells delicious,' I joked, but actually taking it a step further I licked the end of the knife.

'What are you doing? That's repulsive.' Terrie recoiled. 'You'll start barking and begging for treats next.'

'I just had to test it. Actually, it's not that bad.' I panted and ran around on all fours chasing a squealing Terrie.

Finding out that I liked dog food had an advantage: it was the one foodstuff Peter didn't keep strict control over. Which meant Terrie would nick a tin and some biscuits if we came home hungry in the afternoons. Then we'd run like the wind back down to the park and sit under our favourite tree to eat it. I had buried Dad's old army tin opener under a bush nearby.

'I can't believe we've become this desperate,' said Terrie miserably, as she nibbled on a few of Sam's biscuits.

I had an idea. I flashed her a movie-star grin, my eyes wide. 'Mmm, I love the smooth meaty chunks in Pal,' I laughed, smacking my lips together.

She giggled. 'You look like you're from a dog food advert.'

Some days rain was a problem. We had literally nowhere to go. We'd sit huddled together under a big oak tree, staying close for warmth. Although many kids around our way didn't have much money, I bet few were so hungry they had to sit in the rain under a tree eating dog food.

Soon after, one August day, we managed to get inside and up into the attic. Peter hated us going up there, it was strictly forbidden, although he was always popping up and down there to see his increasingly large collection of videos all stacked in date order. But we managed to get in, slide the ladder back up and play up there. We were playing 'Snap' and trying to slap each other's hand as we slapped the card down.

While I was slapping a card on the roughly planked floor, the ceiling shuddered. The door had been slammed. We both stopped playing our card game and froze, our hearts beating so loudly we could hear them. 'He's back,' I hissed. 'Shhhhhhh.'

We sat hardly daring to breathe. Then we listened as Peter mooched around. As he started chatting to the dog, we stifled giggles. 'You're a smelly boy,' he was saying, as Sam whined around him.

'He's not the only one!' I whispered, forcing Terrie to stuff her jumper into her mouth to stifle laughter.

He only stayed for a few minutes and then something hit me. 'Terrie, have you noticed how Peter has been leaving his diary in really obvious places?' I said.

'Yes, I suppose he has,' she replied.

He usually kept it near him but over the past few days he'd been leaving it on the stairs or in the hallway. 'I think he's actually doing it on purpose. He'd put in his diary he was out all day today, but look, he's back, sneaking around looking for us, I bet!'

'Well, how do we get round that one?' Terrie asked.

I grinned at her as a very easy solution fell into place. 'I'm going to ring BSM and ask for Peter's shifts for the week, then we'll know for sure.'

'What?' gasped Terrie. 'That's too risky, surely?'

'No it isn't,' I said. 'What person at BSM could possibly think Peter's family were checking up on him?'

The next day I called Shirley, Peter's manager, and cheerfully asked for his shift pattern. She happily gave it and I got away with it. It was such an obvious thing to do, I was certain she'd never check.

Later that evening when Mum got home from work, Peter was in a bad mood. Mum had made him steak as a special treat for tea but he just sat staring at it. Then he sliced off a piece and looked at it like he was looking at a week-old turd. 'This isn't how I like it!' he snapped. He shoved the plate hard across the table away from him in disgust. 'I want you to do it again and this time it needs to at least resemble a steak and not require a pint of water to rehydrate it.'

Mum looked up from her steak. 'We don't have any more,' she said. 'You'll just have to have mine.'

Peter had started to complain more and more to Mum about her cooking. The previous night he'd told her he didn't like the beans on toast. 'Make it all again but put it NEXT to the toast,' he'd cried. 'Beans on toast make the toast soggy. It's horrible.' Mum's eyes filled up as she went back to the kitchen to redo the meal. Now tonight she was going hungry.

Later that evening, Peter was sitting on the sofa eyeballing us as we watched *Hawaii Five-O*. Then he dug his finger into a nostril, pulled out whatever had been residing in there, rolled it between finger and thumb and flicked it at me. 'Make me a coffee,' he barked.

Glad to, I jumped up. Then I rushed back with it. It was one of my special froth-a-chino's with an extra addition – a small squirt of washing-up liquid.

Peter took big slurping sips as usual. Then he stopped half-way through the cup. 'Urgh, this tastes of washing-up liquid,' he said.

'Oh, sorry,' I apologised, trying to put my most apologetic voice on. 'Terrie probably didn't rinse it properly last night.'

Terrie glared at me then, but I lifted my eyebrow at her. Not only had that been a decent enough explanation, I was thrilled Peter had downed a few gulps. Putting washing-up liquid in a drink gave you a terrible tummy.

Chapter 16
'Fresh Hell'
Paul

*T*he following week it was raining so hard we decided we couldn't stand being wet any more. After checking with BSM we knew Peter definitely would be in all day, so we walked to Nan and Paps instead. We were so happy to see them, it was such a relief. Nan couldn't believe how soaked we were and dried us off before making us some chips. She made proper crinkle-cut ones, all fried in a deep-fat fryer – the sort that was likely to reduce life expectancy. 'We've got frozen Mars bars for afters,' she grinned – one of Nan's favourite 'stand-by' desserts.

We all sat around, chatting and relaxing, when suddenly a red car slowed past their house. I spotted it through the front lounge window. 'Oh my god, it's Peter!' I cried. 'Sorry, Nan, but we're not supposed to be here!'

Pap looked up. 'Oh dear. I'll go and keep him busy.'

Terrie and I jumped up from the table as Pap pushed 50p into our hands. 'Go out the back and over the wall,' he said.

We raced off and leaped over walls like hurdles behind their terraced house, apologising to neighbours as we went. We managed to get on the bus and make it back before Peter did. It turned out he just had a last-minute driving lesson in the area.

The next day Terrie was helping me make mud pies in the garden, enjoying a few hours of peace as Peter was out doing a couple of lessons. As we laughed, throwing mud at each other, Mum was sunbathing nearby. It was like the good old days just after Dad had left, the three of us hanging out together. It was almost possible to forget about Peter. But as we flicked mud at each other, a shadow appeared at the back door. I instantly recognised Peter's shape. At first, however, I hadn't spotted what he was holding in his hand.

Then we heard a sharp crack. I dropped my mud pie and stood up. 'Oi, you two had better run for it!' Peter cried, firing a ball-bearing gun up into the air, setting some birds off in the trees.

Terrie and I leaped to our feet, the hairs on the back of my neck standing on end. I was petrified and saw the whites of Terrie's eyes as she stared back at me.

'Oh my god,' she gasped.

Mum sat up too. 'Peter, stop!' she said, trying to warn him off, but he completely ignored her.

'Go on!' yelled Peter. 'Run!'

The garden was only small, but we started running around the perimeter, assuming that's what he meant. Then Peter raised the gun and started taking aim. Like two trapped rabbits running for our lives, we kept crashing into each other, or the fence, as we desperately tried to get away in panic.

'Quick, Terrie,' I screamed as we bashed shoulders. The garden really wasn't big enough for this. Breathing hard, I felt sick to my stomach, adrenaline racing through my veins. Then a terrible pain like someone had smashed several nails with a hammer into my shin hit me.

'Oooooowwwwww,' I screamed, clutching my leg. The pain took my breath away.

'Your fault, Paul,' laughed Peter. 'Not running fast enough. Little wanker.'

Terrie came running over to help me, but then Peter took aim again, sending a steel ball through her hair. 'Arghh!' she screamed, clutching at her head. He'd missed this time, but only just. She helped me to my feet. I had to half hop, but ran, crying now.

'Faster, faster,' screamed Peter, taking a few pot shots past us at the fence. His eyes were darting around, as we jostled like trapped fish in a barrel. Then finally, after 10 minutes of us racing like a pair of mad dogs, Peter told us it was over, and we collapsed panting like greyhounds at a race, rubbing ourselves where he'd hit us. My head was buzzing as I gasped like an animal.

'What a twat,' Terrie cried.

Mum was glaring at Peter. 'What do you think you're doing?' she yelled.

'Aw, shut up, it's just a fucking game for the little wankers!' he screamed at her.

Peter's new 'game' started suddenly, whenever he fancied it, and whenever we were happily minding our own business in the garden. He even accidentally shot Mum in the toe once; she cried out in pain, but nothing stopped him. Not until he'd grown bored with it did the game end.

That night I avoided Peter, but after the gun incident I knew he was in a mood, so while we did the washing up I smeared a thin layer of butter over the handle of the metal spatula. Sure enough, it worked, slipping out of his hand as he swung it back above his head later preparing for a power swipe, hitting the window and cracking it. He went even madder but it was worth every second seeing the surprise on his face and wondering how he was going to explain it away to Mum.

The next morning it was school. I woke up wishing I still had a few more hours as my bum and legs were so sore still from running around to avoid the gun. I was exhausted too. I couldn't remember the last time I'd had a proper night's sleep.

As my alarm rang out I heaved myself up, desperate to stick to the schedule to avoid yet another bruising. Peter didn't let up on checking my bags, coat and even buttocks and it remained the usual tricky experience of trying to get my 'contraband' items to school and back in one piece. But I'd also successfully found a new way of keeping things safe. For months I'd got away with keeping things in my locker instead of bringing them home. Peter was none the wiser.

Then one day, out of the blue, Peter announced that he was taking me to school and was going to check my locker. How he had found out about the locker I don't know, but this was likely to cause me a few problems. I had invested some of the bottle-top money a few months prior into some Warhammer figures. I paid a friend called Chris to paint them and I then resold them for a modest profit. This gave me a steady 'off-the-books' income. There was a collection of books and toys, including my prized yo-yo, plus a few miscellaneous items like stickers and magazines, all stored in my locker. The house of carefully placed cards I had built was all about to come falling down.

We reached my locker, just outside my form room, and Peter's face lit up like a Christmas tree – all his birthdays had arrived at once. 'You're going to get a thrashing straight after school,' he grinned as he started grabbing everything.

'You can't take them, they're not mine', I yelled desperately. 'I'm looking after them for a friend who has no locker!' I blurted out, knowing he wasn't going to believe me.

'You lying little …' Peter was saying in hushed tones as he was interrupted by a voice.

'Morning, Paul. Can I have my things back now? I've just collected my new locker key.' Glenn, a classmate, said, waving a very shiny key in front of me.

At this point Peter went a bit red and mumbled something about 'when I get home', while stuffing the items back into the locker and storming off.

'Jesus, Glenn,' I said, 'you couldn't have picked a better time to step in. I owe you BIG TIME.'

'I could see you were in a bit of bother,' he replied happily as he walked into class. 'Pleased to help.'

Shortly after this, I decided to set up a second locker. Now when Peter came for spot checks I could safely store all my prized possessions in there.

This worked for a while, but after about a couple of spot checks I realised Peter was likely to get suspicious again. The last thing I wanted was for him to find the second locker. So I 'accidentally' I left the key to the second locker in my bag. As Peter rifled through it as part of the morning bag check, he pounced on it. 'Ah-ha!' he said, pushing his glasses further up his greasy nose. 'And what's this, Paul?'

'A key for a locker,' I said, putting on my best miserable voice. 'Erm, it's my friend's.'

He glared at me. 'Is it now?' he cried.

'Yes!' I insisted.

'I don't believe you,' he said, his piggy eyes narrowing.

'I swear!' I repeated.

'Every ACTION has a REACTION, Paul. Remember?' he said. 'Now tell me the truth.'

I scuffed my feet on the carpet. 'Okaaaay,' I said. 'Sorry, it is mine. I have a second locker at school. I confess.' I held my hands up, like I'd seen people in films do as they confessed all. Thankfully Peter sucked it up just as I'd wanted him to.

He narrowed his eyes. 'You little fucker. Think you can get this past me, eh?' He grabbed my arm and pulled me close to his face. 'I'm coming to school with you,' he snarled, jumping in the car. He glared at me all the way there and marched me to the lockers again. He loved making a spectacle in front of my classmates.

'Which one is it?' he snapped, as I pointed. Fumbling for the key, he couldn't wait to get it open. Throwing open the door, he found a couple of books I'd already read and some stickers that were duplicates.

'You sneaky little bastard,' he said under his breath, scooping out my belongings. Then he slammed it shut and locked it, dropping the key into his pocket with a jubilant flourish. 'Nothing gets past me, and you'll be punished for this!' He turned and walked out as the bell went.

I paused for a few moments to make sure he'd gone, then smiled to myself. Inside my shoe was another key, so I shook it out and then opened another locker: my third one, filled with all of my favourite belongings Peter knew absolutely nothing about! Now I'd let him find my second locker he was unlikely to believe there was a third.

When I'd explained my new locker system to Terrie she was so impressed. 'Blimey, Paul, you think of everything!' she said, grinning.

That weekend was boiling hot; we were having an Indian summer. Peter had said he'd been waiting to find a suitable punishment for finding the second locker, and he'd decided today was the day to dish it out. He went to the garage he rented at the back of the house and returned with something that looked like a spaceman's suit. 'This, Paul, is a Nuclear and Biological Chemical Warfare suit,' he smirked. 'And you need to put it on.'

'Eh?' I said. 'What for?' I was confused. Does he know something that I don't, I thought, looking at the sky.

'You're going to go outside and creosote the whole fence and the new shed this afternoon. And you need to wear this. To protect yourself from the fumes.'

The suit was very thick and rubbery. It came complete with a black rubber gas mask. 'Put it on,' growled Peter. 'And get outside.'

I swallowed hard. I knew why he wanted me to wear this and it had nothing to do with protecting me from creosote. Even with a pair of shorts and a T-shirt on it was roasting outside. This wasn't going to be easy. But knowing I'd no choice I started to pull it on.

He stood over me, helping do the buttons and zips, pulling them tightly shut. Within seconds I felt suffocated. He jabbed me in the back with his index finger. 'Outside,' he barked, the sound of his voice muffled now.

Slowly, feeling like a space monster, I waddled to the back door. I hadn't appreciated the punishment 'allowing' Peter to find that second locker would involve.

Peter thrust a pot of creosote and a paint brush into my hands. Clumsily I grappled for it, the rubber chafing as I tried to get a handle. 'Now get on with it!' he snapped.

I looked down the fence. It was about 30 feet long. It would take hours, and to make it worse a shed lived in the corner of the garden so for about 10 feet I'd have to work in a confined space. I started to pace my breathing as I bent over stiffly to dip the brush in before pulling myself upright and slapping the liquid on.

Sweat was pouring down between my shoulder blades and I could taste salt on my top lip. I wanted to cry but I knew tears would only make the condensation in the mask worse so I concentrated on my breath and the paint. Bend, dip, breathe, brush, bend. I tried to focus on a rhythm, knowing the faster I worked the faster I could get out of this horrible situation.

After half an hour I started to feel faint. My mouth was dry as sandpaper as waves of sickness washed over me.

Now and then Peter came out to see how I was doing. 'Bloody hell, is that all you've done?' he screeched. 'Faster! Work faster!'

'I can't!' I blurted out. 'Please, Peter. I feel like I'm gonna pass out.'

Peter muttered to himself and went back inside. I wondered what he was going to bring out next. I half expected the ball-bearing gun. Instead he came out with a strange-looking bottle.

'This is the bottle designed for the suit,' he smirked, unfurling a long bendy piece of 'straw' from the front of the mask. He attached it to the top of the bottle and ordered me to 'suck'.

The water was warm and tasted all plasticky, but I greedily drank, desperate to stop the thirst. After just a few mouthfuls Peter pulled it away. He looked pleased with himself for 'allowing' me to drink without even letting me take off my mask.

Two hours later I'd finally finished and felt myself half collapse, as far as that was possible in a stiff rubber suit. I was drenched, my hair sticking all over my forehead with sweat, but I'd managed to complete the task.

Peter rushed out when he saw I'd stopped. 'Oh, so you think you're finished, do you?' he asked, pacing up and down, inspecting every inch. 'Here,' he said, pointing to one spot. 'Do here again. Come on, get yourself on it.'

He had me 'redo' a few spots to his standards for another half an hour. I think in the end it was too hot for him to stand outside too, so he'd had enough and told me I could stop.

Pulling that rubber off felt like being released from a torture device. I fell on the tap in the kitchen and drank three glasses of water, one after another. Afterwards, I stood for a few moments, trying to gather my strength, unable to quite believe what Peter had put me through. I was basically being tortured by a psycho, and nobody, nobody was doing anything about it. I'd tried to tell Mum, my teacher, I'd even tried to tell the staff at the family centre, but nobody believed me. I dreaded to think what punishments Peter would come up with next.

Chapter 17

'Betrayal'

Terrie

I loved Paul for always trying to be one step ahead, but even with his quick mind he couldn't always counteract Peter. Watching him out of the bedroom window suffer in that nuclear suit was one of the worst things I'd seen, but worse still was my own helplessness. I longed to scream at Peter to stop it, but what good would it do? God knows what the neighbours thought. They must have heard Paul moaning, and the ball-bearing gun and the flares Peter randomly set off too.

For Peter it was more important to capture me alone, of course, and he was becoming more and more opportunistic. Mum, Paul and I all had an appointment with our dentist so we caught a bus down to the bottom of the racecourse. All we needed was a check-up and teeth clean, so Peter picked us up afterwards.

First he dropped Mum back at work, then Paul at school, before driving me on. I was looking forward to going to school. I had art and I'd been throwing my frustration into my work. My stomach lurched as I realised we'd gone the wrong way – we were heading back to the house.

'No, Peter, PLEASE!' I begged. 'Just take me to school. I don't want to go home.'

My heart was racing as he didn't react. The fucking igno-rant bastard was ignoring me. The thought of going home alone with him was terrifying. Peter pulled the car outside our house and opened my door for me, as if playing the role of dutiful stepdad. He gripped my arm and escorted me to the house, ensuring I didn't run off. To anyone looking it would just seem innocent.

But as he clicked the front door behind me, he didn't waste any time. 'Get your clothes off,' he ordered.

'No!' I shouted. 'I want to go to school!' Suddenly I'd had enough. I wasn't going to do this. Not this time.

Peter grabbed a handful of my hair, twisting it around his fingers. 'Do as you're told. You know it's not worth fighting me,' he said.

But this time I stood still. No, Peter, I thought. No.

Without warning he punched me hard in the stomach. I doubled over, gasping and feeling hollow inside. He grabbed my hands, pushed me to the ground face down and jumped onto my back, sitting on me, so I could hardly breathe, pushing my mouth and nose into the carpet.

'Urgghhhhh!' I tried to scream, kicking at him as his knees pinned down my hands.

He flipped me over, and I let out the biggest scream I could produce, as he fumbled for my tie. Unfurling it off my shirt collar, he stuffed it into my mouth. Then he ripped open my white school shirt and used a blade to cut my bra in the middle. Grabbing hold of my nipples he twisted them as hard as he could. Then he slapped my breasts, and started biting me viciously.

The pain was excruciating as I screamed. But as he kept biting something strange happened. As I breathed through the pain my tears stopped falling, and I found myself just staring at him as if my body wasn't my own.

He spun me back over, ripping off my cardigan and blouse. Then he grabbed some rope and tied my hands together and grabbed my head and banged it repeatedly on the floor, until I started spinning. Next he pulled off my knickers. Now naked, he roughly tied my ankles together and my hands behind my back. My heart started thudding as I began trembling so much I could barely breathe.

Finally he stood up and took a few steps back as if to admire his handiwork. 'Feel vulnerable, do you, Terrie?' he asked. 'What would Mum do or say if she came home and found you like this, eh?'

I tried to keep still and just breathe, but feared his next move. Like a tightly coiled spring inside, I felt my body tremble like jelly.

'Scared, are you?' he continued, a smirk playing on his lips.

'NO!' I said, my voice muffled by the tie. Quaking in terror, I was on the brink of total panic again. My chest felt so tight. I truly wanted to die.

'How would you feel if you woke up and found Mum and Paul had been suffocated, or their throats slit?' he asked sinisterly.

'You bastard,' I thought. He knew that would be my darkest fear.

'Please just give up on me,' I begged my body. 'Just die. I don't want to be here.'

Peter pulled back his foot and gave me a sharp kick in my sides.

'Urghgghhh,' I tried to scream, in pain. I breathed in deeply through my nostrils to manage it.

'Don't be defiant,' he said. 'You'll only regret it.' He paused for a moment. 'Maybe I'll leave you there for Mum and Paul to find you,' he mused. As I listened, waiting for his next move, I concentrated on trying to keep my breath even.

'Don't panic,' I told myself. In and out. In and out.

Suddenly he crouched down and started biting my legs and bum as hard as he could. Then he moved up to my shoulders and arms. Next he briefly moved away, then suddenly pushed something cold and hard inside of me. A sharp pain clenched my insides as if I'd been poked by a needle. He kept pushing and pushing, and I winced with pure pain as he viciously poked me with something that looked like a sword.

Thoughts of school popped into my head. Art was my favourite subject. I imagined the girls lining up outside and filing in. Mr Mutton the teacher, with his fiery red hair and beard like a lion's mane, would be organising paints, asking everyone to be quiet. That lesson we were due to draw an alien scene.

More pinches to my bottom and legs jolted me back. My guts churned as bile rose into my throat. More panic set in, as I imagined choking on my own vomit.

'Breathe,' I told myself firmly. 'Just breathe.' In and out. In and out.

I took breaths as deeply and slowly as possible until I could feel my heart rate slow as a new strange calm descended. I could still feel Peter's teeth on my skin, but somehow now I was breathing through this pain. The tears stopped again.

Suddenly my mind became blank, as a sense of sheer calm took over. I knew he was still chomping at my skin, but I was just here, breathing calmly, almost as if nothing was happening. And in a way it wasn't. I'd somehow 'left' my body behind on that carpet, naked and being bitten by a man I hated. The horror of what he was doing was too much to take.

Then he jumped off and walked out as I lay there like a zombie, feeling numb. Until another bite jolted me back to the room again. He pulled the tie from my mouth, but as I gasped for fresh air he wound it tight around my throat.

'Time to die,' he said, simply.

As much as I'd wanted to die moments earlier, I tried to struggle. I didn't want to die. Not here. Not like this. Not at the hands of this bastard. But I knew it was futile, so I allowed my body to relax again. As spots danced in front of my eyes, darkness started closing in. It might have been minutes or seconds, but I opened them to find I was untied.

'Get dressed,' he ordered.

I leaped up and dressed as quickly as possible. 'You're disgusting!' I screamed. 'I hate you and hope you burn in hell!'

His eyes widened with rage as he launched himself at me, grabbing for my neck again. He slammed me up against the wall. 'Unless you want to be responsible for the deaths of your family, watch your mouth,' he yelled.

He raised his knee hard into my crotch. 'Next time it won't be my knee,' he spat. Then he let go. 'Get what you need for school,' he said.

I grabbed my bag and ran out of the house, the bite marks all over my body stinging. Peter followed me and opened the car door. We sat in silence as we drove there again, him looking calm and like the helpful stepdad again. He dropped me at school and I rushed to art. The teacher glanced up as I tried to slip in unnoticed.

'Ah, Miss Duckett, you're late!' he said.

'Sorry, Sir,' I said, looking for a spare seat. It seemed so surreal: just 20 minutes earlier I'd been fighting for my life on my living-room floor; now I looked like a normal schoolgirl starting a lesson. My head was spinning. I took a few breaths, trying to squash the desire to scream at him. 'You're fucking lucky I'm here at all!' I wanted to shout.

But I didn't. Instead I put my anger and frustrations into my art session. Swirling and dabbing orange and black paints on the paper, I tried to think of something other than Peter.

At the end of the session Mr Mutton looked impressed. 'What's this you've depicted, Terrie?' he asked.

'It's a raging, hot, fiery planet,' I said to him. 'A burning hell-hole.'

I'd been thinking of some way to hurt Peter back but decided to bide my time. Then, as the annual Royal Marine Association dinner was coming up, an idea formed. Our Pap was the local Royal Marine Association chairman and it was going to be a big do, so it was the perfect time to cause maximum embarrassment to Peter. It was a drop in the ocean compared to what he'd done to me, but I had to do something. Paul and I agreed: any little thing to irritate him in life was worth it.

I waited until Peter and Mum went out together to a work do – Peter told us he wanted us in bed at 8 p.m. and if he caught us up we'd know all about it. Paul had already scouted around for the camera and was certain Peter was bluffing and he'd not hidden one. So I slipped into their bedroom and into Peter's wardrobe. All of his clothes were horrible. He wore big kipper ties and pointed lapels from the Seventies, as he was too tight to buy new clothes. Careful not to move anything else, I managed to slip a pair of his hideous black polyester flared trousers off the rail, the ones he always wore on special occasions.

Grabbing a pair of scissors I unpicked a few stitches on the seat. And I rubbed itching powder all along the inside seams of his trousers too; I had sold an old pair of earrings to a girl at school to buy some at the joke shop on the way to Nan and Pap's. I'd also bought some sugar loaded up with laxative, but I saved that for another day.

The next day we all trooped off to the drill hall in the barracks, all dressed up. Predictably, Peter had worn the special-occasion trousers, but hadn't noticed the sabotage. As always, Peter ensured we were kept rushed off our feet all day. We'd had to make hundreds of sandwiches and I was told to work in the cloakroom to take tickets, while Paul stood at the entrance taking tickets.

When we arrived I told Paul about the trousers; I'd been bursting to tell him since I'd done it. He bent over double, gripping his sides with laughter. 'This is why I couldn't tell you sooner. Just calm down and keep an eye out for the big riiiiippping.'

This made me laugh harder.

'I'm so glad you're my big sister.' With that, he ran off back to take the last tickets.

Predictably, the hall was packed. Peter was on his best behaviour, taking the ladies' coats and pulling out chairs for them. From a distance, it was obvious why people thought he was a charming man.

'It's so good of him,' one lady quipped, not knowing who I was. 'For taking on the Duckett family, I mean, two kids, and I've heard how troubled they are.'

I felt my insides clench. Peter had fooled everyone, and done a very good job of it indeed. Every last detail had been planned, so even if we did complain nobody would believe us. The thought made me question my own sanity. The world we lived in was so completely warped.

Paul came and sat with me and we sat and ate the dinner we were given by Nan. We sat and watched Peter; we couldn't take our eyes off his backside. Surely, it was just a matter of time. After a few speeches and dinner, the music started. Then I noticed Mum talking to Peter crossly. She was pointing to his backside, rolling her eyes.

Peter then sat down on the chair looking confused. He was furiously rubbing at his crotch.

Paul had been handing out drinks and came sniggering into

the cloakroom. 'Terrie, it worked!' he cried. 'His trousers are completely split. He can't dance now. He's gonna be sat down for the rest of the evening!'

We both cracked up, crying with laughter. 'Every action has a reaction.'

Peter was furious when we got home. He'd no idea how his trousers had split quite like that but he had nobody to blame. Mum was cross too and said he'd probably not be so itchy if he showered more.

A few weeks later Mum managed to persuade Peter to get back in touch with his mum, whom he'd been estranged from for many years. 'She's only getting older, Peter. You don't know how long she'll have left,' she said.

Reluctantly Peter arranged for us all to go and see her at her council house in Hemel Hempstead. Her name was Inge and at 5 foot 8 she was Peter's height with greying hair and neatly dressed, wearing metal-rimmed glasses, and spoke with a strong German accent. 'Call me Oma,' she ordered me and Paul. 'It's German for grandmother.'

I could see where Peter got his obsession with neatness from, as Oma's house was spotless, everything having its place. She was a strict lady, and expected us to be quiet with good manners, but we liked her. She made delicious crêpes filled with mincemeat and covered in a cheese sauce, and amazing German layered cakes filled with chocolate and creams. And she was interested in us, always asking questions about school and our lives.

As we settled down for dinner, Paul and I were famished as usual and tucked in with gusto.

'Cor, this is nice,' said Paul, his mouth full like a hamster's. As our portions at home were always so small and controlled, we always fell on plates of food like starving animals.

'Very glad you like it!' smiled Oma.

'Don't be so greedy,' snapped Peter as I reached for a second helping of cake.

'No, Peter!' barked Oma. 'There is plenty to eat and that's what the food is here for.'

She turned to me, her face softening. 'Eat as much as you like, my dear,' she said.

For once we did.

After that visit she hugged us warmly goodbye and told us to come again soon. Peter didn't touch his mum and coldly bid her goodbye. He was in a terrible mood once we'd got home.

We did start to pay regular visits, however, usually thanks to Mum arranging them. Peter always looked on edge during our visits. I sensed a feeling of resentment towards her. I wondered what she'd think if she knew what her son was doing in private, but it never crossed my mind to actually tell her. After dinner, she always settled down for a glass of Asti Spumante, her favourite, she said. Then we'd go outside and sit on her garden swing if it was a nice evening.

On the third visit, Peter brought his video camera along. He usually took it everywhere but obviously wanted to wait to see if he could get away with it with Oma. We were having a barbecue outside in her back garden. Oma used her dustbin to stoke up some coals and then cook meat on top. She set up a table by the swing and Peter set up his camera directly opposite.

He kept adjusting it so everyone was in shot. When Paul had his back to the camera he ordered him to move. 'What iz all zis filming for?' asked Oma.

'Just testing a new camera,' said Peter.

We all knew very well it wasn't a new camera at all. Peter had become more and more obsessed with capturing every event outside the house. And he liked to play it back in the evening to try and 'catch' me or Paul out for doing something we shouldn't be. He was documenting every second of our lives, but not for the joy of having children. It was his own sickening need to control.

On Christmas Day, Nan, Pap and Oma all came over for their dinner, and they all got on rather well. Pap bought some homemade apple wine with him, and we all cheerfully had a glass, toasting a 'Merry Christmas'. Mum had cooked the dinner and, for once, we were all stuffed afterwards. For a few moments I could even pretend we were a happy family.

Then, as Pap poured me a glass of wine it somehow ended up missing my mouth, and spilled down my top and trousers. 'Whoops,' I laughed. 'I'll just go upstairs and change.'

'Go on then,' said Nan. 'We'll save you some pudding!'

I left the table and ran upstairs. Pulling off my top and trousers, I ferreted in my top drawers to get some more underwear. The wine had seeped right through. As I pulled some out, I heard my door creak open. I stood up, clasping the clothes to my chest as Peter's shadow fell onto me. 'Peter!' I spat. 'Get out!' I was incensed, feeling a little braver too, knowing Mum and everyone were downstairs.

'Quick, leave your clothes off,' Peter said. 'I want sex now.'

'What?' I gasped. 'What, with Nan, Pap and Oma downstairs? You filthy pig. Leave me alone.'

'Do as I say or I'll drag you downstairs naked and tell them all you were coming on to me!' he snarled.

Tears sprung to my eyes just at the thought of Nan and Pap's faces. The shame was too much to bear.

Already he was next to me, twisting my body around. He pushed me over my bed slightly and started to rape me. I shut my eyes, held the side of the bed, desperate for it to be over.

Then I heard a voice. 'Terrie!'

I twisted around to see Mum standing behind Peter with his pants down at his ankles. She was horrified. 'Peter, what the hell are you doing?' she cried in a hushed whisper.

She grabbed me and pushed me into the bathroom. 'Terrie, what's going on?' she cried.

I started sobbing, hardly able to speak with relief. Finally Mum had seen what he was doing. Now she'd have to throw him out. He'd been caught in the act.

Saying nothing, Mum turned on the shower. 'Get showered and dressed,' she said. 'Then go downstairs and act normally.'

I was a bit confused, but guessed she didn't want to spoil everyone else's Christmas too. So I quickly showered and dressed, then fixed a smile to my face as I went back downstairs.

'That took a while, love,' said Nan.

'She'd spilt half an orchard,' Pap laughed.

I sank back into my chair at the dining-room table, breathing out a sigh of relief. Nobody had overheard. Peter had busied himself tidying away and Mum was asking if anyone wanted another drink. The only way I knew anything was wrong was how flushed her cheeks looked.

I tried to guess what she was doing and decided she was just waiting until everyone had left before confronting the bastard.

That evening Peter put on the TV and we all sat watching the Christmas film, *National Lampoon's Christmas Vacation*. I even managed to find myself laughing at it, awash with relief that Mum finally knew the truth.

The next morning I got up and Nan and Pap were already ready to leave. Paul was going with them. Oma went a bit later on and so finally I was alone with Mum and Peter.

Now the moment had arrived, I was almost excited. Mum would have to throw him out. This was it.

After saying goodbye to Oma I shut myself in my room, waiting to go back downstairs and see what Mum was going to say. How Peter was going to react? God only knew.

Then Mum called me downstairs.

'This is it!' I thought. Finally, once we'd got rid of this monster we could piece our family back together. But as I walked into the living room Peter and Mum were sat on the sofa together. Peter's arm was curled around Mum's shoulders. I'd not seen them cuddled up like this for a while.

I just stared at her in total confusion. 'Mum?' I began.

But she interrupted me. 'Peter explained everything to me,' she said, curtly. 'I couldn't understand at first. Couldn't believe it was possible. But actually it makes sense, I suppose. You're young, you're confused and you thought you'd try it on with him.'

I opened my mouth to speak, but the look on Peter's face stopped me. He was absolutely jubilant.

Mum frowned, looking like a crossed lover. 'What did it feel like, Terrie?' she asked. 'Did you enjoy it?'

I just shook my head as the full horror dawned on me. All hope, all faith. It had vanished. I had nothing left. My heart felt like a burst balloon shrivelled to nothing as the reality sunk in: Mum had caught Peter raping me but blamed me for it. 'No,' I said dully. 'I didn't enjoy it.'

I didn't bother to protest. I just listened to Mum ranting about the betrayal and how she couldn't believe it, her own daughter coming on to her partner. But Peter was so deeply sorry. He said it would never happen again. He'd promised her.

I stared at her. 'If I was the one coming on to him how could he promise not to?' I wanted to shout. It made no sense. But then, none of this did.

'Let's just put it all behind us,' Mum said finally. 'Okay?'

I didn't say anything and walked out of the room, knowing now for sure nobody would ever believe me. If my own mother refused to see the truth in front of her, what chance did I have telling anyone else?

Chapter 18

'Best-laid Plans'

Paul

*A*s soon as I was old enough, I couldn't wait to join the army cadets, with meetings held every Tuesday and Thursday night at the Gibraltar barracks in Northampton. Although I was not close to Dad, he'd been in the army, and of course my Pap had been in the Marines too.

And I absolutely loved it. Not only did it help me escape the house, but I learned all kinds of new skills and, for once, I didn't stand out from the crowd. I wasn't Paul Duckett being teased for being poor or having a rubbish surname. I was a Cadet Duckett or, as I became known, 'your Dukiness', learning new skills and being recognised and rewarded for trying hard.

I quickly excelled. Having the chance to do something I loved meant I wanted to do my best and prove to everyone and myself what I was capable of. And do something away from the misery at home, somewhere safe.

I became a good marksman and able to shoot all kinds of weapons with the .303 Bren gun from World War Two being a particular speciality. I could strip and reassemble it to five main body parts in 24 seconds. No one was quicker. I also did well in running and got county colours and came top in clay pigeon shooting. Of course, having to spend a lot of time running home from school or jogging to places instead of paying for buses kept me very fit.

I started to accrue several badges and we sewed them onto a brassard, a kind of armband that we wore proudly at parades. For the first time in my life I felt real pride in what I was doing, and when my instructors noticed and said 'Well done' it was a wonderful feeling.

Sometimes Peter couldn't wait to take me there – it was almost as though he couldn't wait to get rid of me – and would jangle the car keys an hour before it started. 'C'mon, let's go now,' he said. 'Get there nice and early.' But as time went on he realised how much I enjoyed going and he started to say on a whim that I wasn't allowed to go.

Quickly I got a reputation as an unreliable cadet, even if I was a good one. After all, nobody knew whether I'd turn up or not.

Often we went away on camp at the weekends and it was during these days you could go for more badges, learning field craft or camping skills. I loved it. Even in the cold and wet, I felt such a sense of freedom.

One of the adult instructors, Sergeant Major Felkins, knew my dad and he always looked out for me. He always took extra time to give me extra help. I felt like there were people I could really trust; I was safe for once.

But once I made the mistake of saying how much I couldn't wait for the next camping trip, so Peter made me cancel it an hour before I went. I was so upset, but I told Mr Felkins I'd fallen ill, thinking he might not believe the truth.

So when the next camp trip came up, I had a different approach. A week before we went I started moaning about it over dinner. 'Oh God,' I said, clamping my hand to my forehead. 'That camp trip is next Saturday. It's going to be so cold and wet in that tent. I don't fancy it at all.'

Predictably, Peter's face changed into a smirk. 'Well, you'll be going for definite,' he said.

I pulled a face. 'Do I have to?'

'Yes,' Peter said. 'If you choose to join the cadets you learn to participate in everything.'

I slumped in my chair, secretly wanting to punch the air. It worked like a charm. Of course Peter would make me go if he thought I was dreading it. The bastard.

Terrie saw how much I loved it, though, and even if she was a girl and didn't think much of shooting and stuff, I'd always show her my certificates when I got them.

As the months went by I began to collect so many badges, my brassard was looking full. I had a signals badge for radio operating, a marksman's badge, a sabre badge, a 3-star badge – only one below the top level, which indicated I was experienced and senior – plus many others I'd worked hard for. As I was sewing my latest badge on one evening I noticed Peter glaring at me from the corner of his eye. 'What are you doing?' he snapped.

'Sewing on my bronze Duke of Edinburgh badge,' I said.

I knew he'd never congratulate me or show any interest. But I actually felt quite pleased with myself about this one.

'No you're not,' he said. 'Get to bed.'

I sighed and took my brassard with me.

'And leave that thing here,' he said, snatching it off me.

I didn't say anything but lay awake that night worrying what he was going to do with my brassard and my precious badges.

Thankfully, the next morning it was still on the sofa, so I picked it up quickly, hoping Peter would forget all about it. But I'd learned another lesson. Fearing he'd do something to my sash, I decided to get another one. On the spare one I sewed all my future badges away from Peter's prying eyes, keeping it at cadets. I left the other one at home for Peter to find. It was important he didn't see me doing well. I knew he couldn't stand me having even a sliver of happiness or success.

Now I was at upper school I was given the 'privilege' of having a doorkey to myself. 'If you abuse the privilege it will be taken away from you,' Peter warned. I needed a key as I was the first home, and I vowed to look after it. But, being a teenager, of course it wasn't long before I lost it. 'I'm sure it was in my bag,' I protested to Peter.

He smirked. 'That's okay,' he said. 'You'll now pay for all the locks to be changed out of your accounts over the next few months. That way it will teach you not to lose your key, won't it?'

I was so upset. It would take me ages to save up the £100 to change the locks.

Very quickly having the key was seen as a 'bonus' rather than a necessity, and on a whim Peter made me hand it over before school.

'But I won't be able to get in!' I complained one day. It was chucking it down outside and the weather was forecast to be bad all day.

'You'll learn a valuable lesson then, won't you?' Peter replied. 'Under my house, my rules go.'

This happened so regularly that our neighbour Mary noticed and started taking me in and offering me biscuits. I suspected she knew the truth about Peter but she never said anything.

Whenever I lost the key, I had to grovel to get it back and usually Peter would say I'd need to do everything perfectly for at least a month and then he'd consider it. I'd have to go and ask him when he wasn't busy, busy meaning watching TV or drinking coffee. 'Please Peter, can I have my key back?'

'Don't call me Peter,' he snapped. 'Call me God.'

'Please, God, may I have my key back?' I asked.

'On this occasion, yes, you can. Next time you might not be so lucky.'

Not wishing to keep being in this position I got a copy made and secreted it up the drainpipe in the garden, making sure it was the same colour and make as the original.

I used to go via Nan and Pap's every Tuesday and Thursday before cadets. It was another opportunity to keep some money off the books. I'd check out £1 for a return trip on the bus but actually jog the four miles each way. I'd pick up discarded receipts at the bus stops to enter into my accounts – Peter didn't check the dates, just the amount.

The only other time I really went to visit them was on Saturdays. More often than not I was alone as Peter would find an excuse to keep Terrie behind. When I said goodbye to Terrie she always looked a bit upset to miss it.

'I'll stay too,' I said once, even though I didn't know if Peter would let me.

'No,' said Terrie. 'You go on. I'll be okay.'

She gave me a fake smile and I hated to leave her, but there was no choice. I would often jog there on these days too to save money, which never normally raised questions until on one particularly wet and cold day I turned up looking like a drowned rat.

Nan asked me why I hadn't taken the bus. 'Oh, we've not got much money,' I replied, not wanting her to know the lengths we went to in order to have a bit of spare emergency cash.

'Let me give you some, you poor thing. You'll end up catching your death in weather like this!' cried Nan.

'No, you're all right,' I said.

I felt bad taking their money but they insisted. I hid it in my shoe so I wouldn't need to add it to my accounts. Then Nan brought out a huge plate of roast dinner for lunch with cake and custard for afters. 'Do you want seconds?' she asked, holding out the cake.

I always did. Thirds sometimes, or even fourths.

I glanced at the clock. I'd looked in Peter's diary earlier and knew he was going to be off work by 4 p.m. It meant he was likely to come here to check on me afterwards. But I'd an idea so he wouldn't cut short my peaceful visit. Only a few weeks previously he'd dropped me and Terrie off at Nan and Pap's with a warning. 'They've not done their jobs properly this week so they're not allowed any puddings, or sweets.'

Nan had nodded dutifully but as soon as he drove off she pulled out the biscuit tin to offer us one. 'Peter's rules don't apply in this house,' she smiled.

It had backfired on us, however, as Peter burst into the house just after dinner. I had a spoonful of sponge pudding mid-air as I looked up to see him suddenly stood by the table. We were dragged home and given a beating for 'defiance'.

For today's visit I was more determined than ever to relax so I subtly suggested we made a trip up to the allotment where I could assist in a bit of weeding. Peter didn't know where this was, so if he did come looking he'd not find us.

Peter had always been busy in the TA himself, using their dark rooms to develop pictures or clean his guns, but then he made an announcement one day when I returned from cadets one evening.

'Guess what, Paul? I've been accepted as an adult instructor for the army cadets.' He grinned.

I didn't allow myself to react and just shrugged. But inside I was screaming: 'You bastard!' I knew he'd done this simply to keep tabs on me. He'd applied to oversee Tuesday and Thursday evenings too.

Fortunately, though, Sergeant Major Felkins had other ideas and got Peter posted to a unit on the outskirts of town, well away from me, and on different nights too. It still meant that Peter would be attending all of the summer week-long camps, though. And despite there being hundreds of other cadets I knew he'd be lurking around trying to catch me out doing something or other.

During the first camp Peter came on, he was in a different detachment from me, but he was still keeping tabs. Whatever I was doing he'd suddenly appear behind me, monitoring me over his glasses or have other instructors reporting back to him.

I avoided him whenever I could. One evening, when sitting in the NAAFI, a pretty blonde cadet called Lucia came up to me and spent a while talking to me. Our encounter concluded with her asking if I wanted to meet her by the swimming pool later. I couldn't believe she'd even come over to talk to me, let alone want me to meet her.

'Sure,' I beamed. 'I'll be there.' All the other cadets that were around were whistling at me and calling me a lucky twat.

I waited until 8 p.m., the time she'd asked to meet me, before running over. But when I arrived at the pool, nobody was there. Feeling despondent and pretty cold, I was getting ready to head back to my billet when the bushes behind me rustled.

Before I knew it Peter leapt out with one of his colleagues in support, shoving me straight into the pool, fully clothed. Kicking my legs I rose to the surface, gasping, and swam for the edge. It was freezing cold and pretty dark, but I managed to struggle out wondering how I was going to explain this away to the lads. 'You little wanker,' yelled Peter. He thought it was hilarious.

Quickly I realised it was all a set-up. I pulled myself out, burning with humiliation, and trudged back to my billet and the virtually guaranteed taunts and ribbing.

In spite of Peter infiltrating the cadets, it was still the main respite in my life. School was as miserable as ever, my label as troubled child firmly established. Thankfully, however, not all teachers saw my bad side.

One form tutor, Mrs Carter, had noticed something was wrong early on when I started upper school. She'd often let me off for not having the right uniform or being late. I sensed she was sympathetic, knowing something about my home life was amiss. I was truly grateful for her treating me as a normal teenage lad.

The truth was, compared to most of the lads in my area, I was a good kid, except for the odd misdemeanour carried out in desperation. I still had my fascination with science and thoroughly enjoyed it but I had no real equipment to take my interests further. So during a science lesson we had been playing with putting lithium in water and seeing it skip around, and I decided to 'borrow' conical flasks and beakers so I could do some experiments at home. I'm not sure what I was thinking but I figured these wouldn't be missed.

Peter wasn't home that afternoon, so I quickly slipped them upstairs to my room. But that evening Peter had a look in his eye that told me I was 'in for it'.

'I know you're a thief,' he said simply. 'Go upstairs and bring those flasks down.'

Little did I know, but Peter had hidden a camera in another spot in my room and had me hiding the flasks all on film.

'Right, Paul,' he said. 'Tomorrow morning first thing we're going back to school to confess your appalling behaviour.'

He turned to Mum. 'Do you see now, Cynthia? He's a thief as well as a liar.'

That night I barely slept, knowing tomorrow would be hell. The next day Peter was up early, obviously itching to see me get my comeuppance. He drove me to school and marched me to the reception.

'Paul has stolen school property and we are here to confess,' he said, plonking the flasks on the receptionist's table.

I just stared at the floor, saying nothing, as first my science teacher then the Head gave me a bollocking. 'You're to stay in for detention after school,' he said.

By 4 p.m. I found myself back in the science lab breathing a sigh of relief. After all, I'd much rather still be at school than at home, running around, doing my jobs, stressing out. Peter would just have to wait. Strangely on this occasion, however, they'd left me unsupervised, so I'd nothing to do but sit there, staring at the walls and the graffiti on the wooden benches. I was thinking about Peter too and the kind of punishment he was bound to dream up when I got home. I faced a beating of my life that was sure, but for now I'd just enjoy the peace.

Then as my eyes roamed the room I spied a sign with a skull and crossbones on the side that read: 'Dangerous. Highly explosive.' Well, that got my attention, as I guess it would most teenage boys.

I stood up and went to examine the contents. It was ignition powder. Then I spotted a reel of magnesium cable. Suddenly I found myself thinking of an ingenious plan.

What lay in front of me was equipment to make a bomb, something I'd learned in cadets. With a bit of creativity, I could set something up under Peter's car. I just needed to ensure the ignition powder was in a confined space. I wanted to punch the air with happiness. This was too good to be true. It was clear Peter was never going anywhere now. Mum was too broken to leave him and he had a cushy life, doing nothing and living for free. This would liberate us all from him, once and for all. Five years of military-style routines, beatings, total control and being under a microscope had taken its toll on me.

God only knows what my sister was going through. No one else was going to help us; it came down to me, the man of the family, to sort it out.

Excited, I jumped up and picked up the glass bottle of powder. It was quite heavy but I could easily hide that and the reel of cable in my school bag. Quickly I zipped up the equipment and then waited for the rest of the detention to finish. I couldn't wait to get home now and set my plan in motion.

As I reached Churchill Avenue I slid the magnesium and bottle of ignition powder up into the bottom of the drainpipe attached to our stone shed. Back indoors, Peter was predictably on the prowl for me. He was keen to mete out a big thrashing with the metal spatula. This time he kept going until my buttocks began to bleed. 'You're a liar and thieving little bastard,' he shrieked as I clung onto the chair.

But knowing what lay hidden outside kept me going. Knowing it was ready and waiting for my plan to be put into action and the multiple permutations of what I could do to Peter got me through the evening.

Then the phone rang at 6 p.m. Peter answered it and stood smoothing his moustache, as he stared at me. 'Oh right, he did, did he?' he said. 'Well, yes, the police sound like a sensible option … given the circumstances.'

Straight away I guessed the school was on my case, so I had to get out fast. I shot upstairs and grabbed my bergen, sleeping bag and hexamine cooker and ran out of the door. I got as far as a country road a couple of miles away called Boughton Green and climbed like a monkey up a huge tree until I was at least 18 feet up. There I set up a camp in a large fork. I laid out a sleeping bag and fired up my stove to make some tea. I strung a poncho over the top as a roof. For once I was putting my cadet skills to excellent use. After a few minutes set-up I'd created a cosy den, somewhere to hide for the time being. As I sat with a steaming cuppa a police car siren wailed past. But I knew nobody would find me up the tree, so I settled down for the night. I'd no idea what I'd do next but I would think of something. All I knew was when people are searching for you they don't look up, they look down and around.

By morning, however, I woke, shivering, my face covered in morning dew and worried. The fact was I'd no money and nowhere to go. I'd little choice but to face the music. I slid down the tree and walked the long walk home, dreading each step I took, but smiling inside all the same at the fact Peter would have gone mad that I was out of his control for a night and didn't know what I'd done or where I'd been. As I turned the corner of my road and spotted a police car sat outside Number 59, my heart sank further. Peter would be relishing every moment of this.

I rang the doorbell and it flew open as a pair of hands grabbed me off the doorstep. Peter dragged me into the room like a jailor and his recently recaptured escaped convict. The only thing he was missing was a pair of handcuffs.

'You're in a lot of trouble, son,' said one officer. 'What you took is really dangerous and the Chief Constable himself has taken an interest in this case.'

'What have you done with it?' another asked.

'Search me!' I said, holding my arms out.

Peter was happy to carry out that task he had become so proficient at over the past five years, but found nothing. I wanted to carry on playing dumb but the police officers made it clear that having explosives was not a game and the consequences could be very big indeed. Helpfully one of the officers said that if I returned the items no further police action would be taken against me as it should have been locked away and I should have been supervised. I had one chance to use the 'get out of jail free' card. Knowing the game was up I admitted the hiding place. Instantly the officers rushed out to seize it, relief clearly written on their faces as they bagged the items.

Afterwards, Peter looked ultra-calm, as the officers returned from their car to have a brief discussion with him and Mum. Out of the blue one of the officers turned to me and asked, 'Why did you do it, son?'

Before I got the chance to unleash details of the hell I and Terrie had been living, Peter cut in and told me to go upstairs. 'It's okay, officers,' he said, shaking their hands. 'I think we can deal with this as a family. My lad's gone off the rails a little, but we'll do our best to support him from here on in.'

The officers all nodded, taken in by Peter's well-rehearsed caring stepdad spiel.

Afterwards I waited for the thrashing of my life, but Peter just sent me to bed without dinner. Perhaps having police in the house was too close for comfort. Later, as I and Terrie did the washing up, we spoke in low whispers as I told her what happened.

'You're mad, Paul!' Terrie laughed. Then her face fell straight. 'But I really really wish your plan had worked.'

I was starving the following day. With some spare time on my hands and with Peter out at a driving lesson I decided to go 'scrumping'. This basically meant stealing whatever fruit I could lay my hands on. I'd spotted trees heavy with fruit, like apples and pears, in the gardens of lots of the old houses that led onto the back of the oval where I walked Sam. 'They never ever pick them!' I thought. Often I'd watch the fruit fall to the grass, turn brown and get eaten by wasps. For a hungry boy it was a rather sickening sight.

That Tuesday, after school, it was an unexpectedly sunny evening, so I climbed over the fence and then scaled down onto the grass, landing noiselessly. I couldn't see anyone in the windows at the back so I shimmied up the tree and started to help myself.

But after a few minutes a door flew open and an old lady raced down the garden. I underestimated her speed as by the time I'd started my descent she was by the trunk shouting at me. 'Why are you stealing my fruit?' she cried.

I looked at her index finger jabbing at my shoulder as we stood eye to eye. I decided to just be honest. 'I'm really hungry,' I admitted. 'And you never pick it yourself.'

She stopped poking me and looked up at heavily laden boughs. 'How's about you pick all the apples for me and you can keep half of them?' she suggested.

'Okay, cool.' I agreed, both relieved and shocked at her suggestion!

She handed me a plastic bucket and I shot back up the tree and started to pull all the best apples off. After half an hour the tree was much lighter and I was chuffed with my haul. 'Go on then,' she said, handing me half in a bag. 'Go home and enjoy them.'

I couldn't wait to show Mum. I hoped we could bake a pie or something.

I dragged my big bag home, walked in the door, and Mum's face was a picture. 'Paul!' she cried. 'Where did you get that lot from? I've never seen so many apples!'

I laughed. 'I picked them for an old lady,' I said. 'She let me keep half.'

Peter looked up from his newspaper. 'You what?' he said. 'You lying little thieving bastard. I don't believe a word of it. He won't have got permission for that lot, Cynth.'

I opened my mouth to protest but Peter was already dragging me out of the house. 'Come on then,' he bellowed. 'Which "little old lady" was it?'

I took him to the old woman's house and she was still there, in her garden, enjoying the evening sun.

'I'm terribly sorry. We're here to apologise for my lad's theft,' Peter began.

'No! You're wrong,' she replied. 'He kindly helped me pick them all from the tree. I let him take half.'

Peter huffed and took me home. But back home he didn't say sorry or explain to Mum. She took the apples to Pap's later. 'These are gorgeous ones, Paul,' he said. 'I'll get plenty of apple sauce and wine out of this little lot.'

He looked at me with pride and I wondered what he'd think about how Peter had reacted. How I longed to tell him but both Terrie and I knew Nan and Pap wouldn't cope with knowing what was happening. And it seemed too much of a risk in case they didn't believe us. The last thing we wanted was Peter turning our precious grandparents against us too.

Chapter 19

'Thwarted'

Terrie

$\mathcal{P}$eter liked his holidays and insisted Mum put any spare money aside for them. One weekend in April he packed up a trailer tent for the car and we set off for Hunstanton, a seaside town in Norfolk.

I couldn't see how Peter would engineer time for us alone, but then again now he was able to utilise shorter and shorter windows of time. The previous week he'd managed to use a half-hour window before Mum and Paul got home to abuse me. Grabbing some rope he'd tied my hands and feet together, and beat me with the spatula as he contorted my limbs into the shape he wanted. 'This will make you comply quicker,' he said, as he started poking me with a banana. I screamed as loudly as I could, but a thump on the back of my skull soon quietened me down. Only when I told him I heard Mum coming did he stop.

Without much money we were limited in what we had to do during the day. It was either the beach or the pool but both Paul and I were relieved we were away from the routine at home at least. At the big pool, Peter had to take his glasses off but that didn't stop him moving his hands everywhere under the water, as he slid in after me. 'Stay near me,' he growled. His eyes still adjusting to not having his specs on, I took my chance and swam off as fast as possible to the deep end. I knew he would punish me later, but I wasn't going to have him touching me. Not today.

I had a lovely time laughing with Paul, until Peter got his camera out. I was wearing a T-shirt over my costume, keeping as covered as possible as usual. But Peter caught up with me as I was sitting on the side. He was pretending to film everyone and then zoomed up on me. 'Get that T-shirt off, Terrie,' he ordered.

Seeing Peter on the warpath Paul quite sensibly swam off fast.

I folded my arms. 'No,' I said, staring at the water, wishing he'd just go away.

'Take. It. Off. Now,' he growled.

'No!' I said.

Without warning he grabbed a handful of my hair. I saw the concrete edges of the pool loom into vision. Whack! Whack! One, two, three, four, five times … He smashed my head against the side then let go, leaving me spinning, not knowing which way was up, the blue water or the sky through the roof. I'm sure a few people around the pool must have noticed, but everyone looked away quickly.

'Next time you'll do as you're told,' he spat.

I clutched my eye. Already I could feel a bruise coming on. I swam back to the other side, where Mum was sitting reading a magazine. 'Oooh, love,' cooed Mum, looking concerned. 'What happened to your eye?'

'Oh, I just slipped,' I said, trying to sound casual. 'It's fine.'

For the rest of the afternoon my head ached.

That evening we went to a café for fish and chips. After dinner, Paul was looking at the dessert menu and I glanced at it over his shoulder.

'Mmmmm, I'd love a knickerbocker glory please,' I said, looking at Mum.

'Nope,' said Peter swiftly. 'Not after your behaviour in the pool today, young lady.' He gave me a knowing look. We both knew what he meant. I'd not allowed him to take a good picture of my body, so no dessert.

Halfway through the holiday Peter decided we all had to go for a long walk by the sea. We started walking along the beach wall. One side was full of huge rocks and stones; the higher the beach wall rose the less rocky it became on the other side. It was lovely having the breeze on our faces. On days like this, it often occurred to me how outsiders must've seen us as a very ordinary family. As we walked along, Paul was winding in and out between Mum, Peter and me and the edge of the wall.

'Be careful, Paul,' Mum said.

'Yes,' snapped Peter. 'If I catch you winding around me like a cat one more time I'll knock you right off.'

Paul was licking an ice cream as he walked, cheerfully, looking so happy. I admired him for being able to still be upbeat despite everything. As he grinned, the freckles on his face a deeper shade of brown thanks to the sun, I felt a jolt again, of how innocent he was really. And I wanted to keep him that way. A few minutes later we were at the highest point of the wall, I could hear the seagulls, the sea and wind. I was feeling relaxed. As we continued Paul walked near Peter again who, suddenly, without saying anything, raised his arm and shoved Paul clean off the wall. It happened so fast, it was a case of 'now you see him, now you don't', so quick my brain barely registered.

Gasping, Mum and I ran to the edge. Paul was lying on his back about ten feet below, between two jaggedy grey rocks, holding his ice cream high in the air, looking shocked but victorious about saving his precious cone.

Mum let out a nervous laugh. 'Paul, you saved your ice

cream!' But then milliseconds later she started trembling as the reality of what could have happened kicked in.

Paul had narrowly escaped being killed falling that far.

'Peter!' she shrieked. 'Look how close Paul is to those rocks. You could have killed him. Oh my God!' She was becoming hysterical.

Peter shrugged. 'Oh for goodness sakes,' he said. 'I could see he'd land there. I knew he'd be okay.'

But both Mum and I knew Peter was lying. He hadn't looked to see where Paul would land at all. He'd just shoved him.

Mum started shouting. 'Paul, come up here. Come on, we're going!' She was shaking as we skipped off to keep up with her, away from Peter.

'Come on, Cynthia, it was just a bit of a joke,' he shouted.

But Mum clutched Paul's hand and led him away. 'No, it wasn't!' she yelled. 'You could have broken his legs or his bloody neck!'

I was so relieved Mum had finally seen what Peter was capable of. We marched all the way back to the campsite, where Mum started packing up our stuff. Peter followed us all the way. 'We're going home, Peter,' she screamed. 'I want to get us away from you.'

He looked surprised. 'No, now don't be silly,' he began. But nothing was stopping Mum. Not this time.

She got a small bag packed and then started walking us to the station. But when we got there she looked in her purse and it was almost empty. She barely had enough money for one ticket.

'Bugger it!' she cried. 'We'll have to just go back now.'

Slowly we walked back to the campsite. Peter was sat by himself, waiting, as if he was expecting us.

Mum turned away and sat down. 'Tell Peter I'm not speaking to him,' she said.

I looked at Peter and he tried to strike up a conversation with Mum, like nothing had happened, but she stubbornly refused. For the rest of the holiday the pair of them were silent, the air thick with tension. We also drove home in silence, but within a day or two Mum appeared to 'forget' what had happened. I knew Peter must've said something to her, but God knows what. She was too far under his control to break free.

Not long after the holiday, Peter's mum Oma got sick with cancer. She'd already had it three times in her life, and now, in her seventies, she seemed to have given up. We went to visit her in Hammersmith Hospital. It was so sad to see the dignified old lady wither away in her bed. We promised to visit her again.

Peter seemed very removed from all the emotion of his mum's illness, though. In fact, we cared more than he did. Mum had liked Oma too. She had once told Mum all about the war she'd survived and how the Russian soldiers raped her as a young woman at the end. It affected her very badly, she'd confided. I was shocked to hear such terrible events had happened in her life. She seemed like a strict, old-fashioned sort of person, but I couldn't have guessed the horror she had lived through.

She died shortly after our last visit. But as we all prepared for Oma's funeral Peter didn't seem in the slightest bit concerned. In the church, with a few other friends and distant relations of Peter's we'd never met before, Paul and I were sat together near the front. As the service began I could see Paul's body shaking. It wasn't through sadness, but because he was trying desperately not to laugh. That set me off. We were always like that when emotional things were happening around us, as a defence mechanism, even though in this instance we were both genuinely upset to see her go. Both of us started shaking as if we were crying, but actually we were howling with laughter by the start of the last hymn.

Weeks later Oma's will was read out, and she had unexpectedly left us some money. She really had seen us as her grandchildren; it was very touching. But Peter was fuming. Oma had stipulated he wasn't allowed any of her legacy until 10 years had passed. She'd also left her Fiat Punto car, something Peter had had his eye on, to a close friend of hers. Even in her death she'd done something to annoy him.

In spite of still trying to regularly get detentions at school, I loved some of my lessons. Along with English and Art, History was another favourite. My teacher was brilliant and her explanations of the Aztecs and Incas set my imagination on fire. By the time it came to choosing my O-levels I was in a dilemma. I thought Geography might be more useful but I didn't want to give up on History.

To help me choose I went to have a chat with a teacher who used to teach me lower down in the school, someone I really trusted. After we spoke about the subjects she frowned, her face softening with concern. 'Terrie?' she said, gently. 'Are you all right?'

I fell silent and bit my lower lip. Nobody ever asked me this. Nobody ever noticed. Could I maybe tell her? Would she listen? Overwhelmed with emotion, I thought I might cry.

'Is everything all right?' she persisted.

I swallowed hard. 'Actually,' I began, my tongue feeling too thick for my mouth, 'there is something.'

It didn't cross my mind to tell her I'd been raped. That seemed too much. Who would believe that? Besides, long ago I'd decided I couldn't risk Peter killing Mum and Paul. Perhaps it would be safe to say something else, though?

She leaned forward in her chair, listening intently.

'I have a rough time at home,' I began, the words spoken out loud sounding foreign and strained. 'My stepdad ...'

Her eyes were so bright I could almost see my reflection in her black pupils, me sitting in a chair behind the desk, twisting the ring on my finger round and round.

'He,' I continued, thinking of Peter's sweaty face in mine, the cameras whirring, the pain. The rapes. '... is violent sometimes.'

There, I'd said it. That was enough. It had to be. Would it be? I stopped, abruptly, unable to go on.

Her mouth was now slightly agape, and her hands lay on the desk in front of us. 'My precious little flower,' she said softly. 'Leave it with me.'

I nodded. I'd said enough. For those few moments I genuinely had felt like she'd cared for me.

That afternoon after school I waited anxiously for the phone to ring, daring to hope the end of my ordeal was near. But it stayed silent. Over the next few days I half expected to be called to the Head's office. Maybe the police would come? Or Mum would get sent a letter?

But the next time I saw my teacher nothing was mentioned. She acted like nothing had happened. Nobody else spoke to me about it. The phone didn't ring. Only bills dropped onto the doormat.

Then I guessed that even if my teacher had said something no action would be taken. After all, Peter had done a good job convincing the school I was a bit of a troubled kid, hadn't he? Suddenly I could hardly breathe through my anger and crushing disappointment. I'd dared to hope someone would step in. And once again all the proof was that nobody cared.

Shortly afterwards, in a chemistry lesson, a girl called Heidi was chatting loudly about her Monday evening. 'Yeah, so I went to this party,' she boasted. 'And while I was there I had sex with this boy on the sofa.'

'Wow!' another girl responded. 'Really?'

'Yep, right on the cushions. It was well good,' she continued.

All the girls started to congratulate her or ask her questions on what it was like.

I just listened in and didn't say anything. As she boasted, I just felt nothing. That's because it was nothing to me. Sex to me was something horrible and painful, something Peter did to me whenever he felt like it. Why anyone else would want to show off about it was beyond me.

Everyone else sat riveted as if she'd described being high on drugs or learning to fly. 'Wow,' one said. 'Can't believe you've actually Done It.'

'So bloody what, big deal,' I thought. I was actually more shocked she'd been allowed out to a party and on a school night. That was far more impressive. I'd never be allowed to do that.

I'd no idea what I'd wanted to do when I left school. Years previously I'd wanted to be an archaeologist, but life had taken on such a daily nightmare, a different 'normal' existence didn't even seem possible any more. I found it terribly difficult to function at school properly after exhausting evenings either being beaten, cleaning or crying while Peter filmed and raped me. By the afternoons at school I found myself struggling to stay awake. When the classrooms were warm and stuffy I'd often sit at the back of the class, my eyes drooping shut but my mind racing.

A few times teachers would shout my name at me to make me 'sit up', but I wasn't being lazy; I was just constantly worrying. My school reports were full of phrases like 'Could improve but prone to daydreams.' If only they knew what they were about.

I hated myself for having to live the way I did at home, but not only that, the girls at school often gave me a hard time too.

I still heard whispers of 'Terrie Fuck It' wherever I went and I didn't fit in. I'd no money to go out and join the others after school and Peter was too controlling to ever let me out of his sight for long. While everyone dressed in the trendiest clothes, I had to make do with hand-me-downs or the last season's trend. But in comparison to the horror of my home life, school problems were nothing, so I didn't let them bother me.

My relationship with Mum had grown colder over the years too. With retrospect I felt I'd 'lost' Mum at the age of 10. Ever since Dad had disappeared to South Africa the first time and she'd discovered his affair, she'd lost her fun-loving spontaneous side. Instead she was always tired, always working, always stressed. Now she'd betrayed me too, there seemed to be no way back. Peter's sulks were frequent and seemed to unnerve her. I always suspected he was violent towards her when we were not around. However, despite their clearly unhappy relationship, Mum still carried on working, providing for everyone. After all, she had to. Peter wasn't going to do it.

It was a Thursday evening; Mum was getting ready for a works do. She'd been at Rainbow Carpets for a few years now and knew her work colleagues well. She'd made a beautiful Chinese-style dress with little pink flowers on for the special occasion, and Peter was going with her. I'd watched her night after night sewing that dress. It was the only way she could afford anything new. It had a high collar and lovely sleeves, with perfect stitching. It made me feel good seeing her taking time over something for herself for once.

Mum looked lovely as she put on some make-up in the mirror, adjusting her dress. But Peter, despite being all spruced up for the night as well, paced the room, in a menacing mood. 'I'm not going,' he said, suddenly.

Mum looked nervously at me and Paul watching TV. 'Kids, go upstairs,' she said, and we moved fast, but we stopped at the bottom of the stairs and waited, listening.

'Don't be silly,' Mum soothed. 'My colleague will be here to pick us up soon and I don't want to go on my own. He's expecting both of us.'

Then we heard a sickening thud, as Peter punched her. 'Urgh,' Mum cried.

'You stupid cow, thinking you can always tell me what to do, eh?' Peter screamed. 'Telling me to do this and that. Pay for things. Go to places.'

With each sentence came more thuds and moans. I clamped my hands over my ears. Paul's eyes were like saucers.

The door flew open and Mum staggered in the doorway, her face totally unrecognisable from moments earlier. Scarlet drops fell from her nose onto the hall carpet and her eyes were swollen. In a muffled voice, she spoke urgently. 'Call the police!' she begged, looking blindly in our direction. I leaped up, desperate to help.

But as I made a move to grab the phone and dial 999, Peter reached it first. With one swift movement he ripped the phone out of the wall, leaving dangling wires exposed. 'Nobody's ringing anyone!' he raged, and raced to lock the back door. 'And nobody is leaving this house.'

At that moment the doorbell rang. Before Peter could stop her, Mum fell onto the front doorknob and twisted it open. On the doorstep was Mum's colleague. His smiling, expectant face soon dropped as he saw our bleeding mum half-dazed using the doorframe for support. 'Help!' she gasped. 'Ring the police! Peter has just beat me up!'

I wanted to burst into tears with gratitude. Thank God Peter had done this and Mum was taking action. We could be saved now. Someone else had seen what he was like. The police would come and perhaps I could tell them about the rapes too? I wanted to, I really did. Our family would be saved from this hell.

Paul and I were on our feet next to Mum now, as she stared at her colleague on the doorstep. 'Ring the police, we need help,' she repeated, clearer now, her voice louder.

But he wasn't moving. In fact, he was just staring at us all as if we were creatures in a zoo. He started backing away as if he feared contamination. 'Sorry, Cynth,' he said, holding his palms up. 'Not my problem.'

I watched with absolute horror as he turned on his heels quickly, back to the car, in his smart suit, all ready and expectant for his night out, not wanting our family and our 'problem' to ruin his night. All it would have taken was one phone call. But instead we watched our potential saviour disappear into the night. At that moment I hated him more than Peter.

'This is it now,' I thought. 'Peter is going to kill us all.'

Peter had taken himself to off bed. Mum gave us a quick hug and sent us off to bed. Shaking with fear, we ran upstairs and huddled in my room. We watched out of the window as Mum ran off down the road to her friends.

The next day we were up and out very early before Peter got up. Mum came home from work early at the end of the day as well, her face still swollen. 'Did you see that man today?' I asked.

'Yes, and he acted like nothing had happened,' she replied. 'My boss called me into his office, though.'

'What did she say?' I asked, hopefully. Please! I thought. Please say you told her.

'Oh, she asked me if I was okay,' shrugged Mum. 'And when I said I was, she said: "That's all right then."'

I said nothing but inside I was fuming. Why were people so keen to turn a blind eye? Why didn't Mum say she wasn't okay? Could no one hear our cries?

For the next few days Peter skulked around, but mainly stayed in bed out of our way. I knew it wouldn't be long before he'd want to make up for lost time, though. The following Saturday morning Mum was off to work early. She'd started to leave earlier and stay out later in order to avoid him too.

'Hey, Terrie,' she said, as we ate some toast. 'I need you to take Sam to the vet today, remember? He's had an upset tummy again. Also, can you pop into town for a few bits afterwards?'

'Sure,' I said. I didn't have many plans, and I didn't mind having a walk around town to the shops.

Then Peter looked up. 'I'm taking Paul to Mark's today,' he said.

I started to feel sick and put my toast down. If he wasn't working, it meant the possibility of a whole day with me alone with Peter. I went up to my bedroom after breakfast, just hoping Peter wouldn't be back after dropping off Paul. I listened to some George Michael and closed my eyes.

But the sound of a car between songs made me sit bolt upright. He was back.

Peter marched upstairs, straight into my room. 'Downstairs, now,' he barked.

Immediately my limbs started to tremble. As usual, his 'tools' were laid out down the side of the sofa. This time it was a huge dildo. The camera light was already on. He positioned me in full view of the camera and started raping me from behind with the dildo. I started crying in pain, as he grabbed my hair, twisting it hard.

'Just shut up and look like you're enjoying it,' he snarled. Then he started raping me himself. I clenched my fists with anger. I hated this so much. I didn't even cry, I just told him how much I hated him as he laughed.

Suddenly the phone rang. I assumed he would ignore it, but instead Peter stopped moving for a moment. 'It'll be your mum,' he snapped. 'Answer it.'

I gulped. 'You're hurting me too much,' I gasped.

'Just. Do. It,' he cried.

I picked up the phone and swallowed hard, trying to calm my voice.

'Terrie?' said Mum. I could hear the sound of sales people in the background. Phones ringing. Typewriters. Nattering. The sounds of normality, a million miles world away from the pain I was experiencing.

'Hi, Mum,' I said, closing my eyes as I winced.

'Oh, glad I caught you,' she said. 'Did you manage to get an appointment for Sam in the vets?'

'Er, no,' I said. 'I tried but they were full up. No appointments left today.'

'Oh,' said Mum, disappointed.

Peter shifted position and started doing it harder. I felt tears spring to my eyes.

'Okay,' Mum continued. 'Was Paul dropped at Mark's?'

'Yes,' I said, struggling to keep my voice calm. 'Fine.'

'Now later on,' Mum continued, 'we'll nip into town to pick up a few bits, then pick up Paul, and if you can make the tea too that would be great. I was thinking of sausages and chips and beans tonight, all right?'

'Yes,' I half whispered. I cleared my throat as Peter tightened his grip on my hair. 'No problem.'

Finally Mum said goodbye and I made sure the receiver was back properly.

'You bastard!' I screamed. 'I fucking hate you so much. I hope you rot in hell!'

I twisted my head around, to see Peter smirking at me from behind, looking very pleased with himself. He was so sick and twisted. I could see in his eyes how much he enjoyed this: raping a young girl while forcing her to speak to her mother. It was beyond sick.

Chapter 20
'Thumbscrews'
Paul

I'd grown so used to trying to second-guess Peter I now had my own systems in place to try and beat him at every opportunity.

To get around the incessant account reviews, I'd collected a bank of receipts from the used-ticket bin on the front of the bus. Often I asked friends for their receipts for things as well, or picked them up off the floor when I found them. Then I'd keep the stash in a tin on the bottom of my bookshelf at the back. To find it you had to get on your hands and knees and really look, so I assumed it was safe from Peter's prying eyes and cameras.

My day at school had been quite fruitful. My Warhammer business was expanding and a couple of kids in lower years were paying me to write a few computer scripts to cause some mischief for an unsuspecting administrator. I'd got a good fist of random receipts I intended to put into my tin, so I ran upstairs and assumed the position only to find to my shock the tin had been replaced with a whirring camera.

'Fuck,' I thought. 'How the hell did he find the tin?' I muttered out loud. This is just getting stupid, I thought to myself. I pressed stop on the camera and rewound the tape. Adopting my old trick, I hit play and record and ran out of my room and jumped down the stairs. I then re-enacted coming into my room again, this time without spotting the camera. But I knew Peter had found the receipts. And I knew I was for it. Luckily I kept my proper 'off-the-book' accounts in a separate place, in plain sight in an old notebook that looks just like one I used to write all of Peter's orders in. The sort of thing he just wouldn't consider looking in.

All that afternoon I couldn't concentrate on my homework, or my jobs. Over the years I got the jobs on the rota down to just under an hour and a half, but today I couldn't concentrate, which added another hour to the work schedule. I was just dreading what would happen next.

But I didn't have to wait long for Peter to come back home from wherever he'd been and even less time for him to lay into me. He grabbed me by the shoulders and threw me into the living room. While I stood up rubbing my shoulder he put himself in his favourite position lying on the sofa. Straight away I knew what was coming.

'You are standing there until you admit to all the other things you've been hiding,' he yelled.

I win first prize again, I thought. Predictable. Wait for the video to start. Titties and giggling girls. I stood up straight, eyes ahead, my mind racing. There genuinely wasn't anything I could tell Peter about – well, not that I wanted him to know, or that I was in a position to admit without him finding other things. Both Terrie and I had been using the air vents since the contraband rule for sweets had been brought in. We'd carefully unscrew them, remove the grille, then put what we needed in there and screw it back up again. There's no way he can know about my business income as it's still based in the unknown third locker. Maybe he's realised I can fuck with his camera at whim. No, I knew I'd be dead if he knew about that.

'I'm not hiding anything, I swear,' I said, my fingers crossed superstitiously behind my back. 'I swear on your life, Peter,' I said with a glint in my eye and maybe a bit of hope God was listening that day.

'Peter? What do you mean, Peter?'

'God, I mean there's nothing else, God.'

'Try again,' he prompted, after lazily kicking me hard in the thigh.

'Master? Boss? Sir? Lord?' I suggested not knowing quite how he wanted to be referred to that day. In any event he ignored me and concentrated on the TV. 'First prize again,' I thought to myself as semi-clad women appeared on the screen.

By now I'd built up quite a resilience while standing still for so long. But as the hours passed it never failed to make the small of my back and the soles of my feet and shoulders ache like hell. Peter would go about his business, ignoring me, acting like I wasn't there, except for on occasion smacking me or punching the side of my head. 'Stand straighter!' he'd bark.

Inevitably my brain just switched off, and I focused on the digital clock. I'd taken up computer programming a year or so ago and found I was pretty handy, and times like this were perfect for me to run lines of computer code through my head, building new programmes and testing it all virtually. Little was I to know that this skill was training my memory and logic processes and would prove to be one of the most important skills I would come to rely on throughout my life.

Peter put on *Hit Man and Her* highlights, drooling over Michaela Strachan as he watched.

'Heh heh, look at the tits on that,' he grinned. He'd made a compilation tape of all the 'booby bits', as he called them.

I'd been standing there since 4 p.m.; it was now 9 p.m. Five hours of standing make you really tired. I needed to turn off and go into autopilot if I was going to last any longer.

'You gonna tell me?' Peter shouted, interrupting my thoughts.

I shook my head. Slap.

'Stand there longer then,' he said.

Mum had been home for a while now but she didn't sit in the living room. She often sat in the kitchen when things like this went on – unable to bear watching, I suppose, or maybe frustrated that she'd lost control of Peter a long time ago.

Time ticked on; every now and then Peter asked me to confess, or slapped me hard. Then Mum came down at 11 p.m. 'That's enough, Peter,' she cried. 'Let him go to bed now.'

'No!' said Peter. 'Why should I when he needs to learn?'

'He's had enough! That's it, Paul, go to bed. Go on,' Mum urged. 'He can't stand here all bloody night.'

Exhausted, I breathed out, and then went to walk past Peter to bed, but he shoved his arm out, into my chest. 'Stay there, you little wanker!' he shrieked. He grabbed my shoulders and started hammering his clenched fists into the side of my head, hitting me as hard as he could.

I fell to the floor as he carried on beating me. All I could see was the carpet and his scuffed shoe coming towards me.

'Get off him, you bastard,' Mum yelled. She grabbed a hair-brush from the side and started whacking Peter over the head with it. But he just turned and slapped her hard, then fell on me again.

'You little wanker,' he yelled, punching me as hard as he could. He dragged me into the kitchen and opened the drawer to grab any implement he could lay his hands on. I screamed as he pulled out a meat tenderiser.

'No!' I yelled, putting my arms up to my face. But in his rage nothing was going to stop Peter. He smashed it onto my arms and back, until he'd worn out his anger.

'Now get back out there and stand up straight,' he said.

Shaking and sobbing, I found my standing place again. Peter then sat on the sofa near me, and carried on watching the video as if nothing had happened.

Then he paused the video and nipped off upstairs to the loo. I knew I had between 30 seconds and 20 minutes, so I looked to see where my feet were on the carpet to memorise my position, then dived to the tape machine. Swiftly I ejected it, my heart banging, then pulled the tape inside, slightly stretching it, and pushed it back into the recorder on pause.

Peter came back, glaring at me as he walked past to take up his viewing again. As he pressed 'play' the tape made a terrible noise as the heads in the player ate the stretched tape and wrapped it around the insides. 'For fuck's sake!' Peter cried as I smirked.

'Good,' I thought, laughing to myself. 'If I'm going to stand here bored then so the hell are you.'

Glaring at me, Peter tried to remove the tape, but it was jammed stuck. Giving up, he slumped back on the sofa. 'I'll fix it tomorrow,' he mumbled.

I watched as his breath quieted and he dozed off. I slouched a little, easing the tension in my back. I longed to lie down too, but part of me knew Peter might have set an alarm or could wake up any time, then I'd get another thrashing of my life. Weighing it up, it would hurt less to just keep standing there.

Eventually a bluey-grey light began to seep through the curtain edges, gradually turning to yellow, and the birds began to chirrup. Within an hour the whole dawn chorus began and Peter stirred, his moustache twitching. My head was spinning with exhaustion and I felt sick with hunger and tiredness, but I'd done it. I'd stood there all night long and not admitted to a single thing.

I waited until just before 7 a.m. before I ran upstairs to get in the shower so I didn't miss my schedule. I couldn't wait to go to school. I was utterly exhausted, but relieved to escape the house.

Strangely, the receipts and the tin were not mentioned again. I guess he was hoping to catch me on camera but I had already relocated a new waterproof tin under a slab in the garden.

That weekend we were due to go to Nan and Pap's house, and this time Terrie was allowed to come too. Peter said he was doing some developing in the TA darkroom and would pick us up after.

'Make sure you leave the house promptly when I pick you up. I don't want any messing about or waiting around,' he said.

Just before we set off, I slipped out of the house while Peter was in the shower. With lightning speed I let down two of his car tyres. Then I slipped into the cupboard where he kept the tyre pump and pierced the pipe so it wouldn't keep any pressure, or if it did it meant five pumps for every usual one. While I was doing this I'd directed Terrie to keep turning the cold water on and off so Peter's shower became decidedly uncomfortable!

'Ahh, now we can enjoy a whole afternoon completely uninterrupted by Peter,' I said to Terrie. 'It will take him a good few hours to sort that one out.'

'Not only that, Paul,' she giggled, 'but he'll take a while to sort a shirt out. I managed to slip into his bedroom and loosen the thread on his shirt buttons.'

That afternoon, for the first in a long time, Terrie and I were able to relax and enjoy ourselves, even daring to pretend we were normal kids with loving grandparents.

* * *

For about six months I'd been practising hard for the silent marching display with the army cadets. As a senior cadet with exceptional marching skills and coordination I had been selected with eight others to appear in public at a big show in Northampton.

The march involved a synchronised display of around 50 individual moves which needed to be performed in unison without any prompting or verbal orders. It was pretty tricky. Every week we practised for hours, and over six months it all started pulling together. All of us were in Gibraltar Detachment and when we practised cadets from other detachments watched us in amazement. We looked good and felt great.

On the big day, I had to get my uniform into tip-top condition, painting the belt and special cuffs bright white, making sure my uniform looked crisp and clean and finally my boots shone bright. Then I got my brassard, the one I'd secretly hidden from Peter, and hid it in my coat, so I could wear all my badges with pride when I arrived. After a couple of hours I looked as smart as a pin. All spruced up, I waited in the hallway as Peter finished in the bathroom upstairs. As he came down he glanced at me. 'Where are you going?'

'Er, my drill for the public open day,' I said. Already a horrible stinking feeling formed in my stomach. He knew full well what today was.

'No you're not,' he said, flippantly. 'Go upstairs and take all your kit off.' Then he turned his back to me and walked off into the kitchen.

I clenched my fists into a ball, as a rising rage caught in my throat. I felt so disappointed I wanted to cry, but at the same time I didn't want to give Peter the satisfaction. Whatever I wanted in life, anything good, from a yo-yo to doing cadets, he wanted to sabotage. I never forgave him for that day and I don't think the cadets ever forgave me.

But despite Peter's cruelty behind closed doors he continued to morph back into Dr Jekyll when it came to everyone else – apart from the local kids, at whom he shot flares over the fence if he saw them near his car. Happily for me he still blamed them every time I did something to sabotage it.

Peter loved to show off to friends and neighbours with his 'dos'. One weekend he was planning a barbecue and talking about who to invite. 'I've heard you've got a little girlfriend, Paul,' he smiled slyly.

I shrugged. I'd started seeing a 13-year-old girl from cadets called Michaela. It was all very innocent. I was just thrilled she showed me any attention, as I was certain if she knew me from school she'd not like me as much and think I was strange. Fortunately she just knew me as a great shot and talented cadet that a lot of people respected.

'Why don't you invite her to our BBQ on Saturday?' he suggested.

Naively I thought it would be nice to have her there and agreed to ask her to come.

The morning of the barbecue, Peter spent ages buying in meat and choosing a play list for the music. Of course it meant more work for Terrie and me mostly, and he ordered us to clean and re-clean the entire house. It never ceased to amaze me how much effort he put into the food for other people. I spent the entire morning skewering a mix of meat and vegetables on bamboo skewers to create a mountain of kebabs – Mum's signature dish.

'Now, you lazy little twats,' Peter said, an hour before everyone arrived, 'I want to see everyone's glass filled to the brim at all times, do you understand? I will be filming the event as well in case you think you can slack off. I also want the washing up and bins taken out before the end of the afternoon. Okay?'

Right on cue, guests started turning up, including Michaela. She was a lovely girl, and as she arrived she kissed me shyly on the cheek. Peter warmly welcomed her into the garden and then started chatting to her, his piggy eyes running up and down her body.

'Hey, Michaela,' he said, pointing to the bread rolls on the floor by the grill. 'Could you pass those up for me, please?'

Michaela promptly bent down and as she did so Peter craned his neck at the same time, very obviously looking right down her top. She wasn't wearing a bra. Mortified, Michaela quickly stood up, clutching her T-shirt neckline to her. 'Hey!' she said, a bit annoyed. She went bright red as Peter laughed his head off.

'Don't let me put you off,' he leered.

'Pervert,' I thought. Understandably, Michaela was mortified. She barely ate a thing, and because Peter had me running around I got very little chance to speak to her other than to apologise to her. Not long after she made her excuses and left. I never heard from her again.

Later things went from bad to worse, as Peter rewound the film he'd recorded and accused us of not filling people's drinks fast enough, so we got 500 lines each: 'I must do as Peter says and make sure guests are fed and watered.' I came up with the ingenious idea of sellotaping two pencils together to write them faster, but when Peter caught me he made me re-do them again.

That night I was sent to bed early. Peter loved to carry a punishment on, sometimes for a whole week if he was in the mood. Luckily, I had my torch. I often sat up until the small hours, reading away. I always had to keep an ear out for the stairs, though, as Peter had already caught me a few times. The first time I shoved the book under the sheet, but he pulled the bed apart until the book plopped out. The next time I pushed it under my mattress, but after he couldn't find it under my sheets he looked there and I got a hard beating when he'd found it.

My current place was a bit more ingenious, though. I kept a pile of clothes on the other side of the room to give a soft, soundless landing for the book. As soon as I heard a squeak of a stair, I'd chuck it and watch it fly through the air to its noise-less landing. Then I'd happily let Peter pull my bed apart and he'd never find anything. That night I read until I heard the house fall silent. By 1 a.m., when I was certain everyone had dropped off, I slipped out of my bedroom window, ran to Peter's car and threw his 'L' magnetic plates from his car into the bushes. Tomorrow morning he had an early start and I'd enjoy watching him play 'hunt the L plates' first thing before I walked to school.

I was exhausted, though. Unless I was asleep, which was sometimes hard to come by due to the stress, my brain was always busy. It was like trying to play a constant game of chess and stay 10 moves ahead of your opponent, and I know Terrie was feeling the strain too. That evening, as we cleaned our teeth, we whispered to one another about how we were coping.

'I can't take it any more, Terrie,' I admitted. 'Honestly, I've had enough.'

She spat out her toothpaste and dried her mouth. 'One day we will be old enough to move out.'

'But it will happen sooner for you than me!' I cried, a bit louder. I loved my sister, but I longed to be her age. The pain in her eyes proved to me once again just how much she cared, but it didn't feel enough. I knew she would leave me one day and that night I went to bed more depressed than ever.

I lay awake, wondering how I could escape. The thought of everything Peter had forced on me over the last five years: the grinding down, the mind games, the constant list of chores, not to mention the beatings and near-death incidents really depressed me. But what depressed me more was that I potentially had another five years of it. I couldn't take that. There had to be a better way, somewhere I could get some peace and relax. Somewhere I could be a young teenager. The problem was I just couldn't think of anywhere. There wasn't anyone I could turn to.

No matter how far I walked down my tunnel of life I just could not see any light. Now with the prospect of Terrie moving out sooner rather than later I would be on my own in this hell-hole. There only seemed to be one more real way left now.

I'd heard from school we should never ever eat red berries, and the bushes around the council estates in our area were full of them. So the next day after school, depressed, exhausted and dreading facing going home, I pulled as many as I could off the bushes. Without thinking, I ate them one by one, then a few at a time, until my cheeks were filled like a hamster, as I walked home, swinging my bag. They tasted bitter, nasty, and happily I thought how likely they were to do some serious damage. Fingers crossed. I gathered a few more fistfuls and decided to save them for later.

In bed that night, I squished up the rest into a glass and then slurped up the juice. Then I lay back on my bed and just wished for a speedy path to peace.

No more Peter. No more beatings. No more coffee breath. No more standing to attention. No more fear. Eventually I nodded off, and then everything went thankfully dark. Next thing I knew I woke to find sunshine streaming through my curtains. Turning my face into my pillow, I sobbed, unbearable emotions bubbling up inside of me. All I wanted was for this to all end. Was that really too much to ask? After everything he'd done I couldn't stand another minute, not another day of this hell. But, piercing my bubble of pain, the alarm pinged off and it was time to get up. If I didn't move fast Peter would find a way to punish me again, for being late. With no choice, I hauled myself up, not ready in any way to face another day.

Clumsily, I ran into the bathroom to clean my teeth. Looking in the mirror I should have seen a young boy, but what I saw was an old man. The berries hadn't worked. I'd have to think of something else. 'Paul, you've survived, so you'll have to hang on for a bit longer,' I told my reflection. 'This can't go on forever.'

Peter's voiced boomed from downstairs. 'You're one minute over schedule,' he yelled. 'Get down here now for your breakfast before I tan your backside.' Anger clenched my insides. Peter wouldn't win. He couldn't win. I mustn't let him win. He won't win.

Chapter 21

'Work Life'

Terrie

$\mathcal{P}$eter nagged at me continuously about what I was planning to do for money after school. I wanted to go to college, but Mum couldn't afford for me to stay in education. Not that I had any idea what I wanted to do; it had been hammered into me that I was stupid and useless for so long that I had come to believe it.

'Now you're almost 16, you need to contribute!' he raged at me. His hypocrisy was breathtaking. He'd contributed absolutely nothing to our house for years. How did he get away with this?

But just a few weeks after my last exams, I got a Saturday job at Tesco on the cash till. On the morning of my first day, Peter pulled me aside. 'Every penny counts, remember, Terrie,' he said. 'Every penny must be accounted for.' As if I could forget.

When I arrived at Tesco, I was shown to a till by a supervisor who explained how it operated. It was very simple. Left alone, I paused for a moment to absorb this new position. To many it looked like a boring, mundane job, but to me it represented something else. Now I could sit here for six hours, completely away from Peter and his attacks. For me, life as a checkout girl was bliss. At the end of the day, I felt alive for the first time in years. Already I was looking forward to the following Saturday.

The supervisor offered me overtime and I snatched every hour I could get. I just didn't want to be at home. I worked 9 a.m. to 9 p.m., Monday to Saturday. I even managed to get four and a half hours' work on a Sunday. A few girls from school also joined, but I found it easier to ignore them. Being at work, rather than school, made us equal.

I earned around £45 per week. Half had to go towards board for Mum, which I didn't mind doing. Then Peter decided on shares to go into my bank accounts. He also demanded to know my full schedule and noted it in his diary.

So my new life began. Peter, however, was keen to remind me I still hadn't escaped. He'd often pop in to the store to buy some milk or tea bags. He'd queue at my till and glare at me in silence as he handed me the exact change. His eyes never left my face as I handed him his receipt.

Often I'd catch his silhouette loitering outside the glass doors if my till was near the shop front. One day Teresa, who worked the tannoy on reception, told me a man had been asking after me.

'What did he look like?' I asked.

'Greasy black hair, smelly breath,' she said.

'Oh, that's my stepdad. What did he want?'

'Times of your shift patterns,' she said.

'Can you tell him you can't give out that information?' I pleaded.

She nodded, with perhaps a hint of the relief I felt. 'No problem.'

I walked away smiling, a surge of defiance lightening my step. Things were changing. Peter's hold was slipping and, thanks to my job, I felt like my escape was edging closer. I still couldn't afford to move out, but for once I clung to the hope it was possible.

A few months after starting at Tesco, I woke feeling badly bruised after Peter had viciously raped me one Sunday afternoon while Mum and Paul were at Nan and Pap's. I'd been in so much pain all week, even just sitting at my till hurt. Thoughts of running away again had never left, but now I was working I couldn't stop thinking about it.

I'd told Tracey, a girl I'd befriended at work, how violent Peter was towards me the previous lunchtime. It never occurred to me to go into any more detail. Nobody ever spoke about sexual abuse at that time. Plus I was so ashamed, filled with embarrassment about what this man got away with doing to me. Where would I even start? It seemed unbelievable. But Tracey had listened and then made a suggestion. 'Why don't you come and live with me?'

'Oh, really, could I?' I'd gasped.

'Why not? Get a bag packed and come tomorrow.'

So, after work that evening I put the plan into action. It was Friday and pay day, so I picked up my money, posted my board for Mum through the letterbox and then ran to Tracey's house, down the road by the park.

I was so relieved to get there. All I needed was a few weeks to plan my next steps. However, when Tracey's mum got home from work she had different ideas. 'You're not stopping more than a night,' she said. 'We cannot afford to keep you too.'

I felt embarrassed and a burden already. Tracey didn't look me in the eye all evening and by the morning I decided it wasn't going to work. I thanked her mum and trudged home.

Peter slapped me hard when I came through the door. 'Don't even think about trying that again,' he yelled.

But weeks later I did try again. This time I followed Sally, another girl who worked at Tesco, home after she offered me a bed in the squat where she lived. But within an hour of arriving, Peter had tracked me down and was banging on the door with the car engine running.

Back home Mum was weeping on the sofa, a shredded tissue in her hand. She'd been ill recently with haemorrhoids and spent days in bed depressed. In spite of everything I felt very sorry for her.

'Terrie, are things really that bad you have to keep trying to run away?' she sobbed. 'Julie from your work rang and said you'd been telling people that Peter beats you. Why would you do that?'

I stared at her incredulously. How could she not believe Peter hit me? She'd either seen or heard it enough times. He even hit her! This was madness. I just sat dumbstruck, thinking how badly Peter was going to take this out on me later.

'And your mum has been ill,' tutted Peter again, as if he only ever had Mum's best interests at heart.

The next time he raped me he was more vicious than usual. He had a collection of weapons to use on me, lined up as usual by the side of the sofa.

'Bet you wish you'd not tried to run off now, don't you,' he laughed, as I screamed with pain.

There didn't seem to be any escape. Ever.

I was so happy and cheerful at work, talkative and interested in people and their lives. As a result people liked me and I got invited out in the evenings a lot. At first I didn't go, but then I plucked up courage to ask Peter and to my surprise he said yes. But I quickly imagined he was only allowing me because I'd tried to run away twice now. Maybe he was giving me a little freedom to stop me trying to get away?

'But you need written permission to be allowed out,' he added at the last minute. 'At least a week in advance.'

'Okay,' I said.

We'd go to nightclubs and I was amazed people genuinely seemed to enjoy my company. I spent most of the evenings dancing, enjoying my freedom. I always had to be home for 10 p.m. on the dot, unless agreed the prior week. That usually involved me stripping off naked in front of his camera before he'd agree to me going out. However, Peter warned me, if I was a second late the door would be locked.

Then, one day, a guy called Patrick who worked on the trolleys came over. He was lovely, with dark hair and a cheeky smile.

'My mate Kerry sent me over to ask you out,' he said. 'But instead I am going to do it for myself. I think you're gorgeous.'

I blushed furiously, not knowing where to look. I'd never ever been interested in any boys and couldn't quite believe what I was hearing. How could anyone fancy me? I felt invisible to boys. Besides, I had no idea how Peter would react. I doubted he'd approve – after all, I was his property. Somehow, though, I managed to smile and not seem too surprised.

'I'll see,' I found myself saying.

But Patrick didn't give up, and when he asked me to the cinema I said yes. I pretended to Peter I was working late and sneaked off. While watching our film, Patrick held my hand and gave me a polite kiss at the end. It all seemed too good to be true.

Before long we were inseparable. Then he asked if I could join him and some work colleagues at the local nightclub, Cinderella's. I knew I'd have to ask Peter's permission, so I told him I'd think about it. I still hadn't told him about Patrick but I decided it was best if I just blurted it out rather than him catching me with him.

'Peter, do you mind if I have a boyfriend?' I said, while bringing him a coffee through as he watched TV.

He glared at me over the top of his glasses. 'What?'

'A boy has asked me out from Tesco,' I said.

'How old is he?'

'17.'

Peter rubbed his chin. 'Yes, okay.'

I almost dropped the coffee in shock.

'Remember, you'll still be doing what I want too, though,' he warned. 'Okay?'

'Yeah,' I shrugged. How I hated him.

'Yeah? You mean yessssss,' he hissed in my ear. 'Say yes!'

'Yes, Peter,' I sighed.

'Yes, God!' he snapped.

The first few times I went out, I always came back a few minutes early. But inevitably I was late once when my taxi got held up in traffic. Peter was waiting behind the door for me, itching to punish. 'You're two minutes late,' he barked, grabbing my hair. Smacking me a few times, he punched me in the stomach before ordering me to bed.

Quickly I learned to weigh up the length of my lateness verses the consequences. For example, if I was two minutes late, or half an hour late, I usually got punched hard a few times, so I might as well enjoy half an hour extra if I faced being hit anyway.

Then, one day, the door was locked and the house was quiet. It was raining and 11.30 p.m. I was very late and knew I faced something awful, but I actually felt relieved he'd locked me out.

I climbed over the gate, down the side of the house, and went into the shed in the back garden. Shivering, I found a piece of tarpaulin and cuddled up underneath it on the hard floor. The reality was I felt safer in here away from Peter. In spite of the spiders and chilly air, I slept in the shed better than I'd done in ages.

As Patrick and I grew serious, I lost my 'virginity' to him at a party one night in someone's house. I knew very well by now what sex was about but in my head it seemed a whole world away from Peter and his filth. This was gentle and loving. Somehow I managed to not even think of Peter the entire time.

Afterwards, Patrick told me he loved me and I just lay there being held by him, feeling like it was heaven. Days later, however, Peter asked me if I'd slept with Patrick yet.

'Yes,' I said, not wanting him to know, but not feeling brave enough to lie.

He raped me shortly afterwards, telling me not to get any funny ideas. I still belonged to him.

'You're a total pervert,' I cried. But my insults bounced of his rotting dirty skin.

Life at Tesco was still going well and I was moved to the Wines and Spirits section, but a union lady called Jean kicked up a fuss about me being under 18, so then I was transferred to the bakery, which I loved.

For the first time in my life I stopped being hungry. The boys from the butchers would sometimes give us some frying steak and we'd sit and eat fried steak rolls at 4 a.m. before we started. I'd always been stick thin but I began to put on weight. My favourite things were freshly baked rolls filled with garlic butter, or doughnuts. With the extra food I had more energy and started to feel better than I had ever done before. The best thing was it was a shift pattern that constantly changed, so it gave me more even freedom.

I'd tell Peter I was working earlier or later than I was and he'd jot it in his diary, taking my word for it. It meant that some mornings I would say I was starting work at 6 a.m. when it was really 8 a.m. Then I would walk into work instead of getting a taxi. That way I could save £2 a day. At one point I tried to work as many hours as possible, simply to stay out of the house for as long as I could.

Although Peter seemed okay about me seeing Patrick, he decided he needed to make it known who I belonged to. After raping me one afternoon following a depraved filming session with a carving knife, he pulled out a Bic razor.

'Open your legs,' he snapped. Then he bent down between them and started shaving off all my pubic hair. I squeezed my eyes shut, pretending my body didn't belong to me. It felt completely separate to my mind now on occasions like this, like I was a mannequin whose job was just to lie still and be manipulated until it was over. 'There,' he said, smiling up at me, looking pleased with himself.

I didn't say anything. I brushed myself down and got dressed. 'I hate you so much,' I said. My words seemed so pointless, though. Despite being old enough to have left school, to have a job and some semblance of independence, I was still a helpless sexual plaything in Peter's eyes. His property. And I could still see no end to it.

Chapter 22

'Triggered'

Terrie

Now Peter had less control over my day-to-day activities, he came up with other ways to spend time with me. He said he wanted to start teaching me to drive. It made sense to everyone else, as that was his job. 'You can pay me a fiver a lesson,' he said.

I didn't say anything. Most teenagers would jump at the prospect of driving but I knew what that meant ... yet another excuse for us to be alone. Peter was known in the area as a patient, good instructor, but with me he was immediately bad tempered and aggressive when I got things wrong. Before we set off Peter taped his camera to the inside of the car. As always he wanted to capture every second of my torment. We set off, and already I was in confusion over which pedals were which.

'I said brake on the right,' he screamed, punching me hard on the arm.

I started to shake with nerves.

'You're such a silly bitch,' he said.

As I drove, shaking, trying to remember where to put my hands and feet, Peter reached over and started poking me. Then he slipped his hand up my skirt into my knickers.

'Concentrate!' he barked as I stalled the car.

The lessons became a few times a week and despite Peter yelling at me I quickly improved. But as my confidence in my abilities grew, his attacks grew worse, and he always filmed every moment.

On one of our final lessons, Peter took his video camera and started filming me in a lay-by. He aimed the camera at my crotch as he stuck his hands into my pants.

'Get off, you fucking pervert!' I shrieked. I so badly wished another car would stop, perhaps a police car.

'Stay still. I just want a good shot,' he insisted. Then he pulled down his own trousers. 'C'mon, get your head down,' he ordered. He got what he needed and switched the camera off. 'Right,' he said. 'Now we need to go over your three-point turn again.'

I was so determined to pass first time, I managed to do so after just about ten lessons. The relief of knowing Peter couldn't use teaching me to drive as an excuse for more time alone together was incredible.

He also cranked up the hours he monitored me outside the house. One evening I was leaving work with Patrick at 6 p.m., arm in arm. I'd told Peter my shift finished at 8 p.m., so it gave us a few blissful hours together. But as we approached the glass doors to leave I spotted Peter's silhouette.

'Where are you going?' Peter snapped, pleased he'd caught me. 'You're supposed to be finishing at 8 p.m.?'

'Ummm,' I spluttered, thinking on my feet. 'Actually it's my break and we're just, er, going for some fresh air.'

Peter glared at me as Patrick made his excuses and left. We waited until he'd gone and then met up around the corner again. It had been a narrow escape.

Coming home from work, I had to be careful what I said about my day. Often I'd been laughing and joking all day with the other girls, ribbing the lads or taking the mickey out of customers. We all had such fun. By the time I stepped over the front door, my serious mask was back on and I made sure I looked quiet and sullen.

If Peter ever saw me in high spirits he'd start quizzing me closely, asking what extra tasks I'd done around the house, or telling me off for something. He couldn't stand anyone being happy and high-spirited.

On one shift, I was walking past the bakery counter when a sharp edge caught my skirt, ripping it. 'Oh bugger!' I laughed. The split caused a hole so big you could see my knickers. My colleagues spotted me and we broke down in giggles. Then someone else brought over an apron. 'Here, cover your modesty with this,' she suggested. Giggling, I wrapped it around me.

As usual the work day zoomed past and all too soon it was time to go home. Mum was already back and as Peter was out of the room I shared what had happened that day. 'You'll never believe where the hole in my skirt was,' I laughed. She saw the funny side too. But then Peter appeared at the door. He'd obviously been earwigging.

'Ooo, you've got a hole in your skirt, eh, Terrie? Let's have a look,' he grinned.

I sighed. It was typical of him to notice something like this. Bloody pervert. I twisted my skirt around to show him.

'No!' commanded Peter. 'Don't turn the skirt around, YOU turn around so I can exactly where the hole is.' His eyebrows were raised, as he squinted his piggy eyes in expectation. My cheeks flushed. I didn't want to turn around. I didn't want to do as he said. Not this time.

'No!' I cried. 'I don't need to do that. You can just look at the hole like this.'

Peter looked at me. 'Yes you do,' he said. 'Or you'll be standing to attention, young lady, until you do.'

I shrugged. 'Bring it on,' I said.

He grabbed me and dragged me to the living room.

'Stand there, eyes ahead, back straight, arms by your sides,' he said. 'And if you fucking move you'll know all about it.'

I moved into position. I wasn't going to show that bastard my skirt. I'd decided. I'd prefer to take the punishment, whatever that meant. It was 4.20 p.m. when I got into position. I stared, eyes ahead, and felt more resolved than ever. The hours started to pass. I'd had a lot of practice of this over the years; after a day's work I was tired, but adrenaline kept me going. By 11 p.m. Mum had had enough and disappeared off to bed.

Peter laid himself out on the sofa, still glaring at me. 'Tired yet?' he smirked.

'Nope.' I just stared straight ahead, determined not to buckle.

Eventually Peter drifted off. A while later I heard movement by the lounge door. I crept over quietly. It was Paul. He'd got a glass of water and a cheese sandwich for me. I wolfed them down quickly and gave Paul a hug. Then I crept back to my place on the carpet.

Sleeping fucking beauty was still snoring away. I stood there until 5 a.m. It was starting to get light outside. I needed to get ready for work. I was utterly exhausted.

'Make me a coffee before you leave,' his dry rasping voice commanded.

I didn't acknowledge him, but walked to the kitchen, switched on the kettle and made him a cup of coffee, stirred in my packet of laxative sugar and took it in to him.

'Don't forget your routine.'

I completed my routine, even the extra parts I'd added in: rubbing his toothbrush around the rim of the loo and weakening any seams of clothes out drying. Then I headed off to work, relieved to be out of that house.

If I thought I'd got away with defying Peter, he was quick to remind me otherwise. I got home one day early after a very early morning shift to find the house empty with him waiting for me in the living room. My heart quickened as I spotted the camera.

'In here,' he barked.

I glanced down to the towel to see what he wanted to use on me this time, and what I saw filled me with unimaginable horror. There, glinting at me under the living-room lampshade, was Peter's ball-bearing gun.

'No! No!' I screamed, shrinking backwards.

Peter leaped up and slapped me hard, dragging me onto the sofa. 'Get your clothes off!' he shrieked.

Sobbing, I pulled off my work top, eyeing the gun as if it were a deadly snake.

'You're not going to,' I began, struggling to string the sentence together. This was just too hideous for words. Even for Peter's evil standards.

'Yes I am,' he grinned. 'That gun is going inside of you.'

My knees buckled as I sat down naked on the sofa, trembling all over. My body had already tolerated so much, but not this – this was too sadistic, too cruel. What if the gun went off? I wanted to vomit with fear.

'Pick it up and put it in you,' Peter ordered, filming.

Shivering, I picked up the shiny metal handle and closed my eyes. Bile rose in my throat so I swallowed hard. The thought of the trigger going off didn't bear thinking about, as I tried to shut out the consequences, although already I could hear the shots.

Peter reached down and pushed the nuzzle into me harder.

'Right in,' he snapped.

I thought I would pass out with fear, as I cautiously held it, desperate not to brush the trigger. It might have been seconds but felt like hours as I tried to do whatever Peter said in order for it to stop. Then, finally, he had filmed enough and picked the gun up himself. Toting it in the air like Clint Eastwood, he grinned manically.

'I am going to rape you now,' he said. I felt a now-familiar sensation of a switch flip in my head. My limbs went floppy, as he grabbed me and I just glared at him.

'Fuck you, I wish you'd die,' I said, as he did whatever he wanted to my body. I no longer felt attached to it at all.

That night I was so sore I could barely sleep. Images of bullets and guns kept me awake all night as I had nightmares of being shot from the inside out.

Peter continued to keep a tight rein on things, and not just the money. That summer Tesco had a workday trip to Skegness and he insisted on coming along too, with Mum and Paul. I sat with my friends at the back of the coach, and thankfully when we arrived Peter took Mum and Paul off on their own. We did run into them on the beach, however. As usual Peter had his camera. I couldn't understand where he was pointing it to film. Then I looked and saw girls with big boobs on donkeys bouncing around.

'Bloody pervert,' I thought.

Peter kept a close eye on me on the coach home. Every time I joined in with the laughter I made sure it wasn't too loud. I didn't want to pay for having a good time when I got home.

Predictably Peter's new rule of needing a week's notice and written permission to socialise was subject to last-minute changes. One afternoon I came home to ask if I could join my Tesco workers on a trip to an ice-skating rink. It was ten days before so I hoped it was plenty of notice.

'Can families come too?' he asked.

'Not in this case,' I said.

'Okay,' he said. 'But have you got your bank book?'

We always did accounts on a Friday, so I didn't have it on me, but assumed it would be in my bag as usual. 'Yes,' I said. 'I'll just go and get it.'

Rummaging through, I realised it wasn't in there. I tried to think where I'd left it. It must've been in my locker at work. 'I'll pick it up tomorrow,' I said.

But at work, I had a look and it wasn't in the locker either. Frantically I looked through my bedroom, pulling apart the drawers and looking everywhere. 'Maybe it fell out of your bag on the bus?' I thought helplessly. But I knew it was unlikely.

'I can't find it,' I finally admitted to Peter that night.

'Oh, well, then you can't go,' Peter said simply. 'You know you need your accounts book. You've lost it and that's that then.'

I sat seething. I so badly wanted to go. Where had the book gone?

All week I weighed up what the consequences would be, and decided, yes, it would be worth the risk. I was going to go on this trip, have a great time, and whatever happened when I got home, so be it. After work four of us walked out together to find the coach. Everyone was excited, and Patrick was coming too. As we left Tesco I half expected Peter to be behind the glass doors or be waiting outside. I was so relieved when he wasn't.

As everyone walked chatting away to the car park I tried to join in, but instead my eyes scoured for signs of a moustache and glasses. But nobody was there.

'Brilliant,' I thought. 'I'll just have fun and face the consequences afterwards.' I dived onto the coach, glancing up and down the empty seats. No sign of Peter. I spotted a few friends at the back and stood up for a chat. Then I felt a hand on my hair. It wasn't playful, it was a grab at the roots. Instantly I knew who it was.

'So you thought you could get away with it, did you?' Peter snapped. He grabbed me by the back of the neck, marching me down the aisle of the coach.

'Ow, Peter, ow. Stop it!' I cried. I was so embarrassed, in front of everyone.

'I told you you weren't allowed,' said Peter, aware everyone else was listening, so sounding like an authoritative stepfather. 'Now, off you go.'

Everyone just stared as Peter half led and half dragged me to the car. It was mortifying. But nobody questioned it. Not even the coach driver. After all, Peter was my stepdad. It just looked like I was in the wrong.

When we got home Mum was at the door, looking worried for me.

'Terrie has been trying to go off for a nice evening trip when really she doesn't deserve it,' he ranted. 'She's been a very diso-bedient girl.'

'Oh Terrie, that's so silly,' said Mum. 'What did you do this time?'

'Only lost her bank book,' tutted Peter. 'Well, now she's grounded for a whole month.'

I went to my room and sat and cried. I rarely got the chance to do anything as exciting as ice skating. It was all so unfair. Two days later I got home from work and found my bank book sitting neatly on top of my chest of drawers. I knew exactly who had put it there.

Sadly my happiness with Patrick wasn't to last. It was a Saturday in work when I first found out; we'd been together for several months and everyone knew we were an item. At lunchtime one of the other checkout girls came over. 'Patrick has been cheating on you,' she whispered. 'He was seen kissing a girl last night at the bus stop.'

I was devastated. We broke up for a bit in September 1986, but then we got back together just before Christmas that year. I found it hard to let people go, and I forgave Patrick. It was then Peter revealed new plans for me.

'Right,' said Peter. 'I'm going to set up a hidden camera and

I want you to bring him back here and fuck him on the sofa for me to film, okay?'

I nodded. By now I was so used to Peter's twisted world, I just said yes without question. And it didn't even feel that bad. After all, having sex with Patrick voluntarily was a million times better than being raped by Peter. Even if we were being secretly filmed.

I did as I was told. I asked Patrick if he wanted to come to my house as everyone was out for the day. I made sure we were facing the camera as I came on to him. He didn't need much persuasion and I tried to shut out all thoughts of Peter perving over the images later. Part of me hated myself for doing this, as it was a huge betrayal; the other part was just relieved to have a night off being raped. Plus, I didn't dare think what would happen if I refused. Peter would make me pay tenfold later.

A few months after our reunion Patrick asked me if he was my first. He presumed I was, as he knew I'd never ever had a proper boyfriend before. I looked at his lovely face and felt so secure, something inside of me desperately longed to be honest. We sat down on the grass, as I glanced up at the sky, hoping against hope this was a good decision.

'No,' I said, taking a breath. 'Actually you're not. Peter has been raping me since I was 13.' I don't know how I expected him to react, but it was immediate and not what I wanted. Patrick bolted upright as if someone had poked him with an electronic cattle prod.

'You what?' he said. His face twisted into a look of total revulsion. 'Ugh, God, that's horrible and disgusting,' he said, jumping up. My eyes filled with tears as I scrambled for words to say, to try and make it better. To even take it back.

'I'm sorry,' I said, not sure why. But yes, somehow I thought he was right. I was disgusting. His reaction confirmed everything Peter had told me when I was just 13. Nobody would believe me. And worse, people would think it was my fault. And Patrick, a man I loved, threw my trust that it could be anything different right back in my face. If he'd punched me hard in the guts it would have been less painful.

He didn't even turn to look at me as he left. I knew it was over then without him saying anything. I watched as his back disappeared across the field and vowed to keep my horrible secret to myself. I was more alone than ever, and if this was the reaction of someone who claimed they loved me what would the reaction be of others? I pulled my knees to my chest and sobbed, shame and despair washing over me.

Chapter 23

'Cycle of Life'

Terrie

As my eighteenth birthday approached I longed to escape more than ever. Now that I was almost a legal adult I knew I could do it. But for the moment half my wages were still being handed over, so I wasn't in any financial position to afford to move. But what I could do was go on holiday. I'd managed to sneak some money to the side and save for a few months, so I asked my friend Tracey if she'd like to go away to Torremolinos for two weeks.

Although Tracey and I got on well enough, she wasn't the brightest girl and she struggled with confidence herself. But honestly, knowing she was as insecure as me made me feel less intimidated about being her friend.

She jumped at the chance to travel, so I put a deposit down. If I scrimped and saved a bit more I could just about pay for a ticket with a little spending money left over.

At first I didn't tell Mum or Peter, but then Mum announced she'd planned a big birthday party for me. I didn't believe her, however, as she didn't know any of my friends or their phone numbers. 'Oh, I've booked a holiday actually,' I said casually. 'With a friend.'

Peter's ears pricked up. 'Did you now?' he asked.

'Yes,' I replied evenly. I hadn't planned what to do if he said I couldn't go.

'You could have been more considerate and spoken to us first,' he said.

I shrugged. 'It was a last-moment decision.'

To my amazement they seemed resigned to letting me go, and I was ecstatic. I couldn't wait. Even if it was just a couple of weeks, I was escaping Churchill Avenue.

Tracey and I set off from Heathrow airport, excited as two schoolgirls. The intense relief of not having to look over my shoulder or be touched for two weeks was almost overwhelming. Once we landed, we trundled off on a bus to our apartment and it was everything I'd hoped for. Sun, sea, sand, and no Peter.

Our routine began the next day: getting up late, swimming and shopping and then dinner. And a few days later my eighteenth birthday arrived. 'Tonight it's going to be "Buy one get one free" happy hour again downstairs in the bar.' I grinned. 'I think we should make good use of it.'

We went down and ordered some Snowballs and Bacardi and cokes. Then, for some reason, I thought it was a good idea to move on to wine. We ordered a bottle, which Tracey opened with a flourish and a toast to my birthday. I rarely drank alcohol and very quickly felt my head and everything else start spinning.

I woke rolled in a sheet, my arms wrapped snug against my body. Moving made me ache. I opened my eyes and sunlight flooded in, hurting my head. 'Trace,' I mumbled, sitting up and looking for her – and my confusion only grew. I was on the floor, most of the bedclothes wadded against the wall to one side. She was laying on the bed, still wearing her black dress. 'Come on, aren't we going out yet?'

I couldn't understand why she was asleep. We were supposed to be making the most of my big night. Tracey groaned, then opened her eyes too and looked at me, propping herself up on her elbow.

246

'Terrie! We didn't get that far. It's morning time. I've had the night from hell.'

'Eh?' I gasped, feeling nausea creep up on me. 'Wait a minute. What happened after the wine? What did I miss?'

'When we left the bar downstairs I had to drag you out of the lift. You couldn't keep your feet under you.' She sighed, shaking her head. 'You were bawling your eyes out, wailing about how you wanted to die. You tried to climb over the balcony rail,' Tracey went on. 'I had to grab you and drag you back. God, it was scary.'

My head started to hurt more. 'I don't believe it,' I mumbled, chuckling a little. It all felt a bit surreal.

'Believe it,' she replied. 'You were well gone. I had to lock the balcony door.' Tracey wasn't smiling or laughing. 'You passed out sick on the bed. I moved you down there so you wouldn't choke.'

I felt embarrassed. It was true I'd never been that drunk before, but would I really try to top myself? I didn't want to think about it. I tried not to drink as much for the rest of the holiday. It scared me what alcohol did to my subconscious. Tracey had seemed genuinely upset. I couldn't trust myself again. Instead I concentrated on the simple pleasure of being free, away from Peter.

As our return date approached, there wasn't a bone in my body that wanted to go home. Spain had given me a much-needed taste of freedom. Now I knew it existed, it was worth holding out for.

The weekend I came home, I was apprehensive about walking through the door. Mum seemed very quiet and the atmosphere in the house was even more tense than usual.

'We need to talk,' Mum said, her face looking stern. 'I found some videos while you were away.' She paused and glanced at Peter sitting next to her. 'Naked ones of you, having sex with Peter.'

I cringed inside, my tinnitus became very loud and I felt like I was far away looking down on myself. 'Okay, this is it,' I thought. I was confused why Peter was still there. I thought she'd have thrown him out by now. I was relieved that it was finally all going to be over, as excruciatingly embarrassing as it all felt.

'Peter has explained everything,' she continued. 'He has promised me he'll be stronger in the future and won't be weak to your advances.'

'*What?*' I felt sick. What lies had he been telling her? I stared at him, appalled, and he gave me a hateful sneer. 'But Mum, that's not true.'

'Now, Terrie,' Peter broke in, 'you know what happens to liars.'

I studied Mum's face and lurched a bit inside, my stomach feeling bottomless for a dizzy moment. Her expression was clear. She believed him. Absolutely. She had already closed her mind to anything I could say in my own defence. Whilst I was away, he had succeeded in poisoning my own mother against me that thoroughly.

Mum continued coldly, 'The videos have been destroyed and we'll not speak of it again.'

I stomped off to my room, feeling sick. What the hell? The fucking weasel had my mum wrapped around his slimy dirty fingers. Was she really convinced I could be that vile, or was she in such terror of being abandoned by another man that she was willing to believe anything? I couldn't afford to dwell on the question. Either way, one thing was clear: There was no hope left in this house for me. None at all. My resolve to escape hardened that much further.

* * *

I moved on from Patrick quickly, and often got asked out by the boys at work. But usually I would only go on one date. I was starting to run out of excuses as to why I didn't want to go on a second date, but I knew if I saw anyone regularly I risked Peter demanding to film me having sex again.

One evening after work, Mum and Paul picked me up to go swimming at our local swimming baths. I was standing in line to collect my wristband when a lifeguard approached me. 'Do you have a boyfriend?'

I shook my head.

'Okay,' he grinned. 'I'm Mark.' He was 17 and lovely, with brown hair and a strong, slim, swimmer's physique. Shyly, I grinned back and went off to swim. Afterwards he ran up to me and dropped me his number. He was so lovely I decided to call him, leaving it a few days at least so I wouldn't look desperate.

We went out many times, to the cinema or to pubs. He was just a lovely, decent guy. But within a couple of weeks Peter had realised something was happening.

'Have you slept with him yet?' he asked.

I shook my head. I wasn't ready to. I wanted to get to know him better first.

'Right, well, I want you to bring him back on your day off and do it on the sofa. So I can get it on film.'

I wanted to scream at him and tell him no way, but I knew it was pointless. If I did that he would be even more brutal the next time he could get me alone. I felt terrible, but on my next day off I asked Mark back to the house. He couldn't believe his luck when he found himself on the sofa with a girl so ready and willing. Afterwards he seemed happy enough, but inside I felt full of remorse and guilt. I was assisting a pervert to get his kicks, even if I had no choice.

I ended it with Mark the next day. He was left feeling a bit bruised as I didn't explain why. I just never wanted to put him in that position again. I wanted to protect him from Peter's sordid little world. After that I never dated any boy more than once. I ended up seeing *Top Gun* three times on 'first dates' with different men. If Peter asked me to have sex with anyone I could claim it wasn't a serious enough relationship.

But then in March 1988 I began dating Richard. He was tall, quite handsome and 18 like me. It wasn't that serious, but I liked him a bit more than the others, so I broke my rule and saw him a fair number of times, and we slept together. Over time it became clear to me he was a bit controlling; he told me to wear a skirt on one night out, and tried to dictate when I could dance. There was no way in hell I was going to end up with someone controlling me. Peter was also growing suspicious about the number of times I'd seen him, so I planned to end it. Thankfully, I didn't have to. Richard announced he was moving away for work.

'I'll call you when I'm back in a couple of months,' he promised.

'Okay,' I said, secretly relieved it was over.

Within a month of him going, I missed a period. As someone who was regular as clockwork, I instantly thought the worst. As I sat in the loo at work and watched two blue lines form on a test, I stared, just disbelieving. I knew it was Richard's. The condom had split the last time we were together. There was nobody to tell and nobody to help me. I decided to just ignore it completely. I carried on like nothing had happened, eating as little as possible, hoping it would all just go away.

Over the next few weeks I felt like a zombie. My mind raced, trying to work out what to do. I'd no idea. I knew I needed to leave Tesco before I started to show. I was sad to say goodbye, but I desperately wanted to keep my friends from noticing I was pregnant and now it was almost impossible to hide. My work colleagues were surprised at my sudden resignation.

'Why're you leaving?' asked Elaine. 'I thought you loved this place.'

'Oh, I just decided to move on.' I shrugged. 'It's been a few years and I don't want to get stuck in the same job.'

I covered up my shame with a smile and promised to keep in touch with everyone there. I couldn't give up work completely, as we needed the money, but I got another job almost straight away, working for a company that provided hostesses on trains. They had a hut on the station where they were based. I wore baggy clothes at the interview, careful with my posture to hide my condition. I landed the job and set off on my first day.

I spent hours walking up and down the aisle of a train all day, selling cans of drinks, tea and snacks. I rather enjoyed it and agreed to work every hour they'd give me, as more than ever I longed to be away from Peter. During the first two weeks of my new job, I worked over 200 hours. But when I went to collect my wages the boss would only pay me for 40 hours. I argued for my proper pay but he refused to give in. So I took the money he was offering and resigned. I snuck back to the station late at night with Paul and we put superglue into the lock securing the chain around the hut.

Straight away I went out to look for another job. I found a cashier's job in a garage five miles away from home. I hit it off with the old guy running it and he said I could start right away.

As the months rolled by, I acted normally, going to work cheerfully and pretending nothing had happened. Because I was eating so little I'd barely put on any weight at all. But at seven months my belly could no longer be so easily hidden.

* * *

It was Peter who first noticed when he made me strip one afternoon for a filming session with a vibrator. He had thought for a while that I was just putting on weight, overeating, when nothing could be further from the truth. But there was no hiding it now.

'You're pregnant!' he gasped.

He looked completely stunned, in a way I'd never seen him before. I'd fooled him for months. Pretending I was having a period. I had even been cutting the inside of my vagina, so there would be fresh blood on my sanitary towels.

'Yes,' I said, shrugging. I couldn't bear to look at him. His piggy eyes were all wide behind those glasses, absorbing my big belly.

He didn't ask me if it was his. I didn't mention it either. He just looked very shocked and sat in silence for a few moments, still fiddling with his camera. I wondered for a moment or two if he'd finally leave me alone now.

'Okay,' he said finally. 'Let's get on with this then.'

And he carried on raping me, hurting me as he did it as hard as he could. I felt so sick. I could tell he was enjoying my pain.

'You evil bastard,' I said afterwards. 'You don't deserve to be alive. I hate you so much.'

'Oh well,' he shrugged. 'But it looks like you're going to have to tell your mum about that.' He pointed at my stomach.

I didn't want to, but he was right, and later that evening I told Mum the news.

She looked horrified. 'Who's the father?'

'Just a lad I've been seeing, but it's over now. I don't want anyone to tell him. There's no point. I'm not keeping it.'

The next day Mum took me to see a doctor. I was very calm in the surgery as he talked through my options. 'It's too late for an abortion,' he said. 'But you can have the baby and have it adopted. Or keep it, obviously.'

'I'm having an adoption,' I said immediately. My heart was breaking as I spoke but I remained resolute. This wasn't one of many options: it was the only option. I couldn't even protect myself from Peter. How would I ever be able to protect my baby from that monster? I started crying as the doctor filled in a form.

'I'll let the authorities know,' he said. 'A social worker will be in touch to let you know the process.'

We drove home in Mum's car in awkward silence. At last she turned to me. 'Terrie, you could get a job during the evening, and then I could look after the baby,' she suggested. 'We could manage between us.'

I shook my head. 'No, I'm having it adopted,' I said, sadly, feeling broken. As I clutched my bump, feeling the baby kick, I knew there was no other way.

In his twisted way I could tell Peter enjoyed my pain during the pregnancy. Despite everything, I longed to keep my baby safe, but I dared not fight him off. As he raped me, leering over my body, I felt more rage than ever before. My innocent baby trying to grow inside of me was at risk from Peter's evil even before it was born.

And there was nothing I could do but let him carry on. I just squeezed my eyes shut, almost holding my breath until he'd finished. The more pain I showed, the more pleasure he took, so I desperately forced myself to look as blank-faced as possible.

I had to tell my boss I was pregnant. I was going to need time off when I went into labour, so I decided to explain the situation. 'I'm having the baby adopted,' I said taking a deep breath. 'So after the birth I should only need a week off and that's it.'

'Adopted?' said the manager. His face changed. He looked rather moved. 'Really?' he said, frowning at me.

'Yes,' I replied quietly.

'Straight after the birth?' he continued, glancing down at my bump.

'Yes, straight away,' I said. 'It's for the best.'

'Well, you can have as much time as you want …' His eyes shone and I thought he might cry.

'I just need a week,' I said.

'So the baby's going to a couple that can't have one,' he sighed, with his thick Scottish burr. 'All the angels in heaven will shine down and look after you, for doing such a wonderful thing.'

I struggled not to dissolve into tears. I didn't want to tell anyone else, but the next time I saw Nan and Pap I knew they'd notice. 'Nan, I'm pregnant,' I admitted, patting my belly.

Her lovely soft round face broke into the biggest smile. 'Oh my! Terrie!' she cried, wrapping me in a hug.

'No,' I said, trying to hug her back but feeling like a fraud. 'I'm having it adopted.'

Her face dropped. It was heartbreaking to see. It struck me then what it meant. I was also giving away their first great-grandchild. 'Okay, love,' Nan finally said after a long, painful pause. 'Are you sure?'

I explained I'd never been so sure, and the subject was dropped. I knew if I broke down in front of her it wasn't going to help either of us get through this.

Days later I went to see a lady from the adoption agency, who talked me through the procedure.

'Do you want to see baby after he or she is born?' she asked, making notes.

'No.' I shook my head. I closed my eyes. I'd tried so hard not to think whether it would be a boy or a girl.

'Would you like to hold the baby?' she asked.

'No.' I bit my lip. I knew absolutely if I saw this baby or held it I was at risk of changing my mind, and there must be no chance of that happening. The only way to keep it safe was to give it away.

I swallowed hard and closed my eyes. I didn't want to think about what was to come. How hard it would be to let go. I had to be strong.

'Okay,' said the lady, looking at me strangely. She briskly went on to explain the baby would be in foster care for six weeks before being settled with a new family. Already one had been found. She told me my baby's new parents' first names.

'They're a lovely couple,' she said brightly. 'They run a small farm in the Home Counties.'

I swallowed hard again. That sounded like a much nicer start in life than what I could provide. Away from Peter. That's all that mattered.

'Do you want any photos of your baby?' she asked, still ticking her boxes.

'Yes, please,' I said. That was one thing I longed for. Just a couple to remember him or her by.

'And one after the baby has gone with its new parents?' she asked, absorbed in her notes again.

'No,' I said. 'After all, the baby will belong to the new mum and dad then, won't it? It won't be my baby.' I trailed off. I couldn't allow myself to ever think of this baby as mine. 'Just two pictures will be fine,' I said, taking a deep breath.

She nodded. 'Do you want to give the baby a name?'

'No!' I almost snapped.

This was torture. How could I have the right to give my child a name when I couldn't give him or her a home? I so badly wanted this to be over. It was all too much. I went to work the next day and just tried to forget all about it.

* * *

As my due date approached, the hospital booked me in for an induction. It had to be perfectly timed for the adoption.

None too soon, 10 November 1988 arrived. I was to going to have, and then immediately give away, my baby. Hardly sleeping a wink all night, I lay awake worrying about the pain and what was to come. But most of all another emotion kept me up. Guilt.

I packed a small bag and Peter dropped me off at the hospital, barely saying a word. I mustered my dignity and strode across the car park to the maternity ward among the excited new mums holding their partners' hands. *Always hold your head high*, I could hear Nan as she had coached me repeatedly. *Walk with a purpose, no matter how you're feeling. No one can see what's inside, so don't be scared.* Finally I found the right department and gave my name to the receptionist: 'Terrie Duckett.'

The nurses all looked up when she repeated my name. They ushered me to a side room and explained they were going to place a drip in my arm to kick-start my labour.

'Can I have painkillers?' I asked. Despite all of the pain I'd endured over the years, I wanted to suffer as little as possible with this.

'You can have an epidural,' one said. The nurses moved around me efficiently, dressing me in a gown, stabbing needles into my arms and setting the room up. 'I'll sort one out.'

Nobody asked if I was okay, or even looked at me. I could see nurses whispering at their station. A couple of them glanced over and quickly looked down at their notes when they saw me looking back at them. Nobody wanted to meet my eyes. I stared at the cannula in the back of my hand, wondering when this torment would be over. 'Just a few hours, Terrie,' I tried to comfort myself.

Very suddenly the pains began and I was gasping, bent double over the bed. It really was worse than I'd ever imagined. Tears slipped down my face as I clawed at the bedspread trying to manage the agony.

I called for a nurse, but nobody heard me. I pressed the buzzer, but everyone seemed to have vanished. 'Please!' I called, as one finally passed by. 'Please can I get my epidural now?'

She looked at me blankly, then agreed she'd be back. I waited a while, groaning as the pain gripped me every few minutes, until finally nurses arrived. Nobody said a word as they lifted the back of my gown to inject me. I caught my breath and gritted through the discomfort of setting up the spinal block.

The pain of my body hardly mattered. What I needed was to protect my mind, to lock away this experience, and this part of my life, in a part of my brain where it couldn't hurt me. The epidural, I surmised, would leave the pain a blur in my memory. If I didn't feel the baby being delivered, then maybe I could let go – pretend it was never mine, move on with just a passing glimpse of what could have been.

'Can someone ring my mum and let her know I've gone into labour?' I managed to ask between deep, tightly wound breaths.

'Okay,' said one. Secretly I hoped Mum would turn up to be by my side, and hold my hand. But two hours later I was still alone. There was only me among the chilly, distant nurses, wrestling with rising terror, struggling not to despair. The pain waiting for the anaesthetic to take hold was nothing beside the realisation that Mum wasn't coming to help me through this.

Mums were meant to love unconditionally. Why didn't mine? Did she really hate me this much? There was no radio playing soft music to soothe me. No smiling midwives and nurses. No one to tell me it would be all right. There was only me, barely understanding what was happening, having to be strong the way I'd always been, by setting myself apart from what was happening to me. I must have seemed such a cold bitch.

Labour seemed to take ages, but by 4 p.m. I was finally told to push and my baby emerged into the world. A midwife held him up and tried to place him on me.

'It's a boy,' she said.

'No!' I cried, twisting my head. 'It's in my notes I didn't want him passed to me.'

She stood there for a moment, with this bundle in her arms, as my eyes roved around the room, looking anywhere, at anything, except my baby.

'Please take him away,' I sobbed, turning my face into the pillow.

Wordlessly she carried him off. But soon a nurse pushed him next to me in a clear plastic cot. I still tried not to look, but I knew it was hopeless. I turned and saw a peaceful-looking, beautiful newborn next to me, all snugly bundled up in a white blanket.

I felt like dying.

'I put in my notes I didn't want him around me,' I whispered to her.

'You need to give him a name before we take him away,' the nurse replied. 'It's protocol.'

'Paul,' I said, tears now slipping down my cheeks. 'Name him Paul.' He was the one good, pure thing in my life.

Chapter 24

'Taking the Bullet'

Paul

A few days after Terrie returned from hospital, I knocked on her door for the third time that day, but she still didn't answer. I wanted to see if she wanted a glass of squash, or anything. She'd barely eaten since she'd got back from hospital and we hadn't spoken.

I'd found out she was pregnant when we were on holiday camping with Nan and Pap a few months ago. She was so withdrawn, more so than usual, which truthfully I didn't think possible. Wanting to cheer her up as she walked off to find the Portaloo, I ran up behind her. I threw myself onto the floor to try and rugby-tackle her, like I always did when I wanted to wind her up. But Mum yelled out in panic as she spotted me. 'No, Paul, don't!'

I stopped and looked up. 'Why? What's up?'

'Terrie is having a baby.'

Terrie's face didn't move a muscle as she looked at me. I knew it wasn't good news.

'Oh, okay,' I said, not quite sure what to make of the surprise news.

I didn't ask any questions. I didn't actually have any feelings about it. In many ways I struggled to feel proper emotions now. After so much pain with Peter I'd often watch events unfold in front of me rather numb, like someone looking in on someone else's life. Terrie shrugged me off and carried on walking. Now they'd mentioned it I could see she waddled a little bit like a pregnant woman. My sister, pregnant? Didn't seem right somehow. She didn't even have a boyfriend, at least not one I had seen.

Time whizzed by and it was time for Terrie to go to the hospital. She went off with just Peter. Mum kept saying it was 'for the best' as she made tea that night, but I didn't know what she meant by that, as she roughly peeled the potatoes, faster than usual. 'She won't be bringing the baby home,' Mum said by way of explanation.

If she wasn't bringing the baby home then where was she taking it? I wondered, but I knew better than to ask.

The next day, we popped into the hospital for 10 minutes to drop off some soap and fresh clothes for Terrie. She looked as if she'd been crying but didn't mention the baby, and we didn't see it. There were loads of other babies, though, all wailing with their mums holding them or feeding them. I didn't know where to look. Terrie didn't look at any of them either.

After we left, Mum told me she'd had a boy. 'She called it Paul,' she said.

I looked at her blankly. Again, I didn't know how to react, or why Terrie had given the baby my name. Surely she could have thought of a better one? I suppose maybe I was a little touched deep down. My sister always thought of me, whatever happened.

Two days later my sister came home, and before I even had a chance to say 'hello' she shut herself in her bedroom. Every time I knocked on the door she was lying staring at the ceiling in the same position with her headphones on, tears slipping down her cheeks. I didn't know what to say again so I left her to it. She hardly looked up, even when I bought her a copy of

Smash Hits the next day after school. It had been hard sneaking it past Peter's roving eye. He'd even been letting her off her jobs for this week, so I knew she must've been poorly. I'd no idea babies made you so ill. Finally, after four days, she emerged, looking shaky and pale. She told Mum and Peter she was going back to work at the garage. After that, no one ever uttered a word about the baby again.

I tried to have a chat about it with Terrie shortly after she returned to work, but she made it clear she didn't want to talk about it. 'I just have to forget it, Paul,' she said sadly. 'And so should you.'

'Okay,' I agreed, but I wanted her to know I'd do anything for her if she needed.

It wasn't long before life returned to normal and Peter was up to his usual tricks of ruling everything with an iron rod, including Terrie. He made her join in with the jobs again and started fussing when we weren't cleaning properly. Then one morning he called me outside.

'Hey, Paul,' he grinned, reaching behind him before throwing a 'thunderflash', a fire-cracker-type military weapon used to stun people, directly at me. Leaping backwards, I clamped my hands over my ears as I almost threw up with fright. If it had hit me it would've taken my hand off. Running down the garden, my ears were ringing with pain as I heard something else in the background: the sound of Peter's laughter.

Later I took my revenge with some chilli con carne Mum left on the side for our dinner one day. 'Bring me some dinner through,' Peter barked from the living room.

'Yes, Boss,' I replied.

With speed, I opened a tin of dog food and quickly mixed some into Peter's mince, something I always did if I had the chance and dinner was brown and wet. 'I bet Peter loves the smooth meaty chunks in Pal,' Terrie giggled.

Peter didn't seem to notice he was bolting down a quarter of a can of Pal with his chilli.

Terrie seemed more herself the next day. As Peter rushed around to sort himself out for work, he went to put his shoes on and his lace snapped. Terrie was standing at the kitchen door giggling as he cussed and went to the cupboard to find another. She'd obviously tampered with it just to irritate him and make him late. As we left the house for school I gave her a high five.

Slowly I climbed up the ranks in cadets, but it was much slower than my colleagues, thanks to my reputation of being unreliable. My determination set me apart. Despite me missing weekend camps and evenings I eventually became a Lance Corporal, although the rest of my badges gave away that something was wrong – any other cadet with my collection of badges was a sergeant by now.

I was an incredible shot on the .22 rifle, sometimes using my own rules to win – this is where living with Peter paid off, it made me think about different ways to achieve the same result in as efficient a way as possible.

There was a competition to win a case of beer for whoever shot five polo sweets off a plank of wood suspended at the bottom of a 25m indoor range quickest. I'd already proven myself as someone who could shoot a polo hanging from a piece of string 25 metres away with a .22 rifle, so this was going to be a good one for me. As all the lads had aimed perfectly at the actual polos and mostly hit them, I thought about the criteria of the competition and aimed instead at the wood, resulting in all five polos flying off in just under a second. I won, but only by the letter of the competition rather than the spirit.

The following weekend we were taken to an outside range so we could do live firing. We were each issued 10 rounds of

5.56 live ammunition. Each time we had used it up we were issued more. At the end of the day we all lined up and stood to attention and, as an officer passed, shouted out a declaration, 'I have no live rounds or empty cases in my possession, Sir!', which I duly did.

I didn't consider myself to be lying, because I wasn't. I didn't have any on my person, but I did have one in my webbing, which is worn around your waist, ready to take home. The idea of finishing Peter off, or at least doing some damage so he would stop hurting me, was one that never went away. Now with live ammo at my disposal it was all too tempting. I didn't have a gun but if I used a hammer I could get the bullet to explode, hopefully with Peter somewhere in the vicinity. But as both a cadet and a person who prided himself on honesty and working hard, the fact I had live ammo in my bag rankled with me for the rest of the day. As much as I wanted to hurt Peter I knew I couldn't – not in this way. It was wrong and it would make me as bad as him. I wrestled with my conscience and it clearly distracted me when I got back to barracks as Sergeant Major Felkins noticed I was 'out of sorts' and asked me if I was okay. By the end of the day I decided to hand the live round over, removing temptation. I told my detachment commanding officer, Lieutenant Hill, who then called in Sergeant Major Felkins.

'How did you come to have a live round on you and take it off the range?' they asked, concerned.

I stood up straight to attention. 'I'm not sure, Sir,' I confessed. I couldn't go as far as admit I wanted to use the bullet to kill my stepdad. 'It was an error of judgement and poor checking on my part, Sir.'

I got a dressing down and was dismissed as they discussed my case. Stealing ammo was a pretty bad offence and I got stripped of my rank, referred to as being 'busted', and ended up being probably the most over-qualified rankless cadet in the battalion.

Chapter 25

'Hope'

Terrie

$\mathcal{J}$lay on the sofa, two days home from hospital. Everyone was out for the day. Thoughts of my baby had been whirling constantly in my head. He was the first thing I thought of when I woke up and the last thing I thought of at night.

After the nurse had taken him away, I was stitched up and taken off to recover in the maternity ward with other mums and their new babies. As we passed the beds, most had pink or blue foil helium balloons hovering above with fresh bouquets in water by the bedsides. All I could hear was the cooing of delighted relatives or mumbled pleas from new mums for a takeaway or cup of tea.

My bed was bare and empty. I didn't know what to do, so I just sat on the starched sheet, gazing into the middle distance as if in a trance. I felt completely numb. Then one of the new mums in her slippers and dressing gown shuffled over to me. She slid up on my bed and curled her arm around my shoulders. It was the first kindness I'd seen all day, and it filled my eyes with tears.

'I know what you're going through,' she whispered. 'Three years ago I was in your position. But I promise this is the lowest point and things can and will get better.'

She pulled me closer to her, gently rubbing my back.

'Look over there,' she said, pointing to her bed, with a baby in a cot next to her. 'That's me today and one day that will be you.'

I didn't know if she knew I'd had my baby adopted, or presumed he'd died, but it didn't matter. I broke down in tears. She'd been the only person to show me any compassion, and it meant everything.

I curled up in a ball and tried to sleep, but voices roused me. It was Mum and Paul. Mum thrust a bag of toiletries in my hand. 'Thought you might need these.'

'Thanks,' I said dully.

They only stayed few minutes, none of us really knowing what to say.

'Right, we'll get off then,' Mum said. 'Peter will be here to pick you up tomorrow.'

I barely slept a wink that night, I was in so much pain with my back and stitches.

First thing the next morning Nan and Pap came in to see me. My heart surged in two directions at once when I saw them. They had always been my comfort, but as much as I loved them, I had to hide the dread that came upon me as well.

I gave them both a hug, and we chatted for a little while about work and what Pap was up to. But I knew why they were there. My baby would have been their first great-grandchild. Nan wanted to see him before it was too late, though she wouldn't tell me outright.

'Gladys, we should be heading off,' Pap said at last. They hugged me tightly. 'Come and see us after the weekend.' Nan's eyes looked watery.

I could barely speak.

My heart was in my mouth as I walked them out of the ward; Nan saw the baby room and made a beeline straight for it. *Give me strength*, I pleaded silently to no one.

But I followed her, feeling sick, heart pounding. There he was, lying in his cot quietly, his name on the band on his wrist. *Paul Duckett*.

I wanted to cry.

Nan picked him up. She cuddled him gently for a few brief seconds and put him back down in his cot.

That was my baby boy. He looked so lovely: a dainty little mouth, blue eyes staring back at me, my elfin chin. I took a deep breath. I couldn't stop myself. I reached out and with my index finger and thumb I gently squeezed his hand.

'You'll be better off without me,' I whispered, too low for Nan and Pap to hear. 'I promise.'

Then we all turned without another word. As we walked away it felt as if a piece of me was being left behind.

At first light the next day, I was up and waiting to be collected by Peter. Back home, I went straight to bed. I put my headphones on and listened to George Michael sing *One More Try* over and over again. I was in pain, not my body, but my soul. I was broken. It hurt to breathe. I needed pain-free peace.

I waited until everyone had gone to work and Paul to school I then lay on the sofa downstairs. I played *One More Try*, listening and connecting with the words. I really had had enough of danger. I wanted – needed – to find some peace.

Sobbing, I opened my work bag and pulled out several bottles of paracetamol. Paracetamol was supposed to be good for pain. I lined up the bottles and took a bottle of Martini from the drinks cupboard and washed down every last pill. Soon, I thought to myself, soon I'll get the peace I need, all the hurt will stop. I tidied the empty bottles back into my bag, and put the Martini back in the cupboard.

'Half left,' I muttered to myself. 'Let the fucker punish my corpse.'

I felt a bit queasy, so I slowly worked my way up the stairs and snuggled under my duvet. I laid my head on my pillow, pressed 'play' on my Walkman and closed my eyes.

The birds woke me first, then bright light through the curtains, and then the sound of Peter pissing in the loo. I wanted to scream. I pulled my pillow over my head, hoping it was all one last dream before my mind shut down once and for all. But it wasn't. I was alive. I lay there sobbing until I heard everyone go out to work and school.

'Shit!' I sat up in bed, suddenly thinking to myself, I need to top up the Martini bottle with water.

A little later, my head feeling clearer, I tried to doze off. After so many pills I couldn't believe I was still here. 'Maybe it's for a reason,' I thought. 'Maybe, in spite of everything, I am supposed to live.' And that was when I made up my mind. I'd use my second chance now to get away from Peter as fast as possible.

For the next two weeks he didn't come near me. He avoided me at all costs and just barked orders to do cleaning or other chores if he caught me sitting downstairs. Not once did anyone mention the baby or ask how I was.

I returned to work quickly, relieved to be out of the house. I had a new boss called Mohammed, who knew nothing of the pregnancy, so I acted like nothing had happened either. It was hard, though. I ached inside. I hated myself, feeling guilty every single second, fearing so greatly that my baby would grow up feeling abandoned. After how we'd lived our child-hoods, that was the last thing I'd ever wanted.

It was good to be back at work. Mohammed always saw the funny side of things. Even when dopey Dean, my co-worker, filled his butane lighter with petrol and flicked fire all over the shop, Mohammed just laughed it off and told him he'd be docking his wages for the damaged stock.

The same week, I'd almost given him a heart attack. He'd been filling his car in the empty forecourt when I decided to test my new electronic key fob that made all sorts of noises – including machine-gun fire – over the tannoy system. He dropped to the floor like a brick. When he peered over his bonnet, I just happily waved to him.

A few months later Mohammed mentioned to me that one of our customers fancied me.

'Which one?' I laughed. Men were still the furthest thing from my mind.

'He comes into the garage quite often. He's a builder,' Mohammed said. 'His name is Steve. I'll point him out next time.'

Steve was six foot tall with dark spiky hair and a mature way of speaking. At 26, he was seven years older than me, but when he asked me out on a date I said yes.

He was a lovely, caring person, and the fact he liked me enough to take me out was enough for me. I didn't tell Peter at first, but after a few dates I knew it wasn't worth trying to keep it from him.

'How old is he?' he asked.

'26,' I replied.

'26?' he said, swallowing visibly.

'Yes.'

'I want to meet him.' The look on his face told me he didn't approve. I wondered if Steve being older worried Peter. Steve was a man, as opposed to a boy, like the others I'd dated.

'What's he like, your stepdad?' Steve asked nervously as I arranged for him to come over.

'Oh, not that nice really,' I shrugged. 'We're not a close family.' It never occurred to me to elaborate.

And to say it didn't go well would be an understatement. Steve came over one evening before we went out to a club. I went upstairs to have a shower while Steve waited downstairs. But when Peter came home from work he raced upstairs as I unlocked the bathroom door, a towel clutched around my body.

'What the hell do you think you're doing?' he yelled. 'Parading around half naked with Steve here?'

'What?' I cried. 'Steve is downstairs. He can't even see me!'

I knew it was no good speaking sense, though. Peter was in one of his rages. His contorted expression told me he was jealous.

'I just want you out,' he ordered to Steve. 'Now!'

Poor Steve stood up, confused. 'What?'

Peter prodded his chest, then tried to manhandle him out of the front door. Steve's hands went up defensively to fend Peter off. Suddenly Peter fell, clutching his face. Somehow Steve's ring had cracked Peter's tooth and the bracelet he was wearing had cracked his glasses.

'You bastard!' Peter screamed. 'Get out of my house! I'm charging you with assault for this.'

I ran back upstairs to quickly throw some clothes on. There was no way I wanted to remain alone in the house with Peter in this mood. Then I ran after Steve and we escaped to his parents' house. 'Don't worry, you can stay with me,' he said, taking my hand. The relief I felt at someone as kind – and as big – as Steve to deal with Peter was just immense.

His parents lived in a village about four miles away. They were warm, respectable people who welcomed me. His mum made some tea and told me I could stay as long as I liked. But it wasn't long before there was a knock on the door. It was the police. I was scared. What had Peter said? What were they going to do? But instead of looking annoyed the policemen smiled at Steve's parents.

'Hi there,' one officer said. 'Sorry to trouble you, but we've had a complaint from a Mr Peter Bond-Wonneberger. He is talking about pressing charges for assault.'

As he spoke, I realised the police officers knew Steve's family. Living in a small village meant they were very friendly and respected them as law-abiding citizens. In fact, they automatically believed Peter was being over the top in his complaint.

'We advise you to simply pay this chap off and we're sure he'll forget all about it,' the officer said.

Steve was incensed. 'No way am I doing that!'

The police told him to think about it and afterwards we had a chat with his parents.

'I didn't do anything,' Steve ranted. 'Peter was the one who assaulted me!'

But I knew we had no choice but to pay it, so I used some of the money Oma had left me in her will to pay off Peter without telling Steve. I went home a few days later. Peter was still sulking and had gone to bed. Mum explained how Peter had been shocked at how friendly the police had been to Steve's family.

I just grinned. Again, Steve had more power. Not only was he big enough to thump Peter if he wanted to, his family were even friends with the local coppers. More than ever I felt protected by my new boyfriend.

A month later, in June 1989, I went on holiday with my cousin Nikki. I'd not seen her for five years – after Nan Duckett told us she never wanted to see us again, we'd lost touch – when I heard a familiar voice using the phone in our garage.

I tapped Nikki on the shoulder. 'Oh my God, it's you, Terrie!' she cried. We hugged and I confessed how low I felt and Nikki agreed life had been hard for her too. 'You know what we deserve?' She grinned. 'A holiday.'

That lunchtime on a complete whim I booked tickets to the Canary Islands and told Peter and Mum we were off for a week. Neither of them said anything. I think they could tell I needed a break after the baby.

Nikki and I set off together to have the time of our lives. On the first day I managed to dive into the shallow end of the pool and chipped my tooth on the bottom, but instead of crying I laughed my head off. Being away from Peter and the madness for another week was enough for me to be able to see the funny side of anything. Catching up with Nikki felt good too. She hadn't had an easy time growing up either but she had managed to leave home and live independently. I found her so inspiring.

I didn't hesitate to let my hair down. One night there was a competition to see who could drink beer out of a baby's bottle fastest. I had a bit of an edge with all the practice sneaking a quick drink before Peter's camera caught us, and growing up with my Dad had made me ferociously competitive. No prizes for second best – I sucked the hell out of that bottle and ended up winning a bottle of champagne. Shaking it up, I sprayed foam everywhere, cheering my head off. I proved to myself that outside of the house life could be fun and carefree.

We staggered back to the apartment that night well and truly pickled. I would love to be able to say we unburdened our souls to each other in a deep, heartfelt, cathartic discussion. In fact, it's entirely possible that we did. But to be honest, neither of us could ever remember what we said or heard from that day to this.

I woke up the following morning with a sore head, but we were both determined to enjoy the rest of our time away from it all. By the last day I dreaded going home again and deep down I knew things would have to change. Filled with a renewed determination to leave home, I knew now if Peter wanted to stop me he'd have to kill me first.

Chapter 26

'Straightjacket'

Paul

*T*he two years between 13 and 15 whizzed by. Life at home seemed to get worse, with Peter simply dreaming up jobs to take up any free time I had between finishing my rota and bedtime. The plus side to it was that time passed very quickly indeed. My body became hardened to the beatings and very little seemed to affect me either physically or mentally any more. I had become emotionally detached on the outside, but inside I made my plans and applied myself to every job I did and ensured I completed it to the best of my ability.

I continued to achieve well in cadets even after the setback of being busted, going on to be put forward for a regimental award for the most outstanding cadet. I achieved my silver Duke of Edinburgh award and received a special mention from the assessor for my gold expedition. I even got put forward for the 25lb artillery course on the next camp, at which I won a huge framed picture and award for being the top cadet. Neither my mum nor Peter attended the presentation, but by this point I was used to that.

I arrived at the age of 15 abruptly and I had no idea what I wanted to do with my life. Every day was mentally exhausting, without having to deal with big life questions like what I wanted to do after school, or what career interested me. The subjects I chose were simply ones that made me happy or filled my belly. I took up Home Economics and Arts and Crafts, the only boy to do so in the school, but I didn't care. After all, Home Economics meant extra food, and that was all I could think about. If we made rock cakes, for example, I'd knock up six of them for class, but sneakily make an extra two and gobble them, barely waiting for them to cool down.

In my art class I became a dab hand at sewing: blanket stitch, cross stitch, cherry knots. I made a beautiful felt cushion and a satin relief cushion with a farmland scene complete with furrows in the hills. Other lads thought I was mad but it provided me with a form of escapism, even if it wasn't the most manly pursuit. I wanted to stay on in sixth form, but Peter was having none of it.

'You need a job,' he cried. 'You think your mum is working her fingers to the bone for you, you good for nothing.' But all I could think was, you can talk, you fucking lazy useless piece of shit.

He was a total hypocrite, as he wasn't working himself and was living off my mum like a parasite, but I knew better than to argue. Then it was decided I could stay on at school, but only if I got a job all weekend to pay board.

Quickly, I got a job in a motorway service station restaurant. It was long hours, all day Saturday and Sunday, but I'd get paid £86 for the two days, and it had the added bonus of giving me lots of time out of the house, and I was never hungry. Peter said I had to give half of it to Mum straight away. It angered me how much say he had in this – he was quick enough to lecture others, but never had any money himself, except when it came to buying new technology or computers. The only downside was working all weekend meant I'd never be free to join any cadet camps or go and see Nan and Pap.

My first job was to clean the tables, stack the dirty plates and cutlery in the trolley and then place them in the dishwasher. With my colleague Richard we discovered the average time it took most people to do was 14 minutes. So we set about trying to smash the record with a bit of competition. Between us we managed to clean all the tables and load the washer in under two minutes. Soon afterwards my supervisor placed me on the tills and then the grill. 'If you can be as efficient on that grill, Paul, as you are at clearing those tables, we'll have some very happy customers.'

I was so happy to be doing this job; being out of the house all day was bliss, and I already appreciated the extra food I had. For once I really wasn't hungry all weekend. It was no coincidence that both myself and Terrie had ended up working with food as our first jobs! I started my own system on the grill, always making sure extra sausages or bacon was sizzling away so customers never had to wait long. If staff came for some toast, I'd often slip a few rashers under their bread too. I liked feeding other people as much as myself.

One particular weekend it snowed prior to my shift. I turned up at work to find hundreds of stranded motorists. I was going to have to work like the clappers to keep up, but I managed it and enjoyed every second. The manager, Jenny, who let me get away with murder, was grateful as I kept the food churning out and asked me to stay on for another shift to help keep the grills moving. That day I ended up working 18 hours straight and cooked up thousands of breakfasts and dinners. I was exhausted when I finally collapsed in my bed, but it was worth every minute.

Every Saturday a minibus took us to and from work. On the way back I'd place my knees up against the seat in front and, exhausted, would drop off within minutes. By the time we'd reached my stop I'd be deep asleep, and would have very dead legs. At times I'd have to crawl out of the bus and sit on the side of the road while waves of pins and needles passed.

Once I could walk again I quickly picked up the pace, though, so I could get back in time for *Beverly Hills 90210*. I fancied the actress Shannon Doherty madly and it was my biggest weekend treat. Inevitably, it wasn't long before Peter spotted how much I enjoyed the programme. He'd clocked me bursting into the living room in time for the opening credits and so suddenly concocted jobs that needed doing.

'Go and take Sam out for a walk,' he snapped, just as I settled down to watch it.

I sighed, swallowing my anger. Even my one favourite TV programme per week wasn't 'allowed'. I leaped up and grabbed the lead, but the poor dog's feet barely touched a blade of grass in the oval that evening.

Being out of the house at work was a treat in itself, and I always found fun wherever I could. Often this meant Richard and I found ourselves having food fights with stock about to be chucked away. We'd end up splatting eggs on each other's heads behind the supervisors' backs, or chucking three-day-old doughnuts around like bullets. Most of the bosses turned a blind eye, as I was such a whizz on grill.

Going out and having impromptu fun was impossible with Peter. Like Terrie, I had to ask for written permission at least seven days beforehand. And even if I'd got permission, he still took great delight in banning me just a few minutes before I was due to leave. I had few friends, but the ones I did have often went clubbing, getting home at all hours. I'd have to 'discuss' with Peter what time I was allowed out until. If I suggested a time too late, he'd immediately ban me going altogether. As a result I had terrible trouble fitting in. Most of my teenage years were spent sitting in my bedroom. Cadets really was my only respite. Terrie was so lucky she could escape to work now, and Peter let her out at night sometimes too. I was happy for her in one way but insanely jealous in another. We saw even less of each other.

One day I got an invite to a classmate's birthday. It was to be a huge do, with everyone in school going. I'd managed to get permission from Peter after he'd increased my number of chores twofold. But, determined to go, I did everything he'd asked. Then just as I was about to leave he held out his arm at the door.

'You're not going,' he said. 'I want you to take Sam for a walk instead.' As much as I loved the dog, I really hated him too. Taking the dog for a walk had caused me to miss so many things and not taking him for a walk had caused me to be punished so many times. I longed to thump Peter and tell him to take Sam for a walk for the first time in his life, but I bit my tongue and grabbed the dog lead. On my way back, walking past Peter's car I was struck with an idea for revenge. The cone on top with the BSM sign was held by a magnet, so I quickly pulled it off, leaving only a small patch so the cone would only just stay put. That should cause Peter a problem or two and reward him for being such a nasty bastard.

As predicted, the next day Peter returned from work with a carrier bag full of plastic bits, seething with rage. 'The bloody cone came off on the dual carriageway,' he ranted to Mum. 'Smashed into pieces. I'll have to buy a new one now.'

I stared at my dinner plate, desperately trying not to laugh and betray myself.

That New Year's Eve I was finally given permission to go out and celebrate and stay out until a reasonable hour. There was a big do on in town and all the people from school were going. I spent the month doing everything and anything Peter told me to, in order to get permission to go. I even managed to save £40 to pay for the taxi there and back.

On the day, I got ready, not able to relax, as I knew Peter could say no at any point. But I'd done all my jobs, twice over, and had asked for written permission in my notebook. Everything was as he'd wanted it to be. I'd even remembered to call him either Boss, Master or God all week, depending on his mood.

Finally it was time to say goodbye, so I grabbed my jacket and then jumped in the cab. But when I arrived at the club I patted my pocket to find my wallet was missing. 'Oh no!' I cried to the cabbie. 'I've lost my wallet. Oh God, no!'

The cabbie switched on the light as I looked between the seats and the footwell. It wasn't anywhere. I was certain I'd put it in my jacket pocket.

There was no time to fiddle around. It was already 9 p.m., so I asked the cabbie to take me home. I was gutted as I knew the cab fare there and back again would cost me the rest of my money. I'd have nothing left for drinks or food.

The cab finally arrived home and I raced back indoors. 'My wallet!' I said to Mum breathlessly. 'I've forgotten it.'

'Oh?' said Peter, looking very calm. 'You left it on the sofa. Here it is.'

I took it from him. There was no way it had 'fallen' from my jacket – well, not unless it had a little help.

Saying nothing, I looked inside it. 'I won't have any money left now for the night out,' I said. I looked anxiously at the cab through the window.

'Better be more careful with your belongings next time, eh?' Peter said, his eyes not leaving the TV.

I went back outside and on the way back to town explained the situation to the cabbie, who thankfully took pity on me and drove me back for nothing.

* * *

Terrie Duckett and Paul Duckett

When we went back to school after Christmas, I found out my form tutor, Mrs Carter, who had been a real rock to me at school and my form tutor for four years, was leaving. Everyone liked Mrs Carter, but I was especially gutted as she'd acknowledged something was 'wrong' at home and would let me off if I was ever late, or came with the wrong equipment or uniform. I've never forgotten the people in life that made that extra effort. She was so popular we did a whip round in the class and managed to raise £20 to buy her a present.

I volunteered to go and actually buy the gift, thinking I could just hide the money from Peter somewhere because making the effort was my way to repay her.

'What shall we get her?' asked one classmate, Anthony.

'Flowers? Chocolates?' someone suggested.

A few ideas were bandied around and I promised I'd get something suitable. Everyone knew how much I liked Mrs Carter so they trusted me to get it sorted.

I left school with the cash and carefully hid it behind some books on my shelf, away from Peter's prying eyes or camera, which he didn't seem to use as much as it rarely caught anything interesting any more. I planned to wait for a free afternoon when Peter was at work to spend a couple of hours in the shops working out what to buy. But two days later I came home to find Peter holding a load of change. He threw it on the kitchen table in front of me. 'Where's this from?' he snapped.

Oh God, I thought, not Mrs Carter's money. 'It's a class whip round,' I replied. 'For Mrs Carter.'

'I don't think so,' Peter said, smirking. 'You wouldn't have raised that much!'

'We did!' I insisted. 'Everyone loves Mrs Carter.'

'Why wasn't this in your accounts last night?' Peter asked.

'Because it's not my money,' I replied.

'Ha, I don't believe you,' he scoffed.

'It's true!' I was starting to panic now. This was crazy. I wasn't even allowed to buy my teacher a present. 'Why don't you come into school and ask everyone? They'll tell you!'

'No,' snapped Peter. 'You've probably primed everyone to lie anyway, you sneaky little wanker. Tell me where this money is from or I'm going to confiscate it.'

I slumped onto the chair, my head in my hands. This was unbelievable. 'I promise you it is for Mrs Carter,' I said, slowly. But already I knew it was no good. After all, it would be an even better punishment if he took it away now, wouldn't it?

Peter gleefully swiped the coins off the table and walked out. 'Too late,' he said. 'You've had your chance and lied. It's gone now.'

My mind was reeling. How could I explain this one to my classmates? Nobody would believe me. I'd just be thought of as a thief. It hurt all the more as they'd trusted me.

I started to wonder what to do, and then came up with a plan. A couple of days later I went to a shop in town. I found a shop where they sold carriage clocks and managed to stuff one into my bag without anyone noticing. Walking out I held my head high, but my heart was pounding. I hated stealing but there was no way Peter was going to prevent me giving Mrs Carter a leaving present.

Sneaking in before Peter, I got it upstairs to my bedroom and then tried to take the back off to get a battery in. Somehow, though, I managed to bend the door, as it was made from aluminium. But I got the thing working and, relieved, managed to sneak it past Peter the following day by hiding it in the grass out the back.

Everyone in class had been asking what I'd got, so I showed them the clock. 'How much did it cost?' someone asked.

'£19.99,' I lied.

Mrs Carter said goodbye to everyone and then I proudly handed her the clock. She welled up as she turned it over in her hands. With its slightly bent-looking door it looked like something off the back of a lorry. But she just glanced at me and winked, as she told everyone how much she loved it.

Chapter 27

'Gloves Off'

Terrie

*H*ome from holiday, I felt as if I'd had an injection of a new lease of life. Being with Steven meant having a future and the possibility of moving out. But as our two-month anniversary of being together approached, Peter called me downstairs one evening for a 'serious chat' with Mum.

'Myself and your mum have concerns,' he started. 'Steven is a big man and we're worried he might be violent towards you.'

I almost choked as I looked at him, with fake concern on his face. 'You what?' I asked incredulously.

'We're worried he might be a danger to you if you continue this relationship.'

'Nice try, Peter,' I thought grimly. It was quite unbelievable. Smiling, I looked at them in the eyes. 'Don't you worry yourself, Peter. Or Mum. Steve won't lay a finger on me.'

The next day when I returned from work Peter pounced on me as I opened the front door. It had been several weeks since he'd touched me as I'd been away, but Paul was off at cadets and Mum was out with her friend, so he wasn't going to miss an opportunity.

'Right, get undressed!' he yelled, pulling off his clothes.

'No!' I screamed back. And, feeling an unusual surge of strength, I pushed him.

But he grappled with me, and we both fell onto the carpet. With all my might I twisted and turned, lashing out at him. In the scuffle my fingernails caught his cheek. Momentarily he stopped, clutching at the claw marks. 'Argh, you little bitch,' he yelled. He managed to pin my arms down, but I kept kicking out at him.

'Stop it! It's got to stop!' I screamed. Deep inside me, I felt an uncontrollable strength. The end was in sight for me now; I knew I'd escape Peter soon.

'This is never going to end,' he cried. 'It will never stop.'

I screamed in his face. It was a sound I hardly recognised, like a roar. The blood gushed to my head, rising in me from somewhere new. I looked Peter in the eye steadily. There was no fear any more.

'If you want to continue this,' I spat slowly, 'you'll have to KILL ME first. Do you understand? You'll need to kill me.'

I widened my eyes, gazing at Peter squarely. Like always, he was staring at me in his myopic way over the top of his glasses. But this time the cold hardness wasn't there. Instead I spotted a flash of something I'd never seen before: fear. It was just a fleeting moment, but unmistakable nonetheless. Peter knew I didn't care any more. I wasn't frightened of him, and it scared him.

'You're a pathetic, evil little man,' I spat at him.

He grabbed my hands together in a vice-like grip and raped me. Yes, he still overpowered me physically, but afterwards, when he'd finished, mentally we both knew I'd won. When Mum came home from work she noticed my nail marks on Peter's face. 'What's that, Peter?' she asked, pointing at it.

'Oh, I hurt myself shaving,' he mumbled.

The next morning Peter got his diary out and asked what my schedule was like for the following week. 'What nights are you planning on going out?' he demanded, licking his finger to find the right page. 'I need it written down.'

'Every night!' I said casually.

'Erm,' said Peter, trying to glare at me, 'I don't think so. It's one night and it's only if your jobs are done.'

'No,' I cried, almost jeering at him. 'I'm out with Steve every night and, guess what, you can't stop me.'

He said nothing and walked off into the living room. That evening I went out with Steve to the pub. He'd missed me a lot while I'd been away and wanted to talk about our future. 'Let's buy a house and move in together,' he suggested.

I was so happy I could have burst. 'Yes!' I squealed with delight. He wrapped me up in his big arms in a huge hug. I knew I'd found the way out there and then. My dream of escape was going to turn into a reality.

We put down a deposit on a two-bedroom bungalow. I was so excited at the thought of getting my own place; truth was, I couldn't have cared if it was just a cardboard box, as long as it was four walls and a roof away from Peter. We managed to get together a mortgage very fast, and thankfully our new home was chain-free. Within a matter of a month or so it was settled.

The first person I told was Paul, whispering my plans as we washed up that evening. He looked at me blankly.

'You're lucky,' he said, simply. I didn't know how to reply to that. I felt so guilty about leaving him. I wished I could take him with me, but that would never be possible.

'We'll stay in touch,' I promised.

I casually told Mum over breakfast I was moving out the following week.

'Oh,' said Mum. 'Which day are you leaving?'

'Some time this week it'll be,' I said. 'Not sure when, though.'

'Okay,' Mum replied, and then left for work.

Our relationship had never been worse. Without a doubt she was depressed, and things between her and Peter weren't happy. The years of betrayal and delusion on her part had formed a wedge between us, a wedge I doubted could ever be shifted.

As soon as she'd gone, I didn't waste any time having a quick hunt round to try and start packing. I lingered over my LP collection and old childhood mementoes but decided I'd come back for them later. For now all I'd take was the bare minimum. As soon as Steve got the keys, I took a day off work and stuffed as much in my car as I could. I was too afraid Peter would stop me. More than that, I also felt guilt at leaving Paul behind. All I could think of was escaping.

Once I'd got my measly few belongings into our new place I flopped on the sofa we'd had delivered earlier in the day. I sat and relaxed and waited for Steven to come home from work. I was so happy I could burst. I'd made it. It was just too unbelievable to be true.

I stuck some music on the radio and started dancing around the room. Then I went shopping and bought everything that I liked to eat. Just the idea I could do what I liked was overwhelming. As soon as Steve opened the door from work, I grabbed him and jumped up and down excitedly.

'I'm free!' I cried. He laughed along with me, but I knew he'd never understand the truth behind my happiness. I wasn't just an ordinary girl happy to be free of the constraints of her parents. I was free from depraved abuse, the kind he'd never understand. And I wanted to keep it that way. After all, what would his mum and dad think of me? What would Peter say? Would it put Steve off me? No, I was just going to put my past behind me.

Over the next few days I woke feeling like a prisoner who'd escaped. I almost had to pinch myself as my alarm went off every morning. Instead of leaping up to adhere to Peter's schedule, for the first time in seven years I snuggled back down to relax.

The whole day stretched ahead, without any worries of attacks or violence. It was unbelievable. But despite my happiness, it soon dawned on me that consigning Peter to my past wouldn't be as easy as I'd hoped. He might no longer have been physically in my life, but mentally there was little respite. I was haunted. After spending years walking on eggshells, I found myself struggling to relax properly. Often I felt as if someone was watching me, especially if I was on my own.

Night times were the worst. If Steve went out for the evening to work as a bouncer I'd spend the evening sitting next to the carving knife, fearing someone would break in and attack me. So I worked out a system where I shut and locked every door and window carefully before the sun went down. I wasn't able to use a shower or bath if nobody was in. If I ever walked upstairs in the dark, I had to walk up sideways like a crab, with my back against the wall. My constant need to be on alert for so many years had taken a heavy toll. Even when I didn't need to be vigilant, I couldn't switch off. It was exhausting.

I often had nightmares too, of a faceless person chasing me, hitting me or catching me. I'd always wake up exhausted, but thankful that yet again it was just a dream.

I also threw away my watch. Now I didn't have to measure time I was determined not to. But even this was a hard habit to break. If I went shopping I found myself panicking in crowds and mentally planning how long the trip would take. I also realised I had a problem with the sound of other people eating if I wasn't eating myself. Deep inside I felt a strange rage.

Perhaps all those years of not having enough food had also taken their toll?

I might have been physically free but it was going to take a long time to break the mental hold, and it wasn't long before Peter got in touch.

Just a few weeks after I'd moved out, the phone rang.

'Hello?' I answered.

There was silence. Then a sound of heavy breathing.

My heart thudded. I'd no need to ask who this panting noise belonged to. Peter. I didn't want to say his name or let him know I knew, so I just listened for a few seconds. Then I gently returned the phone to the cradle. A few minutes later the phone rang again.

'Hello,' said Peter clearing his throat. 'It's Peter.'

'Hello, Peter.'

'Can I, er, pop over today?' he asked.

'No, thank you,' I said politely. 'Steve is not here and I'm busy. I don't want you here when I'm alone.'

This phone exchange became a regular occurrence. But I never allowed Peter to upset or anger me.

The next day at work, I was serving a customer when a familiar red car with a cone on top crawled past the petrol station. I carried on counting out the change, ignoring it. I knew it was Peter's way of telling me he was still around, but who cared, I kept trying to tell myself. I was going home to my own house with Steve.

Peter came back a few days later, this time slowing right down and peering into the cash desk window, making sure I glanced up.

Then, a few weekends later, I looked out of the front-room window to see his car in our road. We lived in a cul-de-sac, so I knew full well he was going out of his way to display his presence. This time it sent a shiver down my spine, but I held my head high and carried on doing whatever it was I was doing.

Although I'd escaped Peter I knew it wouldn't be long before he'd make other attempts to re-enter my life. And I could see clearly where his new endeavours were leading. Instead of hassling me, he started focusing time and energy on getting through to Steve. He'd started to strike up friendly conversations whenever we popped in to see Mum or if our paths crossed in town.

'How's that car of yours you're tinkering with?' he'd asked Steve, smiling.

Steve loved talking about his car and the pair would spend 20 minutes chatting about exhausts and carburettors. I knew full well that Peter had never shown any interest in car maintenance beforehand, but suddenly he was riveted. Or he'd mention a new DVD player he could help fit or offer to loan us a video camera. Or loan us new films he'd recorded. Steve was hopeless with technical stuff like that, so he was grateful for the help.

Although I could clearly see what was happening, I felt paralysed to act. After all, the only way I could get Steve to stop seeing Peter was to admit what had happened. Whether it was through shame or concern about how Steve would react, I knew I would never say anything. After ingratiating himself with Steve, he'd ring and ask if he could pop over for a coffee.

I shuddered. I couldn't believe his nerve. 'No,' I said simply. 'And don't you ever try and come to my house on your own again either.' It didn't stop him, though. He'd turn up when Steve came home from work, offering to lend us a copy of a pirated film or computer game. Steve fell for it every time.

My guilt at leaving Paul grew as my taste of freedom did. I kept ringing to check if he was okay, but Peter always answered. The conversation was always the same. 'Is Paul there?'

'No.'

'Can I leave a message?' I knew Peter wouldn't pass one on whether I did or not, but I had to try. All I could do was hope my little brother was okay for now. He knew we'd always be there if he needed us, and I also knew it wouldn't be long before he was old enough to move out himself. I tried to console myself with the knowledge that at least he wasn't being sexually abused. I knew he could survive the physical and mental torment, as I had done too. He was a tough little thing.

But the main way I kept in touch with Mum and Peter was through family shopping trips with Nan and Pap. Often we'd all meet up and mooch around for some food shopping before stopping for lunch in the canteen after. Like always, Peter honed in on Steve, always jovial and chatty to him, asking him all about his life, so Steve felt flattered and interesting. It made me want to scream.

Chapter 28

'Shadow in Sun'

Terrie

*B*ut after two months of living with Steve, whatever Peter was or wasn't doing soon took the back seat of my attentions, as I fell pregnant.

I rang Mum first to tell her. 'Mum, guess what? You're going to be a grandmother!' It felt wonderful to be sharing happy news for once.

'Oh, Terrie, I'm so happy,' she cried.

I welled up with tears at hearing her response. This time I could look forward to a completely different experience. Perhaps it would even bond us together?

As my bump grew, however, so did my guilt for giving away my baby boy. I still thought of him every day and still had my precious picture. Steven knew about the adoption as I still had paperwork delivered to the house, but he accepted what had happened and was supportive. The pregnancy was tough on my body as it was my second in as many years. The baby was lying on my sciatica so it was uncomfortable, plus I already suffered back problems from the epidural from the year before. But knowing I was allowed to be a mum to my baby was a consolation.

When I went into labour, Steve only just made it, he'd been in such a rush. I'd been taken in to get things started as I was two weeks over the due date, but thankfully the labour took just 50 minutes and then my beautiful little girl emerged. I was filled with happiness and I knew what I was going to call her the moment I saw her.

While I was in hospital, Mum came in with Paul with cards and presents. We'd named our little girl Tammy, and she was so perfect I couldn't take my eyes off her. Watching Mum hold my baby girl made me well up with pride. She gave me a card: 'To the happy new mum', it read on the front. I looked up as Mum stood next to me, beaming. I opened it to read inside: 'To our wonderful grandchild. Love Nan and Pap.'

I swallowed hard, thinking of my own Nan and Pap. Then I looked at Mum and slowly it dawned on me. Of course, Mum was now Nan, and Peter was calling himself 'Pap'. I wanted to be sick, but I fixed a smile on my face and turned to look at my gorgeous girl.

As soon as I got home, Paul came over to see me and Tammy. It was a rare occasion, and I realised then just how much I missed my baby brother. As he sat on the sofa, holding Tammy, he ended up nodding off, exhausted from living with Peter. We didn't talk much about Peter. We didn't need to. But Paul talked about moving out himself and how he was determined it wouldn't be long now.

'I hate Peter so much,' he said. 'When I leave that house I'm never going back.'

'I know,' I said, patting his arm. 'It won't be long now.'

He was just finishing his GCSEs and hoped to get a job and move as soon as possible.

'I'm so proud of you,' I carried on. 'Proud of both of us. And I'll always be here for you, don't forget it.'

It was soon after Tammy was born that Steve and I decided to get married. This was the February and we set the date for April. The next few weeks were a whirl of plans. Mum decided we could make the cake between us, Steve's mum made mine and the bridesmaid dresses. Everyone automatically assumed Peter would be the one to give me away. They all liked him and, of course, it was natural he would. He'd been my stepdad for 10 years by now. 'He's brought you up since you were 12, so it seems right,' someone said.

Our own dad was still out of the picture, but none of it was right. Peter didn't deserve this honour. My heart was thudding. What could I say to stop this from happening? People would ask questions if I banned him, so I just went along with it.

Next time I saw Nan and Pap they were thrilled with the news, and Nan took me to one side.

'I want you to have this for the day,' she said. I looked down as she pushed something in my hand.

It was a tiny gold chain with a cross on it. 'You can have it as your something borrowed,' she said. I nodded, knowing how precious it was to her.

'I'll take good care of it,' I promised.

'How's all the wedding planning going?' Pap asked.

'Fine,' I said. I told him about my dress and bridesmaids and the car we were hiring to go to the church.

'Peter will be walking you down the aisle, will he?' Pap asked.

'Oh yes, that's a good idea,' Nan agreed.

I smiled tightly. In an ideal world I wanted Pap to walk me. 'I guess he will,' I said resignedly though.

Knowing how involved Peter was going to be on my big day meant I'd started to dread it. The night before the wedding was worse as I'd agreed to spend the night at Mum and Peter's. It was my first visit back to Churchill Avenue since I'd escaped. That evening I was just feeding Tammy, then seven months old, when I went into the kitchen to fill her bottle. I'd not let her out of my sight around Peter. As I stood at the sink I looked out of the window to where Paul and Peter were in the garden. There, in the corner, Paul was hunched by the wall, as Peter stood over him beating him with his fists.

'It's still going on,' I cried to myself. 'Why?'

I knew it was unlikely to have stopped, but even on my wedding night, to see Peter punching Paul like that brought back all my guilt. I wish I could've saved Paul.

Barely able to sleep, I just wanted to get the wedding over and done with. Having to watch Peter play the doting father-of-the-bride would be torture. In the morning I got up early and Mum helped me get ready. Then she and Paul kissed me goodbye and told us they'd see me at the church. I waved them off, thinking how lovely and ordinary we'd all look to outsiders. A family wedding, a proud mum and brother. Behind my smile nobody could see my churning guts.

Being alone with Peter as we waited for the white limousine to turn up to take us to the church was hideous. I just sat in silence on the sofa as he pottered around. He didn't say a word and neither did I. Finally the car arrived, and we walked to it and sat down together.

'It's your big day today!' he beamed cheerfully. 'Don't worry, everything will be all right!'

Sullenly, I turned my head as far to the window as possible and willed the journey to be over. I didn't know what I'd do if he dared try to touch me. But then, I also knew he didn't need to. He was clearly enjoying every millisecond of this. He still had control. A central place in our family. I squeezed my bouquet hard between my hands, praying for this ordeal to be over.

Finally we arrived. Emerging from the car, I fixed the biggest and best smile on my face as a photographer took pictures. How I hated having to push my arm through Peter's crooked elbow. He was the centre of attention too now, waving and smiling, ever the proud stepdad, when all I could think was, 'He doesn't deserve any of this.'

We walked down the aisle, and I managed to get through just a few more excruciating seconds before I could drop his arm, hopefully forever. By the time I'd reached Steve waiting for me at the end, I wanted to collapse with relief. After we'd said our vows, we went to the Working Men's Club next to our bungalow for the wedding reception. There, Peter made a toast. 'To the bride and groom,' he said, lifting a glass of champagne. Everyone smiled at Peter and then turned to us.

'To the bride and groom.'

I chinked Steve's glass, beaming. I'd done it.

Shortly after we'd married, Peter dropped by and handed me a mobile phone. 'I bought this for you.' He grinned, rocking on his heels. 'Help us all keep in touch.'

Taking it, I thanked him in front of everyone, but deep down I was fuming. After he'd left, Steve eyed the phone. 'That was so nice of Peter, wasn't it?'

I switched it on and immediately looked into the contacts list. Only one number had been keyed in: Peter's mobile.

Tammy's first birthday soon arrived and I invited all the family over to help celebrate. As usual Steve and Peter spent a lot of the time together chatting, looking at his cars or cameras and generally just getting on, while I concentrated on my baby and Nan and Pap. Watching my grandparents fussing over their great-grandchild lifted my spirits. Tammy was such a pretty, happy little thing. She brought real joy to our lives. I loved every second of being a mum. It gave me a purpose in life, in ways I'd never thought possible. As usual I avoided Peter like the plague. However, at this particular do he seemed determined to speak to me.

While I busied myself in the kitchen to top up people's drinks and sort out Tammy's cake, he sidled up to me quickly before I'd a chance to leave. The smell of him still caught in my throat and made my flesh creep. 'Terrie,' he stammered. 'I'm sorry. Sorry for everything.'

I just looked at him. Those familiar piggy eyes, this time with a desperate look to them, and his greasy slicked-back hair. I wanted to scream. 'Just don't,' I said, and pushed past him, holding Tammy tightly.

It was pathetic. If he really expected that a quick apology in a kitchen on my daughter's big day would make any difference, he was even more mental that I'd already believed. But I could see his thinking. He longed to stay part of this family. He worked hard to ingratiate himself with Steve and be accepted as Tammy's Pap. Once again he was only sorry for himself.

Just 18 months after Tammy was born, Nan was taken into hospital with heart trouble. She'd been ill on and off for a few months, and whenever she was admitted for treatment I didn't hesitate to take Tammy with me for a visit to raise a smile. On one visit she asked me to come closer to her bed before I left.

'I want you to have this,' she whispered. She pushed the gold chain I'd borrowed for my wedding day into my hand. I'd only given it back to her a few months earlier.

'Oh no, Nan, you don't need to give me that!' I protested. 'It's your special chain.'

'Yes,' she breathed. 'Yes I do.'

I could see in her eyes she didn't have the strength to argue, so I gratefully took it. 'I will keep it safely forever.' I smiled, gently stroking her cheek.

'I know you will,' she replied, struggling for breath.

We hugged and said goodbye, my emotions welling up as I thought just how much I loved my nan. During some of the worst times in our lives, Nan and Pap had been our only oasis of comfort.

The next day Mum and Peter turned up at the door at 7 in the morning.

'What's happened?' I cried, knowing it must be serious.

Mum's face was blotchy from crying. 'Nan died last night.'

My face crumpled as I covered it with my hands. It was devastating. I hadn't been expecting it so soon.

Three days later Paul turned 18. Still in shock from the terrible news, we somehow managed to get through a birthday dinner with Nan's chair left empty next to Pap. Despite the immense sadness of Nan's passing, I could tell Paul was more on edge than ever. Peter kept glaring at him the whole time and he looked even skinnier than usual. Just a few months later, Mum rang to tell me Paul had moved out. He'd been on his way to the TA, which he had joined after leaving the cadets, when Peter banned him from going, but this time Paul defied him.

'I'm going anyway,' he'd said.

'If you leave this house you're not coming back,' Peter screamed.

'Fine,' Paul said.

And that was it. He left that evening with the clothes on his back and never returned. For months he disappeared, not contacting anyone, but eventually I bumped into him on the market square. I hugged him and told him I'd missed him.

He spent ages sleeping on friends' sofas, struggling to get a job. Somehow he managed to finish his A-levels and then found some agency work in kitchens as a chef's assistant. Always a hard-working boy, he applied himself to whatever they found him and then eventually he got offered a council house. Even though Mum insisted she wanted Paul home, Peter decided to knock down the wall between my old room and Paul's to make a giant computer and photographic room.

Eventually we reconnected and I invited Paul over for dinner. I desperately wanted him to know I was there for him if he needed me. Paul looked tired, but I had to admit much more relaxed then when he came over the last time.

He explained how shortly after he'd moved into his new place Mum and Peter had suddenly appeared on his doorstep. 'How are you?' Mum asked.

'Why do you care?' Paul shrugged.

'I'd like us all to start communicating again,' she replied.

He told her not to bother and closed the door. It was all too late.

Then Peter sent him a letter. 'You need to grow up and stop upsetting your mother like this. When you've made this decision, things will get better and we can all start communicating again.'

Paul screwed the patronising, ridiculous letter up and threw it in the bin. He vowed never to have anything to do with Peter again.

Paul tried to rejoin the TA and pick up where he left off. He missed his friends and was considering a career in the army. But he discovered Peter had returned all his uniform after he'd left home and had made sure he had been discharged as being unlikely to be an effective soldier.

'Of course, Peter had to do that,' Paul said, when he told me all about it. 'It was the last big punishment he had control over. He knew the TA was my only real joy in life.'

'We're both free of him now,' I assured Paul. 'It's up to us to make the most of our lives.'

Chapter 29
'The Truth'
Paul

*A*nd that, thankfully, was the last time I heard from Peter for seven years. In 1992, at the age of 18, I'd finally had enough and I walked out and left my old life behind. I walked forward to my begin my new life, never looking back.

Mum left Peter in 2002, but I'd noticed a change in her a few years before. She became more critical of Peter: always complaining about his smells, or the way he sponged off her. She started to develop a life of her own again, built new friendships, joined a spiritualist church, somehow found the self-confidence to move on and, eventually, met someone else and left him. But – although Mum paid all the bills – our house on Churchill Avenue had a mortgage in joint names. Peter won his last battle by insisting Mum buy him out. She couldn't afford to, as all her money was in the bricks and mortar. Knowing this, Peter offered her a derisory £20,000 to buy her out, which in the end she had to wait over three years for. And Peter being Peter, he didn't let her pack or take any belongings from the house either. It was like when things ended with Dad all over again. She left with a small bag and the clothes on her back. All our belongings from our family – albums, old toys and ornaments – were left behind.

But Peter quickly found out he couldn't afford the mortgage on his own, so even after Mum had left she ended up helping him pay for it for two or three years afterwards. She said she felt guilty for leaving him for another man and was worried that if she didn't help him he would lose the house and she wouldn't see the promised £20,000.

Peter remained in Churchill Avenue, but as far as I was concerned it was good riddance to him and that house. All of those terrible memories could stay there with him, although I often thought of what we'd left behind.

After I moved out, I completely cut him off, but poor Terrie had to endure him for years after. For some reason her husband Steve liked Peter, I've no idea why. He kept them in touch.

After Terrie's daughter Tammy, she had a son called Ben, in 1992. Peter was determined to be his 'Pap' too and would constantly turn up with presents and offer to take them places. If he bought Ben a Lego set, it would be the biggest and the most expensive. And he showered computer games on Tammy. Sometimes he'd even turn up outside their front fence unannounced, if he knew the kids were off school, and would wave cheerfully through the lounge window. He'd whisk them off for pancakes and syrup at McDonald's, anything to keep up the pretence of the perfect grandfather. Whatever Terrie did, she could never get Peter away from her family.

When Mum left Peter, things got worse for Terrie. Steve insisted on inviting the newly single Peter around to keep him company. It was only when her own marriage finally broke down in 2006 that she was able to get him out of her life, for good. Both of us were just anxious to leave the terrible years at Churchill Avenue behind. Terrie moved in with me for three years after that, but in all that time neither of us mentioned Peter or Churchill Avenue. Some things just remained unsaid between us and we were both happy with that.

I kept closer in touch with Mum than Terrie did. Her betrayal had all but destroyed their relationship, something I've only appreciated in retrospect. At the time I simply thought Mum and Terrie didn't get along, like plenty of mums and daughters. If Terrie called me while she was over she'd say: 'Oh, is YOUR mum there?' as a half-joke. She rarely saw her.

After she left Churchill Avenue, Mum set up a new home and new life, only seeing Peter occasionally when she caught up with our old neighbour, Jeff. Now that Jeff was in his 90s, Peter had become the model neighbour to him, popping in for regular chats and cups of tea and cake. Jeff thought the world of him. I'd no idea how Mum could stomach having tea with Peter still, but she was only doing it for Jeff.

By this time I'd also married, and had a happy home life with four beautiful kids. Neither Terrie nor me saw ourselves as victims. We just got on with it, focusing on the here and now, on our own children and families. One thing was for certain: we were both firm in the belief that anyone who turned from being abused to abusing their own kids was monstrous. We never laid a finger on our own.

Time passed and then we received devastating news. The man Mum had left Peter for had committed suicide because he couldn't face the financial mess he had got himself into, leaving Mum to pick up the pieces. This helped to bring Mum and Terrie a little closer, and over the years their relationship thawed a little, to the point where we talked about buying a property for Mum, which we would inherit in later years. We'd met a few times over tea to chat about it.

Then, on 14 May 2012, Mum came over to mine for tea and afterwards we got chatting. As we talked she made a comment about Peter, something about not being 'all that bad'. Now, over the years I'd forgiven Mum an awful lot. She was never fully aware of the extent of Peter's abuse, and chose to turn a blind eye to some of the physical chastisement that went on, but hearing her sticking up for him on any level didn't sit right.

'Aw, c'mon, Mum, Peter wasn't all that innocent!' I said, almost choking on my tea.

Mum looked at me funny. 'In what way?'

'Well, one morning, in your bed, for example, he showed us a big plaster on his willie!' he said.

Mum looked agape. 'You what, Paul?' she gasped. 'Why did he do that?'

'I've no idea,' I replied. 'It was some twisted game. He pulled mine and Terrie's pants down pretending to look for pubic hairs.'

Mum frowned in concern. Clearly this was news to her. 'You know Terrie had dealings with him, don't you?'

I laughed. 'I don't think so, Mum!'

'Yes, she did,' Mum said sadly. 'I caught them having sex one Christmas in her bedroom.'

The world seemed to stop on its axis at that moment as I absorbed the awful words Mum had just uttered.

'You … what?' I gasped.

'Yes,' said Mum. 'When she was a teen she started coming on to him and ended up seducing him in her room on Christmas Day! I was really upset. I rang the Samaritans afterwards, and even went to see my GP. Both said it was just her teen hormones and not to worry about it. Peter told me it was a one-off anyway … all consensual. He was as upset as me about it in the end.'

I sat back in my chair, my head spinning like a top. 'Mum, I don't think so! I know my sister and there's no way this is true,' I cried, when I finally managed to find the words to speak. 'Okay, I need to speak to Terrie about this.'

I grabbed my phone, my fingers trembling as I punched in her number. I'd always known Number 59 Churchill Avenue had been hell on earth for us as kids, but Terrie having sex with Peter? On top of everything else? I hoped to God this wasn't true.

'Hi Terrie!' I said brightly as she answered. 'Could you pop over? Yeah, right away if that's okay. Mum's here and we really need to ask you about some stuff.'

I put the phone down and turned to Mum. 'I'm just going to stick the kettle on. Terrie's coming over.'

I took a few minutes alone in the kitchen, breathing as I thought of Terrie. I still struggled to react promptly to big emotions, but something like this was hard to get my head around.

Within 15 minutes Terrie arrived. 'What's up, Paul?' she asked. Her big smile at the door changed, though, as soon as she saw my face.

'Look, this is a bit of a weird one, so I'll just come straight out and say it … Did you ever have sex voluntarily with Peter?'

'Hell, no way!' she cried. 'Never.'

'Okay,' I said, as a sickening realisation was washing through my guts. 'Listen, Terrie.' I sat her down and blew my cheeks out. 'Mum says you slept with Peter willingly. Is that true?' I blurted out.

'No!' Terrie cried.

'Okay,' I said, nervously. 'Well, Mum is under the distinct impression that you did.'

'Yes you did!' Mum argued. 'I saw you, and you didn't say anything afterwards. You didn't try and defend yourself or anything!'

'I tried, Mum. I wanted to. But you didn't listen!' Terrie cried. 'You were brainwashed by Peter for years and he persuaded you about that too!'

'I can't believe it!' Mum gasped.

Terrie was trembling now, her eyes filled with tears. 'Mum, Peter sexually abused me from the age of 13 until I left home. That's the truth of the matter!'

We all fell silent; Mum started weeping, as Terrie stared at her and then me. Looking at my sister, I saw the defenceless little girl, not the 42-year-old woman and mum of two. It was so heartbreaking to know this had gone on, without me having a clue. I couldn't bear it.

'Well what do we do now?' I asked, struggling to get anything out of my mouth. 'Ring the police?'

Terrie looked horrified; she put her head in her hands. 'I've kept this a secret for so long,' she whispered, not looking at anyone.

My guts clenched inside, as I put my hand on hers. 'I don't know what to say, Terrie.'

I wanted to ask her everything. How he did it. How he kept it covered up. Why she never told me. But I could see how upset she was.

'He did it when everyone was out,' she cried. 'While you were at friends or cadets and Mum was at work. He filmed it. Every time.'

Mum was sobbing now. 'You must both hate me,' she said. 'I've let you both down terribly. I was a bad mum.'

We didn't react. It was true. She had. But we needed to work out what to do and do it soon.

'I think we should ring them, Terrie,' I spoke up again. 'Peter doesn't deserve to be walking around like nothing has happened. Not now.'

She nodded, her mouth opening and closing, but no sound coming out. So I reached for the phone and dialled 999. 'I'd like to report a historical rape and abuse please, or several incidents actually,' I said. 'Yes, nearly 30 years ago.'

I got put through to the station and spoke to an officer who jotted down the bare details I had. Then he arranged to speak to us in a formal interview two days later. I thanked the officer and then explained everything to Terrie and Mum. Everyone's cuppas grew cold, as we sat trying to absorb what had happened. It was true, my nightmare childhood had actually been worse than I'd even remembered.

'I hope I remember everything,' Terrie said, trying to attempt a smile. 'I don't want them to think I'm making this up.'

'I believe you,' I said quickly. 'And so does Mum. Right, Mum?'

Mum nodded, still sobbing into her tissue.

'We're all in this together,' I said. 'We will tell the police everything.'

The police arranged to come and interview us on the Saturday morning two days later. I spent the next day or so in a daze, feeling incredibly anxious and finding it all a bit surreal. Terrie had still only told me the bare minimum of what had happened. She was going to be the first one interviewed. We waited outside the lounge, while an officer took her through events.

She emerged looking strong, and relieved. 'I am so thankful my memory isn't as bad as I thought,' she muttered. 'I just sat down and rattled through everything. I told them they would find all of Peter's videos either neatly lined up in alphabetical order or the whole lot trashed.' We knew him so well.

Terrie had also given a very good description of our old house, to help them with the search. Then it was my turn. When I tried to think back my brain felt fuzzy. Of course memories like the barge trip, or the holiday in Hunstanton where Peter nearly killed me, had stayed fresh in my mind my whole life, and the regime we lived under, the incessant control. But sometimes I struggled to think of details. It felt impossible, but all the same I rattled off the list of what I remembered, which as it happened was far more than I thought.

Terrie jotted down a few things on a notepad to gently remind me of certain incidents, and that helped. As I spoke, officers took notes and ummed and ahhed. They asked questions four or five times back and forth but with details changed; it seemed like they were trying to catch me out, but now I know more I understand they needed to double-check it all.

'It's hard to prove child cruelty in retrospect,' warned one officer. 'It does depend on what evidence we can get. We need to corroborate everything with other sources.'

I told them about Peter's two garages, one behind the house and the one further down by the park. 'It was always stuffed with stuff from the TA, live .22 rounds and flares,' I said. 'You should find the BB gun in there somewhere if you look.'

We just had to wait now to hear of Peter's arrest, but days dragged on and we heard nothing. So I phoned up the police to ask.

'We've been several times to Mr Bond-Wonneberger's premises but he's never been in,' an officer explained.

'Several times?' I gasped. I knew how small the community was, how neighbours talked. Jeff had probably already mentioned to Peter how coppers had been loitering around. 'Why don't you try his place of work?' I suggested, feeling panicked.

Then the next day we got a call to drop in to the police station. They'd not only arrested Peter, but also searched the house. 'The evidence was incredible!' enthused one officer.

'Enough to make this man go down for a long time. We've got him now,' said another, encouragingly.

Terrie and I looked on, not sure whether to laugh or cry. Peter had been charged with 14 counts of rape and child cruelty from the period between 1982 until about 1990. At least 14 rapes of Terrie had been caught on video.

'How did he react?' Terrie asked. 'When you arrested him, what did he do?'

The WPC dealing with Terrie took us aside and explained. She was a focused, caring woman, who specialised in child sex cases. 'He was very calm,' she said. 'We arrested him at Churchill Avenue and when questioned he insisted it was consensual sex. He only looked worried when we told him we were searching his house.'

'What did you find?' I asked.

'Everything was exactly as Terrie had described it,' she said gently. 'We found a huge catalogue of abuse on video and DVD, a gas mask, vibrator, air rifle, a plastic gun, 140 DVDs of indecent images of children, 42 indecent photos of Terrie. And a library of recordings of Terrie from about 14 to 18. As we arrived he also had a video hooked up to four DVD machines copying a recording of Terrie. It was marked: "T & P at home".'

Terrie gasped, covering her mouth with her hand. She looked visibly shaken, as I tried to swallow a rising rage in the pit of my stomach.

'What was the video showing?' she asked, cautiously, as if she couldn't really bear to hear.

'Terrie was wearing a pair of white knickers and a top, and being forced to dance to Madonna,' the WPC said quietly to us both. 'From the photos you gave of yourself, you look like you were probably around 14.'

Peter was actually caught red-handed making copies of himself raping Terrie. It was unbelievable. He still was watching all the videos over 25 years after he'd made them, but more horrifying was the thought he was giving out copies.

Looking appalled, I could guess what was running through Terrie's mind. Peter had become Pap to her children, so some days he could have taken her kids out for treats, and then come home afterwards to watch Terrie's torment on screen for pleasure afterwards.

'God, this is so sickening,' I cried. 'Terrie, why didn't you tell me what he was doing? I would have stabbed him! I would have done something! Anything …'

Terrie shook her head. 'Paul, you were a skinny little nine-year-old boy back then. Nothing you could have said or done would have helped. I wanted to protect you. That felt like the least I could do.'

Chapter 30

'Police Searches'

Terrie

*I*t sounded so strange to hear myself say out loud what had happened after so many years of carrying the pain. The shame and the torment buried inside. Although Paul had escaped Peter being in his life, I'd not been so lucky, and as a result my own kids had spent a lot of time with the monster. The price I paid trying to protect my family from the terrible truth was a heavy one.

The WPC offered to arrange counselling for us both, something Paul and I had never had before. Our philosophy had always been to keep pushing forward rather than look back. But now we had no choice. As we'd spoken in detail, old memories surfaced and the wounds were raw again; I was having terrible nightmares. The good news, however, was that as Peter was caught in the act with his tapes his 'crime' was no longer historical, meaning he'd likely face a longer sentence.

'Did you find everything else?' Paul asked.

'Not his diaries or the BB gun you mentioned,' the WPC said. 'But we have everything we need for a conviction.'

The police corroborated everything we'd said. They'd even contacted the family therapy centre and, although records had been thrown away, they had Paul's referral on file.

'We've also interviewed your cousin Nicky and she backs up the dates and times as well,' she assured us.

Terrie Duckett and Paul Duckett

After Peter's arrest, wheels were put in motion very quickly for the rental company to remove Peter's property. Now he was on remand, Peter signed over everything.

'There's all sorts still in there,' Mum said sadly. 'Those antique silver cups and saucers for Mother's Day you'd bought me. And some pricey ornaments. And of course all of the photo albums.' I'd left all my LPs behind too. Unbelievably, Peter had the rights to all of these as they were in the house.

Now the house was going to be searched, Paul and I wanted to go and see it for ourselves – and we were desperate to try to retrieve the belongings owed to us for years.

We waited for a few more days and then the police announced they'd released the house as a crime scene. After the police had done their search, Peter's house stood empty. Then Mum called. She wanted us to go and see Jeff, her old neighbour.

'He's very shocked,' she said. 'He can't get his head around what Peter has done. I said we'd all go and see him.'

Despite all the upset, we agreed to stick together and turned up at Jeff's house for moral support. As he opened the door, he looked older than ever. 'The police came and arrested him on my birthday,' he stammered. 'It was my 90th and Peter was due to come in for some cake.' He trailed off. 'I can't quite believe what Peter is supposed to have done,' he said.

I wasn't surprised. Peter was always popping in for cups of tea, watching the football with him, and they had even planned to go away on holiday together a few weeks later, as they had done for the last six or seven years.

'Well, he did some terrible things, I am afraid,' said Paul.

Jeff blew on his tea. 'It's hard to swallow,' he said. 'I told him the police had been here a few times, but he thought it was probably about his garage being broken into a while ago.'

310

'Typical Peter,' snapped Paul. 'Arrogant to the last. Of course he thought he'd got away with what he'd really done.'

Jeff offered us some Victoria sponge and then jumped up. 'Oh, Cynthia, before I forget, I've got some post for you,' he said.

'Post?' said Mum. 'From next door?'

'How?' asked Paul.

'Oh, I've got Peter's house key,' said Jeff. 'Peter's solicitor asked me to pick up the post for him.'

Jeff handed Mum the letter. She ripped it open and read it, her eyes widening. 'Right,' she said. 'Listen to this. Peter had two garages. One was in a joint name when I left the property but Peter never changed it back like he'd said he would. That means technically I am liable for the rent and it's still in my name.'

We all looked at each other. 'Let's go down and look at Mum's garage then,' said Paul. 'We've every legal right to.' We made our way down there and found spiders' webs undisturbed everywhere. Everything was covered in dust and filth, obviously untouched. We found Mum's old garden swing, now all rusty, and all kinds of things like old tools and a pressure washer.

'Urgh,' I said. 'It's like something out of Indiana Jones in here, Paul.'

We were rooting through a few boxes when Mum spotted a big piece of tarpaulin at the back. 'Paul,' she said, pointing. 'Go and lift that up and see what's underneath.'

Paul edged his way over there and whipped off the covering dust as spiders scuttled everywhere. It was a hip-height metal cupboard. He slid it open and gasped. 'Whoah,' he said. There were about 80 videos stacked up, each with a label on. Many had worn away but all were written in Peter's handwriting.

Then Paul cried out. 'Look there are decaying smoke grenades and trip flares in here,' he exclaimed. 'It's unstable ammunition as well. A bloody hazard. Right, everyone out.'

Paul rang the police to warn them of its dangers and they sent someone to collect it. After finding all of this, we decided to investigate Peter's other garage. When we arrived it was unlocked. Inside it was also damp, dark and mouldy, but quickly we found boxes with a few thousand slides inside. He also dug out hundreds of negative pictures and a box with Oma's wedding ring and all her belongings.

'Blimey,' said Paul, looking stunned.

The police sent someone down to collect all the piles of live ammo and then admitted they'd released the place as a crime scene. Then it was revealed Peter had instructed the rental company to take the property back and throw away the contents of the house in the process. To save anything we had to move – fast.

Mum called the rental company to explain who she was and our situation and she was reassured we could take what was ours. But a day before the official clear-out we went down to find they had already sent two guys and a 10-year-old lad to come and rake through our belongings.

I ran up to them. 'Please!' I said. 'This is our childhood home. We have permission to collect our things before it's cleared.'

'Who said?' asked one guy.

'Your company!' Mum cried.

'She's talking rubbish.' He shrugged.

Mum rang the rental place again but this time was told that we had no rights and if we wanted permission to have our belongings back we'd need to speak to Peter's solicitor. We made another call but heard Peter's solicitor was on holiday.

'Put everything in writing,' his secretary said. 'And he'll deal with it when he gets back.'

'No!' I cried, eyeing a box filled with photo slides the men were carrying past me. 'It will be too late by then.'

In desperation I ran up to the men again. I hadn't wanted to blurt out my entire story, but there was nothing else for it. 'The man who owns this house abused me for years,' I cried, welling up with tears. 'He's been arrested for serious sex crimes. There might be more evidence we don't know about. Plus, you have a young boy going through stuff he probably shouldn't see.'

The man stopped and looked a little bit more sympathetic. 'Listen,' he said. 'It's more than my job's worth. Unless we find something dodgy needing police investigation ourselves I am just doing what I am told.'

I stood there, feeling so helpless. It was as if we were being violated all over again. All we could do was watch in tears as they walked to and fro, collecting up anything valuable or dumping items in bin bags. Then the man I'd been speaking to cried out from inside. 'Hold everything!' he said, standing on the top of the stairs. He was holding up the BB gun Peter used to shoot at us in the garden. 'This is gonna make you happy,' he said to me. 'I think this is more evidence.'

Finally the emptying of the house was called off and it was declared a crime scene again. Police even put a guard on local Oxfam shops and the tip to try and retrieve goods already taken away.

We scouted around to try and take as much as we could. It felt so odd to be back inside the place. Peter had hardly touched it. Everything was in the same place, nothing decorated or moved since Mum left in 2002, but also almost nothing had been cleaned.

We started in the kitchen, but everything of any value had

gone, all the appliances, even some of the cupboards. Those that were left we looked inside. A shiver went down my spine as I saw how Peter had lived. It was all microwaved food. He had packets of rice in different flavours all very neatly stacked up, standing to attention like soldiers, in perfect order. The bathroom, a place myself and Paul had been forced to clean religiously every day for years, was disgusting, every surface covered in sticky grime.

After Paul had moved out, Mum and Peter had knocked down the wall of his room adjoining mine to make a giant room for depravity. There we saw the desk and the metal cabinet in which Peter had hoarded all the DVDs of me. Then Paul spotted something. On the floor a piece of paper was left with a grid written in Peter's handwriting: it was a catalogue of all his disgusting DVDs. I felt physically sick. I knew the man was evil, but his attention to detail was almost inhumane. He didn't view women beyond being sex objects.

We rushed around knowing we didn't have long. The rental people had taken Mum's antique cup and saucer we'd got her for Mother's Day. Most of my records had gone, too, including my first Blondie album. Then we pulled down the ladder to the attic and had another look up there. Piles and piles of paperwork were wedged everywhere. We found a box containing 3,000 slides. I also found cheque books in different names and more negatives and CDs with 'high-res' images written on the front.

'Oh my God, it's even more evidence!' Paul cried.

We called the police again, and they started a third search, this time as Paul watched them.

'Have you checked the secret compartment of the filing cabinet?' he asked.

'What secret compartment?' asked one of the officers.

'All filing cabinets have secret compartments,' Paul said.

Then he lifted out a drawer and checked himself. Underneath he found Peter's diaries and a packet of photos of cadets, all holding their names and birth dates up to the camera.

Telling my family why Peter had been arrested was harder than I'd imagined. Having to explain to my children that their Pap was actually a monster was one of the most heartbreaking things I faced. I was dreading it.

In the end, Paul organised for us all to get together and then gave me a few drinks for Dutch courage. Tammy cried her eyes out as I tried to explain something no mother should have to tell her daughter.

Other family members were equally incredulous. Steve and his parents, who'd always loved Peter, tried to say they 'knew' something was strange about him. Our cousin Helen was just stunned that such abuse had been happening behind the scenes. Afterwards, Helen sent me a long letter saying how sorry she was and how brave we were. I didn't reply. I simply didn't know what to say.

Chapter 31
'The Trial'
Paul

*P*eter was remanded in custody until the preliminary hearing on 14 November 2012, less than six months after the truth had all come out. This hearing was to find out how he would plead. There was a huge build-up as we waited, but luckily due to all the evidence they had found the case had been fast tracked. Finally we heard Peter was pleading guilty, but our barrister explained that we should not get too excited, as it was just what he was 'intending' to plead. We still didn't know for certain.

Meanwhile, myself and Terrie were still coping with the fall-out. My niece Tammy was in pieces after discovering what her Pap had been up to but she made the brave decision to go to court as well. 'I only have good memories of a good man,' she sobbed. 'I need to see him for who he really is.' It was an extremely confusing time for her.

In a strange way, I admitted to Terrie, I felt a bit sorry for Peter.

'He's suddenly been ripped out of his life,' I said. 'Not allowed to even pack or say goodbye to anyone. The world will never be the same for him now.'

Terrie knew what I meant, but she couldn't feel sorry for him in any way.

'Well, in prison he'll have the routine he's always craved,' she quipped. 'Everything will be cooked for him too.'

I caught her eye and smiled. 'Yeah, you're right. Peter will have a definite schedule to follow now, won't he?'

In spite of everything we fell about laughing. Peter's all-important routine would be all he'd know now in prison.

The date for the court case was set for 21 December 2012, in Northampton Crown Court, and thanks to all of the damning DVD evidence neither of us would need to take the stand. For once Peter's insistence that everything was in order worked to our advantage. He'd literally handed the police evidence of most of his crimes, all neatly labelled.

We were both keen to sit in court and hear everything as it was read out. But our barrister was less sure about us going in. 'They are going to be reading out a lot of unpleasant things,' he said softly. 'I wouldn't advise you or Terrie to listen to it.'

'I've already lived through it,' Terrie replied firmly. 'It's not going to hurt me to hear it.'

The thought of it was both horrendous and necessary. I wanted to be there, not just to hear, but to be there for my sister.

We turned up 30 minutes early and found a quiet corner to sit in, our eyes flicking nervously to the entrance every time someone came in. Eventually, with about five minutes to spare, Rachel and the police officer dealing with our case appeared from a different direction in the company of four other people. We were introduced to the CPS case manager, the CPS barrister and two of Rachel's colleagues. Pleasantries over, and with time running out, the barrister gave us an update.

'Peter is disputing a number of charges,' she began, 'all relating to Mr Duckett, bar one. None of which we have any physical evidence for.'

Basically Peter was denying all the child cruelty allegations against me, in particular the attacks in Hunstanton and on the barge, the two occasions I could have died so easily.

I gave a wry smile. 'I'm pulling out of this whole thing unless he admits to what he did,' I said firmly.

'Yes, me too,' Terrie agreed. 'He has to admit to those attacks.' This was his final attempt to exert control over us, and the situation; there was no way we could let him do that.

'He is also disputing the charge of having sex with Terrie under the age of 14,' she said.

This was a difficult point. The videos showed Terrie looking very similar aged between 12 and 14. Although she knew Peter had raped her before her fourteenth birthday, the lawyers had no proof.

'I'm prepared to let that go,' Terrie said, 'if it makes no difference to the sentencing.'

The CPS barrister asked the CPS manager who was present for advice, who agreed I was right to stand up for myself, and returned to see Peter's barrister. Ten tense minutes later Peter agreed to the child cruelty charges, all except for one – the one where I was almost killed on the barge.

I managed a hollow laugh. 'Go back again and tell him if he doesn't admit to it all we will go to trial and fight him. I know just how much Peter will hate that. The last thing he'll want is a trial where all of his friends and work colleagues get to have their image of him shattered.'

Just five minutes later the CPS barrister returned and said that Peter was not happy and had initially refused to agree to the charges, but his solicitor had had a private word with him and he had now reluctantly agreed to all of the charges.

'I know how that guy's brain works,' I laughed. 'I spent ten years pitting my wits against his. He'll push and push for control, but at the last possible second, when it's too much of a risk for him, he'll crack.'

After waiting around for a very long half hour, we eventually entered the court room and sat in front of the dock where Peter stood. Terrie didn't want to look at him, but I turned to have a glance.

'He looks very old,' I murmured, 'kind of grey and chunky.' He'd aged and not in a good way.

'I don't care,' replied Terrie. 'I am here to finally see justice, not him.'

We both took a deep breath as Peter admitted guilt to all 14 counts, including bestiality. Each count Peter admitted to covered a period of 12 to 18 months and all abuse that happened in that period. Some of those counts were for 50 or 60 different incidents. So every time Peter admitted guilt he was effectively admitting to another year and a half of abuse; it was an important step to allow me and Terrie to move on with our lives.

Before the judge went to view the DVD compilations, our barrister Mrs Lucking opened the case:

'The defendant was a stepfather to both complainants and, to the outside world, a respectable, hardworking man, employed as a driving instructor and member of the Territorial Army. But in reality behind closed doors, he physically abused and assaulted both of his stepchildren and raped his stepdaughter.

'The defendant treated the complainant Terrie Duckett as his sex slave for many years, from the ages of 13 until she was 18.

'Her brother, Paul Duckett, was the subject of an aggressive regime of control and punishments, including physical violence, causing him to suffer physical injury on a series of occasions.

'He too remains badly affected by the defendant's actions. The defendant manipulated the mother of these children and made her too powerless and afraid to assist. The defendant destroyed the relationship between mother and daughter for the best part of 20 years and ensured his ability to control the children by that regime of assaults and cruelty.'

It sounded so serious as it was read out, and we listened, transfixed. Had we really lived through all of this? It seemed unreal.

We were then told how the judge had himself watched some of the worst footage, including Peter raping Terrie with a gun and a sword.

'A sword?' I thought, squeezing my eyes shut.

Not only had Peter kept all the videos, he'd made copies of some of them. Police also found tape after tape of family holidays, but few shots had people's heads or faces in them. He'd filmed Terrie's friend Tracey paddling with her skirt in her knickers on one day out, women's boobs jiggling on donkeys on another, whatever it was he'd found titillating. He even had a video of young females and ponies, with which he was charged with bestiality.

My heart went out to Terrie as she heard all of the evidence. A lot of the horror she'd blocked out. 'I don't remember the sword,' she said, in shock. 'My brain literally blanked that out. And the rapes while I was pregnant. It's all too much to bear.'

The extent of what Terrie had been through was unbelievable. I was in total admiration of her bravery, her courage. Never had I felt so proud of my older sister and her strength. She'd been through so much and yet had hidden it for so long, protecting me.

The child cruelty charges were then read out and they arrived at the piece about the kitchen implements Peter used:

'He hit the children with the metal spatula so often it became the shape of their bottoms,' said Mrs Lucking.

Suddenly, through all the horror, I glanced at Terrie and as usual just one look at her made me want to laugh. Visions of Peter leaping around hitting himself with the spatula flitted across my mind and I just wanted to burst out giggling. Knowing it wouldn't look good to others to laugh in such a place, we kept our heads bent to stifle giggles, feeling as if, once again, we were just two children. We knew everyone would assume we were crying, but really hearing that part had the opposite effect.

Our faces fell again, however, when we heard what they said about Mum. In many respects it was heartbreaking as we heard what our barrister had to say:

'The complainant's mother was spoken to by the police, and in short, described herself as an absolutely dreadful mother and plainly finds it very difficult to explain the events and recollect the full events to the police.'

After hearing most of the evidence and before he passed sentence, the proceedings were halted for an hour to allow the judge time to watch the entire compilation DVDs of the rapes in his private room. Terrie and I left the room, both feeling numb. We sat outside trying to take in everything we'd heard. Finally we were allowed back in. The judge began his summing up.

'Her distress at your behaviour is, in my judgement, entirely genuine and chilling,' he said. 'You assaulted her, you frightened her and you had sex with her despite her obvious and genuine terror.

'This was sick, sadistic, planned and perverse behaviour. For more than three decades you put your own extreme and twisted desires above all else. You are unaffected by the suffering of others, especially those who trusted you as a family member. You did not care what pain or humiliation your victims endured. The word "depraved" simply does not do justice to what you have done. I am confident the scars you have inflicted, both physical and psychological, on your family or your stepfamily will never ever heal.

'From the age of nine you made Paul Duckett's life a misery by the regime of control and violence and there is no doubt that the cruelty you meted out was in the highest category. You made him do physical labour dressed in a nuclear, biological warfare suit, you shot at him with a ball-bearing gun, you searched him in an intimate way just short of sexual abuse … You punished him by beating him either with your fists or a metal spatula.'

The judge continued, reading the pre-sentence report, and then when he finally spoke his words were damning:

'You have manifested perverted or psychopathic tendencies or a gross personality disorder and, if you are left at large, you will remain a danger to people for an indefinite time. For these reasons I am satisfied that the appropriate sentence to pass on you is one of life imprisonment.'

But, as he continued speaking, the sentence got shorter and shorter. Firstly Peter was given a third off for his guilty plea.

'But he only pleaded guilty after all the evidence was found,' I whispered to Terrie. 'How can that be fair?'

This reduced the sentence to 11 years.

Then the judge stated he was fixing the term for custody at five and a half years before parole.

'What?' Terrie gasped. I was as shocked as she looked. Peter was also to join the sex offenders' register for life.

I leapt to my feet. 'This is supposed to be a court but it's more like a circus!'

I followed him out and we waited ages for the police and barristers to come. 'How could he get so little?' I raged.

Eventually it was the CPS barrister who approached us and ushered us into a side room. She was keen to reassure me. 'In the court report it states Peter has psychopathic tendencies and will remain a danger to people,' she said. 'He will therefore never get out of prison.'

'Can you guarantee that?' I asked. 'Would you stake your career on that fact? Isn't it an independent parole board who decides? I would put money on it that Peter will now make himself a model prisoner to increase his chances of release.'

'Yes,' agreed the barrister. 'However, if the board reads the report …'

'But nobody can guarantee he won't get out,' I cried. 'That's the truth, isn't it?'

Everyone went silent and we knew then what the answer was.

Afterword

Terrie and Paul

*A*s brother and sister we have always stuck together, no matter what challenges we face. We stand as a testament to show that, no matter how your life starts out, you can take control of your destiny and steer your own course. Fight each battle as it comes and slowly you can win the war.

Today we are proud owners of multiple, diverse successful businesses. We own one of the largest dolls' house companies in Europe, Mytinyworld – maybe it's something to do with having very few toys growing up. We work extremely hard and, most importantly, we still remember how to laugh. (Paul does occasionally chase me around our warehouse, though not with a belt, but with packing tape.)

It hasn't been easy thinking about what's inside our heads. We've never let ourselves think about everything as one whole life, just snapshots of horror.

But we wanted the book to show that no matter how much suffering you go through, or for how long, it is possible to survive and build a normal life. Our own beautiful families and the lives we have made are testimony to that.

For so long we held our heads in shame at the thoughts of the crimes done to us. Peter might have robbed us of our childhoods, but he couldn't destroy our bond as brother and sister.

It's never too late to seek justice, or for the truth to emerge. The police did listen and our voices were heard.

Now it's time for us to hold our heads high and talk about how we survived, as we finally understand it's not *our* shame to carry.

Moving Memoirs

Stories of hope, courage and the power of love…

If you loved this book, then you will love our
Moving Memoirs eNewsletter

Sign up to…

- Be the first to hear about new books

- Get sneak previews from your favourite authors

- Read exclusive interviews

- Be entered into our monthly prize draw to win one
  of our latest releases before it's even hit the shops!

Sign up at

www.moving-memoirs.com